The Empire of Security
Safety of the People

This new volume explores the meaning of security in relation to, and in the context of, ideas that are fundamental to both international and domestic political order.

William Bain argues that the word 'security' is devoid of substantive content when divorced from ideas such as sovereignty, war, diplomacy, great power responsibility, self-determination, globalization, cultural diversity, intervention, and trusteeship. In other words, 'security' cannot be made to yield a real core or an intrinsic content because it discloses no essence that awaits discovery. This clear and accessible book draws on an impressive range of history, philosophy, and law to investigate these and other questions:

- How do norms of sovereignty inform an ethics of international security?
- Is security something that can be achieved through the recognition of identity?
- Are all states, great and small, of equal moral importance?
- Does the enjoyment of security demand cultural homogeneity?
- Is the body of international law that addresses questions of intervention still relevant in a post-11 September world?
- How might security be understood in light of wars that are fought in order to kill rather than to win?

This book will be of particular interest to those conducting empirical and normative research on questions of security. It is also an excellent resource for students wanting to develop an understanding of security in contemporary world affairs.

William Bain is a lecturer in International Relations Theory in the Department of International Politics at the University of Wales, Aberystwyth, UK.

Routledge advances in international relations and global politics

The Empire of Security and the Safety of the People

Edited by William Bain

LONDON AND NEW YORK

First published 2006
by Routledge
2 Park Square, Milton Park, Abingdon, Oxon, OX14 4RN

Simultaneously published in the USA and Canada
by Routledge
270 Madison Ave, New York NY 10016

Routledge is an imprint of the Taylor & Francis Group, an informa business

First issued in paperback 2011

Typeset in Baskerville by Wearset Ltd, Boldon, Tyne and Wear

British Library Cataloguing in Publication Data
A catalogue record for this book is available from the British Library

Library of Congress Cataloging in Publication Data
A catalog record for this book has been requested

ISBN10: 0-415-38019-7 (hbk)
ISBN10: 0-415-66395-4 (pbk)
ISBN10: 0-203-09946-X (ebk)

ISBN13: 978-0-415-38019-5 (hbk)
ISBN13: 978-0-415-66395-3 (pbk)
ISBN13: 978-0-203-09946-9 (ebk)

Contents

Contributors

William Bain is a lecturer in international relations theory at the University of Wales, Aberystwyth. He has published widely in the areas of international relations theory, human security, and trusteeship or post-conflict international administration. He is the author of *Between Anarchy and Society: Trusteeship and the Obligations of Power* (2003). At present he is working on a project that explores the idea of obligation in international society.

K. J. Holsti is currently a Research Associate with the Centre for International Relations in the Liu Institute for Global Issues, and University Killam Professor Emeritus at the University of British Columbia. He is a member of the Royal Society of Canada and, in 2005, was elected a foreign member of the Finnish Academy of Sciences and Letters. He is the author of several books on international relations, the most recent of which include *Taming the Sovereigns: Institutional Change in International Politics* (2004) and a collection of essays entitled *Politica Mundial: Cambio y Conflicto* (2005), which is edited by Adam Jones.

Robert Jackson is Professor of International Relations at Boston University. He is the author of *The Global Covenant: Human Conduct in a World of States* (2000) and *Quasi-States: Sovereignty, International Relations and the Third World* (1990). His most recent works include *Classical and Modern International Thought* (2005) and 'Doctrinal War: Religion and Ideology in International Conflict', *Monist*, 89.2 (April 2006). He is currently studying the role of religion in world affairs.

Jennifer Jackson Preece is a senior lecturer in nationalism at the London School of Economics and Political Science. She has published widely in the areas of nationalism, ethnic conflict, human, and minority rights. Her publications include *National Minorities and the European Nation-States System* (1998) and *Minority Rights: Between Diversity and Community* (2005).

James Mayall was, until he retired in 2004, the Sir Patrick Sheehy Professor of International Relations and the Director of the Centre of

International Relations at the University of Cambridge. He is a Fellow of the British Academy, having been elected in 2001. He is the author or editor of several books, including *Nationalism and International Society* (1990), which won the Political Studies Association's prize for best monograph; *The New Interventionism 1991–1994: United Nations Experience in Cambodia, former Yugoslavia and Somalia* (1996); and *World Politics: Progress and its Limits* (2000). He currently working on a project that explores the impact of the end of empire on international order.

Cornelia Navari is Senior Research Fellow in the Department of Political Science and International Studies at the University of Birmingham. Her main concerns are international theory, including normative theory, and the history of internationalist thought. Her recent work includes *Internationalism and the State in the 20th Century* (2000) and 'When Agents Cannot Act: International Institutions as Moral Patients', in *Can Institutions Have Responsibilities?*, edited by T. Erskine (2003). She is presently concerned with the international relations of liberal states.

Cathal J. Nolan is Associate Professor of History and Executive Director of the International History Institute at Boston University. He teaches in the areas of war in literature and film, the history of war, and the history of modern diplomacy. His most recent publications include the *Greenwood Encyclopedia of International Relations* (2002), *Ethics and Statecraft* (2nd edn, 2004) and *Great Power Responsibility in World Affairs* (2004). His *Age of the Wars of Religion 1000–1650*, the first of two volumes in a fourteen-volume Encyclopedia of *War and Civilization*, is forthcoming in 2006. Also forthcoming is a co-edited Encyclopedia on US Presidential Foreign Policy.

Sir Adam Roberts is the Montague Burton Professor of International Relations at Oxford University, and a Fellow of Balliol College. He is a Fellow of the British Academy and a Member of the Council, International Institute for Strategic Studies, London. His books include *Nations in Arms: The Theory and Practice of Territorial Defence* (2nd edn, 1986); (edited with Benedict Kingsbury), *United Nations, Divided World: The UN's Roles in International Relations* (2nd edn, 1993); (edited with Richard Guelff), *Documents on the Laws of War* (3rd edn, 2000).

Sasson Sofer teaches international relations and political thought at the Hebrew University. He has previously served as the director of the Leonard Davis Institute for International Relations, and as chair of the Department of International Relations, both at the Hebrew University of Jerusalem. He has published widely in the areas of diplomacy in international relations and Israeli diplomacy and foreign policy.

Acknowledgements

This project began life at Shady Island, a favourite seafood eatery overlooking the Fraser River in Steveston, British Columbia. It was there that Robert Jackson and I, reflecting on the tendency of academics to shine the bright light of novelty on questions of security, began to think through a project that took a longer view of things, one which emphasized the importance of history, philosophy, and law in making sense of whatever security might mean in contemporary world affairs. Since that very pleasant evening I have incurred several debts that I wish to acknowledge.

The essays contained in this collection were initially presented at a conference organized by the Centre of International Relations at the University of British Columbia. Generous funding for the conference was given by the Peter Wall Institute for Advanced Studies and additional support was provided by the Centre of International Relations. I am grateful to both institutions for making possible what was an enjoyable and stimulating event. In addition to the contributors to this volume, several others contributed to the success of the conference: Claire Cutler, John Darwin, Jack Donnelly, Suzy Hainsworth, Carl Hodge, Andrew Hurrell, David Long, Emily Munro, Allen Sens, Georg Sorensen, and Mark Zacher. I am grateful to them all.

I am also indebted to a group of individuals who at various stages in the project offered valuable and welcome advice. Robert Jackson played a very important role in helping conceptualize the project; Cornelia Navari and Adam Roberts provided insightful comments that helped shape the general direction of the book; and Jennifer Jackson Preece offered the sympathetic ear and the reliable view of things that I have come to rely upon over the years. I am especially grateful to Michael Williams, who provided some enormously useful advice on bringing the project to a close. Lastly, I would like to say a special word of thanks to Brian Job. Brian has given unqualified support for this project from its earliest inception through to the days leading to its completion. Indeed, it is no exaggeration to say that without Brian's support this project would not have happened.

Heidi Bagtazo, my editor at Routledge, has offered much appreciated advice and guidance in steering me through various difficulties encountered along the way. I tended to view these problems in the frame of crisis; in the end, though, resolution required only her skilful and reassuring hand. Harriet Brinton, also at Routledge, was very helpful in resolving a number of issues. My thanks are also due to Avery Poole, a remarkably able and industrious PhD student at the University of British Columbia, who assisted in the preparation of the final manuscript. And to the Greenwood Publishing Group and the Taylor & Francis Group, I am thankful for graciously granting permission to republish material that appears in the essays by Cathal Nolan and Sasson Sofer, respectively.

To my wife Diana I owe an enormous debt of gratitude. She has supported my research, through several moves, too many working weekends, and the demands of family life, all while helping me keep things in perspective. I am forever grateful for her support, and, above all else, for her love and companionship.

Finally, I want to thank the contributors to this volume, who, in addition to producing some excellent papers, have been patient when required, responsive when asked, and, through it all, remained in good humour. It has been a great privilege to work with such a superb group of people.

W. B.
Aberystwyth

1 Introduction

William Bain

Among political theorists, especially those who have given considerable intellectual weight to the study of security in international relations, Thomas Hobbes provides what is surely one of the most succinct and penetrating accounts of the politics of security: '*the safety of the people is the supreme law*' (emphasis in original).[1] From this single phrase Hobbes derives the duties of sovereigns, including the absolute sovereign that is subject to no (true) law and beholden to no (human) will. The sovereign, though 'uncompellable' by any authority on earth, has as his guide the rule of right reason, which dictates that governments are formed for the sake of peace and that peace is sought for the sake of safety. But this condition of safety is not to be confused with the microtheoretical assumption – 'states seek to ensure their survival'[2] – that provides the starting point for neo-realist or structural realist accounts of national security and international insecurity; it is an explicitly normative safety that is tied no less explicitly to the felicity or happiness of persons joined (willingly) in a relationship of civil association. For the word 'safety', Hobbes explains, should be understood to mean, not a base condition of mere survival, but 'a happy life so far as that is possible'.[3] Thus, the Hobbesian sovereign is obliged to attend to the safety of the people by enacting laws – civil association being an order of laws – that are directed to external defence, domestic peace, acquisition of wealth, and enjoyment of liberty. Indeed, it is for the sake of these things, that is, things 'necessary not just for life but for the enjoyment of life', that men institute commonwealths and submit to sovereign power.[4]

The supremacy that Hobbes ascribes to the 'safety of the people' is almost certain to gain the approval of most contemporary theorists of security, despite the fact that he is probably best known in international relations circles for his portrayal (as told by some realists) of a ferocious state of nature in which there is no law, no justice, and no morality. Few would dispute the view that civil association should be ordered to the benefit of citizens; that laws should attend to the welfare of the many; or that the safety of the majority should prevail over the interests of selfish or seditious factions.[5] But the arrangements prescribed by Hobbes for achieving these things are unlikely to appeal to most observers of contemporary world affairs. Moreover, they may not be entirely appropriate in a vastly changed world, for the relative simplicity and prescriptive clarity imparted by Hobbes is all but lost when we turn to more recent thinking about security. The study of security in contemporary world affairs discloses a considerable degree of disarray – some would say confusion – that makes it near well impossible to speak of a coherent field of study that is organized around a clear set of problems, settled methods of inquiry, and an established sense of purpose. There is no agreement on the questions that merit scholarly attention and there is no reliable way of separating authentic security issues from non-security issues. Just as troublesome is the difficulty in obtaining agreement on the proper referent object of security, be it states, classes, systems, societies, identities, groups, individuals, or some combination thereof. Thus, the question 'whose security?' is sure to elicit several seemingly unrelated answers that are often mutually unintelligible to those who offer them.

Barry Buzan's (1991) landmark study *People, States, and Fear* was among the first to systematically probe the conceptual inadequacies of a 'simpleminded' notion of security, state-centric in focus, often indistinguishable from power, and too closely wedded to the policy imperatives of a Cold War rivalry that very suddenly disappeared. For Buzan, rethinking security involved an exploration of different referent objects of security, whereby individuals took a place alongside states, in order to illuminate the 'connections and contradictions' of a ubiquitous and often vilified state as both a source of and threat to personal security. It involved distinguishing between discrete though linked elements of the state – idea, physical base, and institutional expression – in order to make further distinctions between states that are more or less weak or strong. And it involved abandoning the overriding concern with military security that dominated the Cold War mindset in favour of a broadened notion of security which encompassed five distinct 'issue sectors': military, political, economic, societal, and environmental. Taken together, different referent objects and different levels of analysis pointed to a conception of security that acknowledged the obvious intersection of political and military questions, but which embraced as well a broader 'integrative perspective' that sees the idea of security as incomprehensible without also 'bringing in the actors and dynamics from the societal, economic, and environmental sectors'.[6]

With the concept of security broadened to include a vastly expanded list of threats, the staples of 'national security' and 'strategic studies' seemed to be excessively narrow, if not entirely out of place. Talk of missile throw-weights imparted intelligibility as little more than a quaint throwback to an absurdly dangerous Stranglovian world that had receded into the background. Indeed, the insecurity conveyed by the anonymous face of grinding poverty, transmitted instantly throughout the world by satellite television, displaced the chilling assurance of absolute insecurity given in Peter George's novel: 'That's right, *nuclear com-*bat! Toe-to-toe with the Russkies' (emphasis in original).[7] The conceptual nomenclature of the superpower nuclear stand-off, which indulged the mind in the intricacies of first- and second-strike capabilities, counterforce and countervalue strategies, horizontal and vertical proliferation, strategic triads, massive retaliation, tacit bargaining, and internal balancing, gave place to several contending approaches to security that endeavoured to escape the closed world of interstate military relations by redefining security to mean something else. Each of the temples erected to an expanded security agenda embraced as its talisman the cardinal belief that the Cold War enterprise of strategic studies, as Steve Smith explains, 'began to look like one story about the world, not the only, let alone the true, story'.[8] And new stories, embroidered with new questions, prompted new and often unexpected answers so that infectious disease and violence against women were stitched into the narrative along with more traditional issues, such as the revolution in military affairs (RMA) and ballistic missile defence.

The multi-sectoral approach pioneered by Buzan opened the way for the so-called Copenhagen School, which conceives 'security' as being constructed in 'securitizing' speech acts that designate issues as existential threats, call for emergency action, and legitimize the use of extraordinary means. A socially constructed security made it possible to think about different security orders, especially a 'post-sovereign' European security order that breaks free of the 'sovereignty-bound political lexicon' that dominates both realist and liberal theories of security.[9] Feminists approached the security problematique by asking a deceptively simple but searching question: 'where are the women?'. Here, answers are sought, not in the masculinized world of states, power, and anarchy, but in the invisible yet illuminating lives of Filipina prostitutes and diplomatic wives.[10] Adherents to the critical security studies approach critiqued this 'traditional' order of things, saying that it reified a realist world that is not terrible real, while gathering around the view that '[e]mancipation, not power or order, produces true security'.[11] The impossibility of an 'essentialistic' danger led post-structuralists to travel a different path, one which emphasized the centrality of disciplinary strategies, their representations, and silences and omissions. Hence, understanding security called for a textual enterprise that involves 'denaturalizing' and 'unsettling' purportedly stable identities in a penultimate step to a celebration of different perspectives.[12] And there are others – human security, constructivist security studies, and a venerable realism married to a 'robust' rational choice theory.[13]

The proliferation of several different approaches to the study of security is probably a positive development and thus should be greeted with cautious approval. In fact, '[i]t may be necessary', as Keith Krause and Michael Williams have argued, 'to broaden the agenda of security studies (theoretically and methodologically) in order to narrow the agenda of *security*' (emphasis in original).[14] But the schisms represented by several incommensurable schools and approaches leaves a deeply fractured academic field of 'security studies' that is bereft of any common understanding of an idea, condition, or practice called 'security'. It is a field fraught with an ambiguity which, far from being anchored by a carefully defined research programme, imparts a sense of coherence only in the form of an unruly collective anxiety. Indeed, it is an anxiety that reduces the field of 'security studies' to not much more than a pedagogically useful name around which a set of loosely related perspectives coalesce around an improbably elusive word 'security'. For security is one of those essentially contested concepts, as W. B. Gallie calls them, which cannot be made to yield a real core or an intrinsic content. There is no essence of security that awaits discovery. There are rival conceptions of security, each of which is authentic in its own right and on its own terms, just as there are rival conceptions of order, justice, equality, freedom, and happiness.

Of course, security is often said to be a contested concept. Buzan argued in *People, States, and Fear* that the contested concept of security gives rise to 'unsolvable' debates; and, more recently, Steve Smith has suggested that the contested character of security admits no possibility of neutral definition.[15] But these views somehow miss the value of engaging essentially contested concepts at all, which, from a scholarly standpoint, involves recognition of genuine disputes and the value they impart. Scholars who seek to answer questions that probe the meaning and value of security must, if they are true to their vocation, remain open to the possibility that such questions beg several fully rational and, at the same time, wholly incommensurable answers. Particular answers advance or defend particular claims but the veracity of these claims cannot be adjudicated with a view to separating those that are true from those that are false. No appeal to a general method or a universal principle can resolve once and for all disputes about security; and, in that respect, emancipation provides no better sight of 'true' security than power or the long barrel of a gun. Indeed, the first step toward understanding an essentially contested concept like security involves 'recognition of rival uses of it (such as oneself repudiates) as not only logically possible and humanly "likely", but as of permanent potential critical value to one's own use or interpretation of the concept in question'.[16] Unfortunately, though, the many temples that have been erected to the new security studies tend to be homes to closed and self-referential debates that are rather suspiciously like the debates they seek to displace.

Understanding the many logical and likely possibilities of security, that is, interpreting meaning and ascribing value, requires a careful and painstaking navigation through the world of human experience. It requires an excavation of the historical, legal, and philosophical inheritance of security in world affairs. So where security is a fundamental human value in an abstract sense, it is something that all human beings desire in some degree and in some situation, the good it imparts is intelligible in the context of time, place, and circumstance. In other words, security is a problem of human relations, the range and character of which are necessarily historical. For outside the world of human experience – the world of desire, thought, circumstance, sensation, deliberation, judgement, emotion, and all else that goes with human consciousness – there is no way of discriminating between contending claims short of anointing a frontrunner while suppressing the field. And while a speedy adjudication of rival claims – recognizing prophets, counting converts, and dismissing heretics – may be ideologically and, indeed, emotionally pleasing, it is in the same proportion intellectually unsatisfying. The activity of understanding security, as with any other essentially contested concept, is a matter, not of application, but of cultivation.

The empire of security

The terrorist attacks on New York and Washington on 11 September 2001 issued yet another invitation to think about what security might mean in a world made exceedingly uncertain by the deadly convergence of failed states, terrorist groups, and the proliferation of weapons of mass destruction. So great are the challenges of this changed world – a world in which the heady optimism that heralded the 'end of history' has dissipated into a pervasive climate of fear – that the tried practices of old are said to be obsolete. A world that is home to fanatical enemies, undeterred by fear of death, demands new ideas and new doctrines in order to ensure the safety of the people. But beyond viscerally personal debates concerning the wisdom and efficacy of the Bush administration's 'war against terror', its (misnamed) doctrine of pre-emptive self-defence, and especially its controversial invasion of Iraq, lies a still greater debate concerning what Henry Kissinger describes as the 'systemic crisis' of the Westphalian order. The fundamental principles of the Westphalian settlement, he suggests, 'are being challenged, though an agreed alternative has yet to emerge'.[17]

Classical theories of international relations tell us that security is something that comes with the independence afforded by sovereignty. Particular arrangements of security are effected through the institutions and practices of diplomacy, the conditions of which are usually instituted in understandings, minutes, notes, declarations, treaties, covenants, and charters. When the craft of diplomacy is insufficient to the task, when a threat of some sort becomes intolerable and a negotiated settlement seems impossible, security is pursued through the activity of war. Great powers, more so than any other political, economic, social, religious, or cultural association, are burdened with the responsibility of defining their interests and, furthermore, adjusting their policies for the sake of 'international peace and security' – something which must be counted among the most fundamental global goods. And for groups who do not live in a state to call their own, especially minorities that suffer under the boot of an oppressive majority, self-determination, and thus membership in the society of states, holds out the possibility of security.

But many of the institutions and practices of contemporary international life, sovereignty and war foremost among them, are more closely associated with pervasive insecurity than with security. Too often the political independence that comes with sovereign statehood results, not in refuges of safety, but in places of shocking violence and misery; and it is the apparatus of the state, more often than external enemies, which poses the greatest danger to the safety of the people. Ours is a world in which governments are often deeply complicit in internal wars that have claimed the greater proportion of five million lives since the end of the Cold War.[18] War too is something that regularly involves, not an activity conducted according to settled rules in pursuit of limited aims, but the infliction of wanton destruction that disproportionately affects civilian populations. Indeed, K. J. Holsti argues in this volume that war in much of the world is unintelligible in its classical Clausewitzian sense: '[w]ar is no longer a continuation of politics by other means, but an end in itself' (p. 47). The profound insecurity associated with these cardinal institutions of international society informs a now well-rehearsed indictment that condemns the entire states system and most, if not nearly all, of its attendant institutions and practices. The state, and by extension the states system, so this critique goes, is neither benign nor neutral in providing security for man or citizen. What is needed, then, as Ken Booth puts it, is a 'reassessment of the relationships that do and should exist between nations, states, classes, economic structures, international organizations, groups of one sort or another (of nations and people) and individuals'.[19] That sentiment, expressed at the end of the Cold War, is no less true today than it was then.

One of the most interesting and perhaps unexpected alternatives to emerge out of the reassessment inaugurated by the terrorist attacks on New York and Washington is that of empire. Indeed, the pages of leading newspapers and academic journals are now filled with talk of empire. So while John Ikenberry frets that 'America's nascent neoimperial grand strategy threatens to rend the fabric of the international community', Charles Krauthammer extols the virtues of America's preponderant power, which, he says, should be used 'unashamedly' to maintain American predominance for the good of the entire world.[20] But most surprising of all is the genuine enthusiasm expressed by various commentators for an idea that until very recently was invoked solely and unambiguously as a term of abuse. To tar something with the brush of empire was to impute hypocrisy, greed, and injustice of all sorts; and to call its name was to summon a sordid history of political domination, economic exploitation, and racial prejudice. Today, the idea of empire has gained a new found respectability, so much so, that in the pages of establishment journals like

Foreign Affairs we read self-confident pronouncements that 'a new imperial moment has arrived, and by virtue of its power America is bound to play the leading role'.[21] America, it is said with waxing conceit, is the new Rome; and to shore up this empire, as one neoconservative doyen puts it, Americans must learn 'to be more expansive in our goals and more assertive in their implementation'.[22]

There are compelling reasons to doubt that history has arrived at a 'new imperial moment' just as there are compelling reasons to doubt that America has embraced a 'neoimperial' grand strategy, not the least of which is that empire consists in something more than the possession of preponderant power and a willingness to use it to create a hegemonic world order for the good of the entire world.[23] The open world championed by a succession of American presidents, a world founded on democracy, human rights, and free market economy, discloses similarities to the liberal imperialism that once flourished during the nineteenth century, but it falls well short of even approximating something that looks like formal empire. America claims no lordship, that is, exclusive executive authority, throughout the entire world: jurisdiction over the *orbis terrarum* is not the aim of the Bush Doctrine or of American foreign policy generally. Nor does America aspire to rule an extended political association composed of various orders and sub-orders of peoples and territories, each of which enjoys limited independence, but which are subject to one legislative authority.[24]

Of course, it is certainly true that a kind of empire lies at the heart of America's founding myth. Americans have long regarded it as part of their unique place in the world to spread a set of uniquely true values that find concrete expression in a long train of historic documents and speeches – Declaration of Independence, Fourteen Points, Atlantic Charter, Truman Doctrine, and Ronald Reagan's denunciation of totalitarian evil before the British Parliament. George W. Bush's national security strategy, a declaration of values and purposes that places America firmly on the side of the 'forces of freedom', provides only the most recent proof of this deeply ingrained habit of mind. But it is very difficult indeed to distinguish this kind of informal empire – if it is to be called that – from the institution of great power responsibility or what in some quarters appears as little more than heavy-handed bullying. In fact, if George Bush's vision of the world were ever realized it would look rather more like Immanuel Kant's pacific federation of republics than an empire of any sort.

But if our world it to be understood in the idiom of empire it is a kind of *imperium* that is intelligible as a paramount knowledge which, in many respects, better illuminates the 'new imperial moment' than the political, economic, geographical relations that usually draw the name 'empire'. It is a knowledge, as Anthony Pagden explains the Roman origin of the term *imperium*, which confers on the world an identity of a particular sort. For citizens of Rome that knowledge was expressed in the form of law; and to know and to live by that law was to be a citizen of the world, outside of which resided 'barbarians' who, while ignorant of the law, could in principle be drawn into the world through some sort of instruction. Thus, the empire of Roman law joined all human beings, or at least potentially so, in what Dante described as a single community of knowledge that rendered intelligible a single (true) human civilization.[25]

In contemporary world affairs this single community of knowledge springs from an empire of security according to which the flourishing of civilization, and not merely its survival, depends fundamentally on security of various sorts. In other words, it is with reference to security, more so than any other idea or value, that international relations is interpreted; and to be 'in' our world is to understand what a condition of security involves, however it might be conceived. For without security all that is beneficial in individual and collective life, all art, all industry, all commerce, and all science, is condemned to a precarious, if not fleeting, existence. Indeed, the collapse of the World Trade Center's twin towers vindicates better than any abstract philosophical argument that security – the safety of the people – is exactly what Hobbes says it is: the supreme law.

Security in the web of language

It is in the context of the empire of security that the chapters in this volume interrogate the meaning of security as it is intelligible in some of the most important institutions and practices in contemporary world affairs. Thus, the chapters do not aim, individually or collectively, at bridging or, more ambitiously, at healing the schisms that leaven the academic field of security studies. No finding is advanced in the hope of distinguishing between the prolix and self-indulgent, as Stephen Walt once described postmodern approaches to security,[26] and the narrow and obsolete, as, for the lack of a more precise adjective, 'traditional' security studies are often described. Nor is any effort exerted in defining a word that is incurably resistant to definition, at least one that has pretensions of providing universal or objective meaning. Essentially contested concepts like security are not 'solved' in a way that suddenly renders them unproblematic. They are disentangled and then clarified in recognition of particular situations, the limits of which are defined, not by rules of logic or principles of reason, but by the peculiarities of a world that is home to both the collected wisdom of experience and the fitful course of fortune. And, finally, these chapters disclose no interest in erecting yet another temple to the study of security that will stand alongside Copenhagen, feminist, and several other 'security studies' neighbours. Indeed, they issue no manifesto for action, no programme for reform, and no call to pull down other temples, no matter what their limitations might be.

The underlying premise running through this volume holds that the meaning of security is substantively intelligible in relation to other ideas.

For the word 'security' is but an empty name when divorced from other ideas that are distinctive of international life. It is in this sense that the rather ambiguous relationship between security and self-determination, as James Mayall explains in Chapter 6, must be interpreted and thus made less so in light of limits imposed by human experience (p. 100). But this approach should not be taken to mean that security is anything we wish it to be; that ascribing meaning is merely a matter of private judgement that in some way or other merely reflects the interests of power disguised by a mask of race, gender, class, or some other attribute. Language is surely central in constituting the meaning of security and issues are certainly 'securitized' through the use of language, but giving meaning in speech acts must amount to something more than what J. R. Lucas describes as a doctrine of linguistic 'squatters' rights'. Language, he argues, 'is as much a web as a lot of labels, and the words "free" and "responsible" gain their meaning as much from their relation to other words and phrases as from the occasions of their use'.[27] The meaning of 'security', like that of 'free' and 'responsible', is also intelligible in relation to other words and phrases; it is intelligible in relation to other ideas that are distinctive of international life, such as sovereignty, diplomacy, war, great powers, and, more recently, globalization. In other words, each of these ideas proposes a peculiar understanding of how human beings might attain a contingent but nonetheless tangible condition called 'security'.

An approach that treats security as a relational idea, the substantive meaning of which is given in the unfathomable genius as well as the sobering limits of human experience, looks beyond the limitations of a 'security studies' that in so many ways is fixed on and therefore confounded by the 'whose security?' question. Several 'new' or 'alternative' perspectives have attempted to answer this question by stressing the importance of individuals as the ultimate referents of security; and they in turn are served with periodic reminders, underwritten by events like September 11, which rehearse a well-known refrain: 'when it comes to the safety of the people it is still states and coercive power that matter most'. The chapters in this volume take no definitive position in either the 'state' or the 'individual' camp, or, for that matter, anything in between. Of course, they evince an interest in many of the same issues that animate the academic field of security studies but the insights they offer are not derived from security studies debates. Instead, these chapters offer a series of different ways of thinking about security with a view to taking some preliminary steps toward separating what is new from what is presented as new. They look to where past meets present and present meets future in reflecting on how we might think about security in a world that is often portrayed as being unable to bear the increasing weight of change. In other words, this collection of chapters probes the extent to which some of the most important institutions and practices of the so-called Westphalian international political order still have anything useful to tell us about the meaning of security in contemporary world affairs.

Taken together, the chapters presented in this volume return what can only be described as an open verdict. Robert Jackson's chapter on sovereignty takes as its point of departure the proposition that the safety of the people begins with safety from other people, the most important historical arrangement of which – at least for several centuries – is the sovereign state. Thus, against Hobbesian scepticism and Kantian universalism, he defends an intermediate course that sees security as something of a joint enterprise in which states undertake legal and moral obligations pertaining to the preservation of political independence and the limitation of the use of force. In this family of nations, or 'anarchical society' to put it in international relations theory terminology, sovereignty attends to the safety of the people by providing the basis for national as well as international security. In other words, the sovereign state is one of the most important historical responses to the reality that 'people must live among each other, but not everybody can be counted on to live in peace' (p. 17).

Holsti raises some difficult questions for this relation of sovereignty and security in a chapter that paints two opposing 'portraits' of contemporary war. Whereas the first conveys an image of war as a regulated engagement in which protagonists kill in order to win, the second conveys an image of war as an indiscriminate enterprise in which the pursuit of (limited) political objectives is cast aside in favour of a different doctrine: winning in order to kill. The human destruction wrought by this second kind of war – a new kind of war that is rather better described as organized thuggery than war properly so-called – leads Holsti to conclude that the classical (international) vocabulary of war, which is intelligible in the discourse of state sovereignty, may be somewhat out of date. Thus, it may be necessary, he continues, to resuscitate or restore states afflicted by 'wars of national debilitation' by resorting to armed force 'in a manner quite distinct from the ethics of traditional peacekeeping operations (p. 58).'

Sasson Sofer tells a similarly conflicted story about the search for security and the institution of diplomacy. The diplomat must chart a course through the perilous shoals where obligation and interest meet, and without ever losing sight that it is an ethics of responsibility, rather than one of conviction, which must carry the day. Absolutism of all sorts is alien to the diplomatic craft, which eschews the glory of triumph for the durability of a negotiated peace that reflects an accommodation of interests. Less clear, though, is how far the virtues of classical diplomacy can be adapted, as it has been in the past, to address questions of security in contemporary world affairs. Sofer laments the mixed blessing of an expanded definition of security, for the long list of threats that are a part of the human security agenda may well be the greasy stuff that loosens the diplomat's grip on the pole of peace. More worrying still is the implication that the *dignitas* of the diplomatic craft – tolerance, self-limitation, and prudence – may have no place at all in at least some parts of the world.

Indeed, where winning in order to kill is the objective of war there is no need for the moderating hand of diplomacy: there is no peace to make.

Cathal J. Nolan examines the relation of security and the great powers, which, in spite of a doctrine of 'radical state equality' that emerged in the rush to decolonization, still form 'the axis around which world history and international relations turns' (p. 71). Consequently, questions of security are answered with reference to the interests and values of these firsts among equals for no other reason than power is still the paramount currency of international relations. Nolan argues that a new international security ethic inaugurated by the United States has evolved into a 'rough consensus around a modified liberal-internationalist view, a more prudent Wilsonianism, which sees long-term national and international security as best achieved by progress toward a confederation of interdependent, free societies' (p. 85). However, the greatest threat to this consensus stems, not from an America invigorated by a muscular foreign policy of 'regime change', but from an autocratic Russia and an enigmatic China. Nolan concludes by arguing that it is the primary obligation of these Asian giants, as it is of all great powers, to put their houses in order and thereby spare the world the calamities that usually accompany the decay and eventual collapse of 'terminally illegitimate regimes' (p. 89).

James Mayall takes up the relation of security and what has been the seductive and often pyrrhic midwife of small states: self-determination. These most potent of ideas, he argues, suggest that the safety of the people is intelligible in a contest between an ever-present 'fear of danger and desire for freedom' (p. 94). However, neither realist nor liberal theories provide a lasting, much less satisfactory, answer to the insecurity experienced by many of the world's nations, peoples, and minorities. Both proceed from common assumption that the search for security runs through the moral and material autonomy that comes with statehood. Indeed, Mayall argues that the necessarily indeterminate meaning of security, as well as that of self-determination, rules out any possibility of resolving such an answer, 'even in principle' (p. 95). For the elixir of insecurity that is self-determination – security guaranteed through the recognition of collective identity – is something more like an alchemist's formula for participatory government as well as pathological nationalism. In other words, self-determination has been no less a source of insecurity than security. Whichever the case, though, Mayall argues that we would do well to remember that 'the nation state, nationalism and the principle of national self-determination describe the political architecture of the modern world and its social and legal justification' (p. 106).

Cornelia Navari considers the challenge that globalization presents to traditional 'statist' approaches to thinking about security. In a borderless world, where people, ideas, and capital move freely about the globe, there is no 'us and them' when it comes to security. The safety of the people means the safety of all the world's people as indivisible threats demand an indivisible security. But Navari expresses considerable doubt that some-thing called 'globalization' tells us very much about security in contemporary world affairs. She acknowledges that the discourse of glob-alization points to a very different kind of security; it asks us to think our-selves away from hidebound notions of state security and toward 'human security' or one of its many analogues. However, less certain is the extent to which security-related issues, such as ethnic conflict, environmental degradation, and the retreat of the state, have much to do with actual processes of globalization. Thus, Navari suggests that it may be necessary to abandon the bridge of globalization theory 'if security theory is to address the normative issues involved in contemporary security practices, or guide us to the requisites of a new, possibly more desirable, set of secur-ity structures' (p. 137).

Jennifer Jackson Preece looks inside states in order to question a paradox that arises when the values of freedom and belonging collide. Whereas freedom entails autonomy of action, belonging entails subordi-nating unfettered action to the requirements of life in society. It is here that paradox gives way to dilemma: the uniformity of belonging may greet the diversity of freedom with suspicion or, worse, hostility. For Jackson Preece this paradox-cum-dilemma points to a tension in the international society approach to security, which, on the one hand, promotes diversity between states and, on the other hand, suppresses diversity within states that threatens the preservation of international order. Neither a doctrine of national security, which subordinates cultural diversity to the supremacy of civic identity, nor human security, which embraces a human rights approach that takes no notice of the diversity exhibited by groups, provides an escape from this dilemma. Instead, Jackson Preece looks to a multicultural approach to security, the underlying claim of which suggests that 'minorities who are recognized and supported by the state, and by extension international society, are far less likely to challenge existing modes of authority' (p. 153).

Sir Adam Roberts explores changes in the practice of intervention, especially the changed language of intervention that is often interpreted as providing evidence of a fundamental conflict between ethics and law. This conflict is usually expressed in terms of progressive ethical sensibili-ties outpacing staid and unnecessarily conservative conventions of inter-national law, which, in turn, is pressed into service to describe some interventions as illegal but morally justified. Roberts rejects this view of things in suggesting that intervention is as much a problem within inter-national law as it is a problem between law and ethics. Indeed, he goes on to argue that a disjunction between different branches of international law, one which addresses prohibitions on the use of force and another which addresses human rights and humanitarian law, means that law may not provide definitive answers to questions probing the legitimacy of particular interventions. Roberts proposes instead an approach that abandons the enterprise of working out a general legal right of intervention for one which charts a course between conflicting legal obligations by recognizing the precedent of a 'slowly emerging and occasional practice of intervention' (p. 184). It is then possible to ground thinking about intervention against the background of a still valid and ethically valuable norm of non-intervention and yet avoid embracing an absolute prohibition against intervention that also involves jettisoning an important part of the legal and ethical inheritance of contemporary international society. For in spite of the enthusiasm evoked by the new language of 'international community', 'human security', and 'responsibility to protect', Roberts argues that 'old realities have endured: military interventions remain problematic and controversial' (p. 159).

William Bain contests the portrayal of trusteeship as merely a 'humanitarian' enterprise that follows intervention in considering the revival of some form of internationally-led tutelage as an arrangement of international and human security. Criticism of trusteeship, especially the kind which condemns what are often described as the pious but disingenuous platitudes of imperial trusteeship, typically proceeds from the supposition that obligation and interest are in some way incommensurable. In short, the claims of personal or human security, so it is alleged, inevitably succumb to the interests of a selfish and narrow doctrine of national security. Bain challenges this view in arguing trusteeship has been justified historically in a way that brings the claims of individuals and those of states into a condition of harmony. One of the most influential statements of this view, Lord Lugard's 'dual mandate', expressed the alignment of seemingly conflicting claims in terms of a reciprocal relationship that joined trustee and ward in common purpose, so that it was possible to say that the exploitation of the natural wealth of Africa should benefit Europeans and Africans alike. More recently the alignment of human security and national security was expanded to include international security, as the preservation of 'international peace and security' was included among the purposes of the now defunct United Nations trusteeship system. However, Bain concludes by arguing that the resurrection of trusteeship as an arrangement of security involves overturning the normative settlement that emerged out of decolonization, 'a settlement that for better or worse accepts the advice offered by Satan in Milton's *Paradise Lost*: "Better to reign in hell than serve in Heaven"' (p. 203).

The society of states is often described as a conspicuously conservative association that prefers the maintenance of international order to schemes aimed at remaking the world in the image of perfect justice. It should be clear that the chapters presented in this volume show a different face, one that is neither a reactionary defence of a Westphalian order that begins and ends with states, nor a declaration that liberates abstract individuals from the heavy-hand of equally abstract states. Instead, they engage a world marked by obvious change without exaggerating either its scope or significance. For the world is never entirely new, despite the popularity of prophecies and proclamations that are the stuff of academic trends, just as it is never entirely like the past, no matter how we might long for the nostalgia of a golden age when all seemed to be right. So while it may be true that many of the practices and institutions of classical international society are being challenged in fundamental ways, it is rather premature to announce their obsolescence, much less their imminent death. Indeed, questions of security are posed in such a way that the familiar, though not necessarily unproblematic, is still intelligible in the nods, winks, and brute force of power politics. However, these chapters make it equally clear that the answers to these questions lay in a great deal more than a world portrayed in nothing but the image of power politics. In other words, reflecting on the safety of the people in contemporary world affairs calls forth a story that is necessarily incomplete without the society of states, but which is also fundamentally about the hopes, aspirations, and, of course, fears of ordinary men and women.

Notes

1 Hobbes (1998), p. 143.
2 See Waltz (1979), pp. 90–1.
3 Hobbes (1998), p. 143.
4 Hobbes (1998), p. 144.
5 See generally Hobbes (1998), Chapter XIII.
6 See Buzan (1991), p. 363 and especially Chapters 1–3.
7 George (2003), p. 443.
8 Smith (2000), p. 74.
9 See Buzan *et al.* (1998); and Waever (2000), pp. 250–8.
10 See Tickner (1992), Chapter 2 and Enloe (1990).
11 See Booth (1991a), p. 319; and Booth (2005), pp. 1–18. For an extended discussion of the critical theory approach to security see Wyn Jones (1999), pp. 92–123.
12 See Campbell (1992), pp. 2–12.
13 For a survey of the intellectual landscape of security studies see Smith (2005), pp. 27–62.
14 Krause and Williams (1996), p. 249.
15 Buzan (1991), p. 7; and Smith (2005), pp. 27–8.
16 Gallie (1968), p. 188.
17 Kissinger (2001), p. 2.
18 Annan (2000), p. 43.
19 Booth (1991), p. 340.
20 Ikenberry (2002), p. 45; and Krauthammer (2002), p. 17.
21 Mallaby (2002), p. 6.
22 Boot (2001). On the comparison with Rome see Bacevich (2002), p. 244; and Nye (2002), p. 1.
23 For contrasting view see Cox (2003), pp. 1–27.
24 See Pagden (1995), Chapter 1.
25 Pagden (1995), pp. 19–26.
26 Walt (1991), p. 223.
27 Lucas (1967), p. 163.

2 'The safety of the people is the supreme law'

Beyond Hobbes but not as far as Kant

Robert Jackson

In this chapter I attempt to understand the ways in which the norms of security and sovereignty are entangled with the aim of learning more about the international ethics of security.[1] I shall be primarily interested in an important body of reflections to be found in the history of political thought, particularly the realist thought of Thomas Hobbes, the pluralist ideas of some contemporary Grotians, and the cosmopolitanism of Immanuel Kant. Together these thinkers indicate that security and sovereignty are fundamentally normative subjects, which, in turn, raise several equally important questions about contemporary world affairs. What operative ethics are involved in a claim of security? How should we account for the relationship between the ethics of security and the legal institution of state sovereignty? Are safe and secure social conditions conceivable beyond the territorial control of sovereign states? These questions, and a few others like them, provide a cue to the direction of this chapter.

Security discourse

The discourse of security is closely involved with that of sovereignty. To grasp correctly that relationship, it is necessary to put the vocabulary of ordinary language to work in our inquiries. No technical vocabulary, such as social scientists are prone to invent, can be an adequate substitute. 'Security' is derived from the Latin *securitas*, which means freedom from care or safety.[2] The word passed into the Romance languages, then into English, with that core meaning entirely intact.

The historical appearance of security discourse in Western languages, as recorded in dictionaries, parallels the rise of the modern state and states system. For the character of complex social organizations – and sovereign states are such organizations – is expressed in a corresponding vocabulary, without which political life is simply not possible. The English language is a rich repository of terminology used to speak and write of such matters. In other words, there is a family of ordinary words and expressions that communicate the essentially human and social world of security: 'safety', 'protection', 'guard', 'shield', 'safeguard', 'defence', 'keep vigil', 'keep watch over', 'guardian', 'protector', 'sentinel', 'sentry', 'under the protection of', 'out of harm's reach', and 'out of danger', among others.

The most important signification of 'security', according to the *Oxford English Dictionary*, is the *condition* 'of being protected from or not exposed to danger'. A condition of 'security' signifies *being* 'free from care, apprehension or anxiety, or alarm', which is 'a feeling of safety or freedom from or absence of danger'. It can also refer to *acts of making* a person or place or country safe from danger or harm: to implement security measures, to render safe, to protect or shelter from harm, 'to guard against some particular danger', to defend. It can refer, as well, to the *means* of protection. In speaking of actions and means we are of course referring to the policies and provisions of security, including especially those which are connected with the sovereign state, such as security policy, police forces, and defence forces. Most of these meanings of 'secure' and 'security' were already well established in the ideas and practices of the sixteenth and seventeenth centuries.

The crux of security for our purposes is captured by Hedley Bull, whose argument is entirely consistent with established English usage: 'Security in international politics means no more than safety: either objective safety, safety which actually exists, or subjective safety, that which is felt or experienced.'[3] Safety is shelter and assurance in our relations with other people. People make themselves safe by establishing armed forces, diplomatic contacts, and other arrangements that are geared to their protection. The protectors stand guard, they give people shelter, and they keep them out of harm's way. The opposite of safety is the condition of being vulnerable to danger, which is created when some wilful and capable people, whether individuals or groups or states, are determined to have their way. This condition of insecurity is addressed when those potentially or actually threatening others are deterred or turned back. Their ill will and power is curbed by our warnings and defences: we put locks on our doors, we build walls and fortifications around the city, and we create police forces and armed forces.

The idea of security does not call to mind something that is natural: it does not exist in the nature of things. People are not armadillos. They are not equipped with natural defences. People create security for themselves and for others: it is entirely a human artifice. People make themselves safe from nature, for example, by wearing protective clothing or building shelter to protect against the elements. But this chapter is concerned with security as a social and political condition: safety from people. People devise their own security or they entrust that responsibility to others, usually a government. Arranging security for people is one of the most fundamental political acts; and establishing and maintaining conditions under which a populace can be safe has long been understood as a *raison d'être* of the sovereign state. Here, we arrive at the core of security in political thought.

The condition of insecurity does not merely happen. It is not a great storm that gathers and breaks. It is brought about by dangerous or menacing people, either individuals or groups (including states) who are not prepared to live in peace and harmony with their neighbours. The inclinations and actions of such people carry the possibility of harm or injury or damage to other persons, families, or possessions; and in the worst case scenario human societies may be ruined and lives destroyed. Such losses, usually associated with wars or the absence of authoritative and effective government, are the most severe that anyone can suffer: they spell destruction, misery, and death. The formulation of security policy implies that there are always likely to be some individuals or groups or countries that will menace us and thus give us a reason to be apprehensive and fearful. Security policy is an attempt to address this problem.

The condition of security also does not merely happen. It does not dawn like a warm and bright summer day. It is made that way by people who are attuned to the presence of other people who might pose or actually do pose a danger. A safe place is protected from such dangers: it is forewarned and forearmed.[4] A safe city or a secure nation is one that takes precautions to address the dangers presented by other individuals or groups or states who cannot be trusted to be peaceful and law-abiding *but among whom we must live*. The well-organized and well-equipped sovereign state, which is forewarned and forearmed, is the usual political–military means by which such protection has been arranged historically.

The language of security discloses a fundamental reality about the human condition, namely that people must live among each other, but not everybody can be counted on to live in peace. If people no longer experienced insecurity or felt insecure they would have no reason to speak and write about it so that the vocabulary of security would presumably fall into disuse. That clearly is not the case at the present time. Will there ever be a time when swords and spears will be turned into metaphorical ploughshares and pruning hooks whereby it will no longer be necessary to take precautions in order to be secure? On any realistic view of human relations – past, present, and future – the answer to this question is most probably 'no'. For the discourse of security suggests that safe conditions must be created and maintained on a regular and continuous basis by the efforts and expenses and measures of the people and governments involved.

In the modern era security has been established via the sovereign state and has become most closely identified with it. Modern people look to the state and count on the state, more than any other organization, to generate and to maintain the social condition of safety. That close relation between security and the sovereign state is a basic and, indeed, defining feature of the modern world.[5] It has captured the attention of outstanding political thinkers of the past 400 years among whom the foremost is Thomas Hobbes.

Hobbes on security and sovereignty

This chapter began with Hobbes' pronouncement: '*The safety of the people is the supreme law*' (emphasis in original).[6] Hobbes is expressing what he considers to be the fundamental justification of law and the state. Safety is the foundation of human society: 'governments were formed for the sake of peace, and peace is sought for safety'.[7] Thus, security is the fundamental human value; and in its absence, or when it is in doubt, human life is more difficult and the possibilities of making something of one's life, either individually or collectively, are greatly diminished. War is the greatest of all sources of insecurity and peace is the greatest of all political ends. Indeed, Hobbes' understanding of the subject is 'deeply pacific' as Hedley Bull rightly emphasizes.[8] Building and maintaining the foundations of a safe society are among the most important 'duties of rulers': 'The sovereign as such provides for the citizens' safety only by means of laws.'[9] Hobbes is of course referring to laws in the deepest meaning as binding and enforceable obligations; and he is also referring to laws in the broadest meaning as the office of authority for their enactment, administration, and enforcement – the sovereign state. By 'the people' he means the civil subjects of an order of law called a sovereign state. In other words, the sovereign state is a protected sphere where people can live and hopefully flourish in peace.

If safety is in fact fundamental to human well-being, and if the enactment, administration, and enforcement of law is conducive to safety, then the law must be supreme and it must be obeyed. The law derives its authority not only from the contractual agreement of the population to obey but also from its contribution to the people's safety. Following that normative reasoning, the creation of civil peace and the provision of security on the basis of state sovereignty is a moral and legal undertaking of a fundamental kind. According to this well-established reasoning security is the *raison d'être* of organized political life, for without security the fruits of human society will not be available. What are states for in the final analysis, if not for creating and defending peaceful conditions under which people may flourish in their own way?[10] Indeed, defence and peace are necessary conditions for the pursuit of happiness; and the primary responsibilities of rulers, according to Hobbes, is to defend against external enemies and to preserve internal peace. That, or something like it, is Hobbes' justification of the sovereign state (emphasis in original):

> By *safety* one should understand not mere survival in any condition, but a happy life so far as that is possible. For men willingly entered commonwealths *which they had formed by design [institutivus]* in order to be able to live as pleasantly as the human condition allows.[11]

These political responsibilities remain fundamentally unchanged.

If we are to understand security as an ethical subject we have to determine what norms are involved that make it so. I think it is reasonable to agree with Hobbes that security is a good in itself as well as being conducive to other goods, especially the good life – a life that makes happiness attainable. Security clearly is in our interests. We would be wise to create and maintain the social conditions of security. But if it is only a matter of interest and intelligence it is not yet fully an ethical subject: the considerations involved would be limited to the rules of skill that go by the name 'prudence'. That is the usual way that security is conceived by social scientists and policy analysts. If it is a right and a responsibility it is a fully ethical subject. However, if security is a right, what sort of right is it? And who has a right to security? The same questions can be asked of security as a responsibility.

It seems intuitively correct that we should consider the desire for security as the sort of concern and action for which any intelligent and prudent person would wish. It also seems consistent with history and experience. A concern for safety arises readily in our perception of the situations in which we find ourselves as persons living among others of our own kind. Anybody who is unconcerned or careless in situations of perceived or actual danger would seem to be either over-confident, to the point of hubris, or perhaps reckless and certainly foolish. So it would clearly seem that security is a matter of intelligence. It would be intelligent to take precautions to defend ourselves against the reality, or even the possibility, of human predators in our neighbourhood. It is intelligent and indeed wise to recognize that we have an interest in being secure. That would be to read correctly our vulnerable human situation. But is that all? Arguably not. Some of the most significant questions about security as a value start where social science and policy analysis usually end.

Hobbes argues that security is not only a matter of intelligent awareness of real or perceived threats; nor is it merely a matter of prudential anticipation and establishing effective arrangements to meet those threats. Security is also a right, and, more specifically, it is a *natural* right of every human being that admits no exception. By invoking the language of rights Hobbes gives an account of security that is intelligible as a fully ethical subject. All men, in virtue of being men, possess 'the *right to use any means and to do any action by which he can preserve himself*' (emphasis in original.[12] This right applies in relations with other individuals, as well as other states, who pose a security threat. So, in a situation of danger in which one's security and survival are at stake, there is a natural right of self-defence, which is one of the most fundamental ethical propositions of human relations – including international relations.

According to Hobbes, it is reasonable to transfer our means of defence to a protector, to some man or assembly of men, who can more adequately provide for our safety than we can manage to do either individually or in collaboration with some personal allies.[13] The protector will henceforth be entrusted with the people's security. To have such a heavy responsibility the protector must be endowed with both the means of security and the authority to exercise such means. The protector must possess supreme command: *terminus ultimus*, sovereignty.[14] This absolute power, crudely stated, forms the basis of the argument Hobbes advances in respect of the social contract.

The protector is the sovereign ruler who, by this political arrangement, acquires the '*sword of justice*' or 'the right of punishing' to ensure domestic peace and the '*sword of war*' or the right to 'compel citizens to take up arms' to ensure national defence (emphasis in original).[15] Hobbes also speaks of the duties of rulers to safeguard the people – something he understands as a fundamental responsibility.[16] To that end the sovereign is conceived as possessing special rights, including the right to make rules, the right to judge, the right to inflict penalties, and the right to command. Moreover,

> it is important for peace and defence that those who have the responsibility to give just judgements of disputes, to detect the Designs of neighbouring states, to conduct wars prudently and to look out for the commonwealth's interests all around, should perform their duties properly.[17]

The ruler must be the sole judge because otherwise controversies and quarrels will ensue which could lead to insecurity and ultimately war. Thus, the social contract establishes the sovereign state on a foundation of morality and legality, not merely intelligent or rational policy, which is absolutely binding on all parties involved in its operation.

Hobbes could not conceive of reliable defence and civil peace under conditions in which citizens, either as individuals or as groups, retained weapons for their own security. To do so would give them excessive independence which might result in civil disturbances or perhaps even a catastrophic collapse into another state of nature. The provision of security depended fundamentally on the state having a lawful monopoly on the means and use of force. Thus, he could not accept that any other body should possess the right to wage war, as in medieval times when popes and certain other clergy, secular rulers besides kings, and some professions – i.e. knights – enjoyed such a right. Had Hobbes lived to witness it, we well might wonder if he would hold the same view of the United States Constitution, which guarantees the citizen's right to bear arms?

Of course the sovereign state is not distinctive from other modern organizations by making use of personnel, finances, technology, equipment, buildings, and other facilities to carry out its varied responsibilities. National governments have grown in parallel with the growth of these capacities and organizations of their civil societies. But where the sovereign state is distinctive and indeed unique, at least in normative terms, is in its *authorized monopoly* of certain means of power, the most important of which are military force to defend against external enemies and police power to enforce the law and uphold civil peace. Max Weber thought this was the only basis for a coherent definition of the state.[18] Thus, a modern sovereign state 'gives no recognition to private armies',[19] as Michael Oakeshott puts it, or to any other armed organization or agent that could wage war within its own jurisdiction and thereby defeat the fundamental point of the entire scheme of sovereign statehood, which is ordered to the safety of the people.

The requirement of disarming people as a necessary step for creating a civil society has been the usual way in the political development of Europe and North America over the past several centuries. Security is commonly a responsibility of the highest priority. A concern for the stability of civil society, the safety of citizens, and the security of their property is an over-riding preoccupation of the criminal law in states that are worthy of the name. Even in countries that recognize a right of citizens to possess weapons, such as the United States (US), there is no doubt about the state's absolute supremacy when it comes to civil peace and domestic safety. As regards national security, that norm usually pre-empts other basic norms of the state, including cherished norms of liberty. For the pre-emptive character of the value of security is such that persons deemed to be a threat to national security may be subject to laws and regulations that override normal legal protections or constitutional rights. This view of security is in keeping with Hobbes' conception of sedition and treason as crimes of war, as opposed to civil offences, whereby citizens who engage in such acts are at war with their own state (emphasis in origins):

> *rebels, traitors,* and all others convicted of *treason,* are punished not by *civil right,* but by *natural right,* i.e. not as *bad citizens,* but as *enemies of the commonwealth,* and not by the *right of government* or dominion, but by the *right of war.*[20]

Security is the normative kernel of state sovereignty; and it is reasonable and accurate to say that on the back of this basic proposition the entire project of sovereign statehood either succeeds or fails as a political and legal arrangement that can provide for the good life. To look upon sovereign states as no more than instrumental arrangements, which of course they are in part, is to ignore their fundamentally important moral and legal foundations. Indeed, this relation of security and sovereignty, which shows a normative as well as an instrumental face, is not far removed from the historical practices of sovereign states which are worthy of the name. For most stable and effective sovereign states have managed to organize themselves and operate on exactly this basis over lengthy periods of time.

Curiously, though, some Western states no longer seem to justify themselves on that basis. The core of these so-called postmodern states[21] would appear to be their liberalism or their democracy rather than their sovereignty. But this view of statehood, while fashionable, is misleading. Liberal states were sovereign before they became liberal or democratic. And in becoming liberal, and subsequently democratic, these states never gave up their sovereignty as it is classically understood. Today, as in the past, these states have the sword of justice and the sword of war at the ready. It may not seem that way during fair weather times of peace and prosperity, but history provides regular reminders that when the great calamities of political life gather and break, for example international wars or civil wars, Western liberal democracies once again show their sovereign character. Successful and enduring liberal democracies are not careless with the security of their people. Even during long periods of uninterrupted peace the Hobbesian sovereign is at the ready to deal with contingencies that might disrupt the peace. This is the foundation of the civil condition, and whatever constitutional forms states take, they are built on these foundations because there are no viable alternatives.

The argument advanced by Hobbes presupposes a condition more fundamental than liberal democracy. For it views democracy, and all other forms of political constitution, as a tottering house built on unsafe ground when separated from the security that comes with effective and lawful government.[22] Indeed, the insight and wisdom of Hobbes' argument has been borne out time and again, typically with catastrophic consequences, by the experience of many African countries since independence. Britain in particular was determined to endow colonies destined for independence with democratic constitutions prior to the transfer of sovereignty. This was not a trivial exercise. It involved considerable thought, planning, effort, and expense.[23] Yet in almost every former British African colony, newly minted democratic constitutions were repudiated and discarded in the covetous and often vicious rush for spoils and power by the new leaders after independence.[24] Unfortunately, the troubled historical record of democracy outside the West more often than not bears witness to that failure of civil politics – e.g. in Central and Eastern Europe between the two world wars of the twentieth century; in Latin America in the nineteenth and twentieth centuries; in Africa and the Middle East since decolonization; and in Russia and some other parts of the former Soviet Union since the end of the Cold War.

The constitutional form that governments may take is of course an important concern, but it is a secondary consideration when compared to the primary concern of having an effective and lawful government in the first place. Without a foundation of security and order, no constitution, democratic or otherwise, can be safeguarded for long. That is a fundamental insight of Hobbes' political thought. Some may object to what appears as a recommendation of an authoritarian form of government. However, his concern for the safety of people and his preoccupation with the blessings of peace cannot lead to that conclusion. He calls for authoritative rather than authoritarian government; that is, government that is both capable and responsible.

Hobbes is preoccupied above all else with safeguarding domestic peace and protecting against war, especially civil war. Peace is the social condition that is most necessary for a flourishing society and, indeed, for a stable political life, where the activity of politics is understood as an alternative to war and as a way of resolving public disagreements and disputes. And the only reliable and trustworthy peace is a civil peace upheld by sovereign authority and power. Indeed, Hobbes points out that 'the greatest [adversity] that ... can possibly happen to the people in general', under the sovereign arrangements he recommends, 'is scarcely sensible in respect of the miseries, and horrible calamities, that accompany a civil war, or that dissolute condition of masterless men, without subjection to laws, and a coercive power to tie their hands from rapine and revenge'.[25] And while Hobbes is concerned with the problem of war generally, he is intent on spelling out the dangers and horrors of civil war above all other conflicts, which destroys the only dependable basis of safety: civil peace.

Security is a fundamental justification of state sovereignty, and the connection between the two is, fundamentally, a legal and moral connection. Sovereignty is the principal way that security has been arranged in world affairs for the past several centuries. State sovereignty is about people looking after themselves in a certain political and military way. It is a self-help arrangement. Sovereigns are duty-bound to provide for the security of the people, and, in turn, the people are duty-bound to obey the sovereign's commands for the sake of that purpose. And if a sovereign government fails to provide for the safety of the people or if the subjects obstruct the sovereign in discharging this duty, they will both be in violation of the supreme law, which for Hobbes is the greatest political sin.

The Grotians on international society

In the Hobbesian scheme of things the possibility of lodging responsibility for security in the relations of states is simply ruled out. A sovereign state is portrayed as a free-standing and self-reliant security enterprise arranged by the government and citizens of a certain territory (and by nobody else) to ensure internal peace and external defence. Security is far too important a value to be entrusted to outsiders. The external standing of sovereign states is that of proud liberty in a state of nature, the outward posture of which is that of 'gladiators; having their weapons pointed, and their eyes fixed on one another'.[26] In contrast, peace is a domestic condition. War can only be subdued and peace guaranteed, with some degree of permanency, *within* sovereign states. But these states cannot establish peace between themselves on a sufficiently solid basis that would inspire confidence in its permanency – they can only obtain such a peace by dissolving themselves and establishing a larger sovereign state in their place. Thus, a system of states presupposes a perpetual condition of war in the absence of an international sovereign that can command the awe and obedience of all its members.

The creation of an international sovereign by way of a social contract among states provides no escape from this state of perpetual war; however, 'there does not follow from it that misery, which accompanies the liberty of particular men'.[27] Owing to the enormous difference between a solitary state and a solitary person – the one being self-sufficient, the other not – there is no compelling reason for states to leave the international state of nature by entering into a covenant with other states. International anarchy is burdensome and demanding but it is also tolerable and manageable. Conversely, domestic anarchy – grim, unrelenting, and ultimately intolerable – compels the creation of the civil state. It is in this context that Hedley Bull writes:

> states may face one another in the posture of gladiators, but the lives of the men in them are not solitary, and not necessarily poor, nasty, brutish, or short. On the contrary, the sovereign powers which, facing outward, create the international anarchy are the same sovereign powers which, facing inward, provide the possibility of social life.[28]

These states are of course at liberty to enter into mutual assistance pacts and to collaborate in other ways to bolster their security. But expedient relations and arrangements between states merely disclose and express the character of the international state of nature. Sovereign governments alone decide what is good and bad, right and wrong, in their relations with other such governments, and such judgements are determined entirely from their own perspective. In other words, there are no *international* ethics properly so-called in the world portrayed by Hobbes. Governments are duty-bound to make that decision by themselves and with the safety of their own people foremost in their minds. However, they are not duty-bound to deliberate in concert with other states and with the safety of their people in mind. The safety of people in other countries is the exclusive and solitary responsibility of their respective sovereign governments.

The purely expedient character of interstate relations means that Hobbes would not regard international law as true law because there is no sovereign armed with the sword of justice and the sword of war to enforce it: *inter arma silent leges*, between armies the law is silent. The '*law of nations*' is part of the *lex naturalis*, which prescribes maxims of prudential conduct rather than law properly so-called.[29] Hobbes sees diplomacy in exactly the same way: it is an expedient means by which sovereigns deal with other sovereigns that have their own interests and desires, some of which cannot be ignored, and therefore demand attention. Diplomacy is not conceived as an institution with special codes of conduct for establishing international comity. The norms of the diplomatic craft, such as the immunity of embassies from the host sovereign, are also part of the *lex naturalis*, which counsels: '*Mediators of Peace should have immunity*' (emphasis in original).[30] In this sort of world states have a strong sense of their own good, but they have a much weaker sense of the good of other states, if only because they do not see themselves as morally and legally bound together.

But in the Grotian way of thinking, it is reasonable and indeed necessary to insist that sovereign states can form associations that enhance their security and which involve legal and moral obligations. This approach is frequently identified by the label 'international society', a conception of international relations as a '*societas quasi politica et moralis*': 'a political and moral quasi-society'.[31] The members of this international society recognize one another as having a valid existence and as being entitled to due consideration. They observe customary international law and they address at least some of their security concerns through international treaties that entail mutual obligations. They interact with regard to accepted international standards of conduct and not merely for reasons of national expediency. They conduct their diplomatic relations with regard to the rights and legitimate interests of foreign governments – including those less powerful than them. International agreements involve undertakings by states to respect each other's sovereign jurisdiction. And there is a genuine law of war that is enforceable, at least up to a point.

For Grotians, sovereign states are juridical entities that are normatively tied to each other by mutual recognition, by common acknowledgement of procedural rules, and by shared interests and concerns. States are independent but not solitary entities. They have relations which exhibit sociality and even consanguinity – in so far as many states are the offspring of other states; for example, the US is the formerly rebellious but now very grown-up and supportive child of Great Britain. Thus, the Grotian view of international relations stresses the importance of characteristics captured in the expression 'family of nations'. Grotians concede that international relations sometimes retreat into being little more than a bare (Hobbesian) *system* based almost entirely on expedient calculations and actions of states. But they also claim that international relations at other times take on the civil characteristics of a *society*, which are manifested in reciprocal rights and responsibilities of member states. Sovereign states can bind themselves to each other without surrendering their sovereignty. Comity and reciprocity can obtain between states that deal with each other, not only as expediency dictates, but also as international morality and legality require. Indeed, international law and diplomatic practice provide evidence of such bonds as opposed to fair weather arrangements to be abandoned at the first sign of difficulty or discomfort. In short, then, international anarchy can be a society of states: an anarchical society.[32]

The Grotian doctrine of international society understands states as legal persons that recognize each other as *valid* political orders.[33]

Recognition is an acknowledgement of juridical personality that can be claimed, granted, withheld, or withdrawn from persons or states. This notion was already evident in the sixteenth century as an aspect of the more general legal and moral idea of 'acknowledging' that a person or country is 'entitled to consideration' or is worthy of approval or regard. To 'recognize' another is 'to acknowledge by special notice, approval or sanction; to treat as valid, as having existence or as entitled to consideration'. At first international recognition did not necessarily imply either equality or independence as different degrees and orders of states were recognized. Acts of recognition usually accompanied peace settlements at the end of wars. By the nineteenth century recognition was a highly formal practice of international law that involved 'the explicit acknowledgement of the independence of a country by a state which formerly exercised sovereignty over it'. And the nineteenth and twentieth century practice of sovereign states divesting themselves of territorial possessions through the recognition of successor states is the immediate source of the current practice of international recognition which implies both equality and independence.

In the outward commercial and political expansion of Europe (later the West) between the sixteenth and twentieth centuries, state recognition came to be represented graphically as a line on the map that marked a fundamental distinction between those political systems deemed to be valid and entitled to full membership of international society and those judged to be defective, unfit, or unqualified.[34] That distinction, which became known as the (Western) 'standard of civilization', was a striking feature of international society prior to the era of decolonization. However, since 1945 recognition has involved an acknowledgement of the independence, equal rights and liberties, and dignity and honour of individual states of which the vast majority are members of the United Nations. This practice of recognition has become virtually universal, and today is usually accompanied by membership of the exclusive 'club' or society of states, of which the most extensive and important formal organization is the United Nations.

Membership in this society of states does not entail any surrender or diminishment of sovereignty. Sovereign states that form or join international associations, normally by establishing treaty relations of some sort, still retain their personality as independent political orders. They do not submerge themselves within a greater political body, be it the United Nations or some other organization. The United Nations is based on member states that founded it, joined it, and sustain it; indeed, the United Nations possesses no authority except that which has been granted by its members. States make use of their sovereign authority in a similar way to establish arrangements of security. By means of treaties, for example, states enter into relatively durable agreements to come to each other's military assistance: all for one and one for all. That is the basic norm of the North Atlantic Treaty Organization (NATO) (Article 5):

> The Parties agree that an armed attack against one or more of them
> in Europe or North America shall be considered an attack against
> them all; and consequently they agree that, if such an armed attack
> occurs, each of them, in exercise of the right of individual or collect-
> ive self-defence recognized by Article 51 of the Charter of the United
> Nations, will assist the Party or Parties so attacked by taking forthwith,
> individually and in concert with the other Parties, such action as it
> deems necessary, including the use of armed force, to restore and
> maintain the security of the North Atlantic area.[35]

All members of NATO possess an equal legal status and they all enjoy
the security guarantees of their alliance, even though the military contributions of individual members vary enormously. That might seem an
excessively formalist view. But the recognition of equal sovereignty is the
basis upon which its member states agreed to join NATO. Article 5 is the
pacta sunt servanda of NATO. Alliances are not based on equal capabilities
of the allies; they are based on equal sovereignty and shared military
responsibilities of the allies. Successful alliances disclose the political will
of the members, not only to achieve a common military aim, but also to
share the military and financial burden within the limits of their capacity
to do so. That is a Grotian world in which states associate and act jointly
without amalgamating and surrendering their independence, the hallmark of which is sovereignty. Indeed, it is in this sense that the security of
states can be reinforced and enhanced by their international security
arrangements. In other words, international peace and security can be a
positive arrangement and not merely an absence of hostilities between
states.

Hobbes could not discern any states other than those that were sovereign and those that were subjects of a sovereign. So he might have seen
NATO as an *imperium* under the control of an American *princeps* or
emperor in which the other members were merely provinces or vassals of
some sort. In contrast, Kant might have seen NATO as the first stages of a
'pacific federation' (*foedus pacificum*) in which states 'must renounce their
savage and lawless freedom, adapt themselves to public coercive laws, and
form themselves in an international state (*civitas gentium*)'.[36] On the one
hand, alliances are outward-oriented political bodies that aim to defend
their members from external aggression; on the other hand, federations
are inward-oriented political bodies that aim to establish tranquil
community among their members.

The states that formed NATO never created among themselves anything even remotely resembling Kant's 'pacific federation'. NATO is not
based on a social contract. But neither did the North Atlantic Treaty
involve any loss, much less surrender, of the sovereignty of its members –
as might be suggested by Hobbes. By forming an alliance with other like-
minded states the members of NATO made international use of their

sovereignty to defend themselves jointly. Alliances involve states with each other in joint or common pursuits; they do not dissolve or submerge the sovereignty of states into either imperial or confederal jurisdictions.

Alliances, especially long-lasting and successful alliances such as NATO, give evidence of the international bonds that can exist over lengthy periods between independent states that have concerns and interests in common. The example of NATO underscores the Grotian argument that national security can be obtained, not only by sovereign states acting individually, but also by states acting together in alliances that involve no surrender of their sovereign authority. By that means the security of one state need not necessarily be in conflict with the security of another state, as Hobbes argues, but may be arranged in such a way that both states are thereby made more secure. The safety of people in allied countries is the *joint* responsibility of their sovereign governments. Here, then, the security of sovereign states can be enhanced by the political and diplomatic arrangements of international society. Sovereignty is still a central institution, but it is now a combined basis for international security and not merely an exclusive basis for national security.

The Kantians on cosmopolitan society

Immanuel Kant elucidates a connected system of public right – civil right, international right, and cosmopolitan right – in order to clarify the ethics of an envisaged political world that is more all-embracing than the independent jurisdictions of sovereign states and their exclusive international society.[37] In other words, Kant wants to transcend the limits of the 'club of states' to which so many 'sorry comforters' of the past have confined their analysis of peace and security.[38] His argument in respect of 'civil right' is not far removed from that of Hobbes: sovereign governments are understood to enjoy a constitutional right to rule and popular rebellion is deemed to be 'in the highest degree wrong'.[39] Indeed, at this point Kant's international thought might be mistaken for that of a classical realist. For Kant, as for Hobbes, sovereign states are conceived as existing in a condition of 'natural freedom'.[40] But, unlike Hobbes who offers no reason for leaving the international state of nature and therefore no prospect of escaping its consequences, Kant wants to get beyond the international state of nature altogether.

Even though Kant starts with the idea of sovereign states existing in an international state of nature, he argues that their inherent right of war is intolerable because it is *provisional* – i.e. makeshift, temporary, and discretionary. It is exposed to the capricious winds of human nature. It is not a dependable legal foundation upon which to build an international community in which the rights of states acquire '*peremptory* validity' (emphasis in original).[41] And it does not have the solidity of a system of constitutional law and order. Thus, Kant strives to transcend the international state of nature by contemplating a way in which the world of sovereign states could become a civil order. The legal foundation he envisages is the civil peace arranged by a union of states organized as a permanent congress, for '[o]nly within a universal *union of states* (analogous to the union through which a nation becomes a state) can such rights ... and a true *state of peace* be attained' (emphasis in original).[42]

This stage in Kant's argument brings individuals into the picture alongside states. International right involves 'not only the relationship between one state and another *within a larger whole*, but also the relationship between *individual persons* in one state and individuals in the other or between such individuals and the other state as a whole' (emphasis added).[43] Incorporating human beings into international law implies a moral community that reaches beyond the state – a community, not only of states, but of humankind as well. And in a single sentence Kant sweeps away Hobbes' dual state of nature (between individuals and between states) and replaces it with a normative condition (international right) that applies to *both* individuals and states.

Kant's notion of 'international right' opens up questions about the ethics of security that Hobbes and the Grotians never fully contemplated. In particular, he raises the question of the security of individuals regardless of the state of which they might be citizens. The idea of 'international right' not only presupposes sovereign states as 'moral persons', it also conceives of them as having responsibilities to each other *as well as* the citizens of each other. Kant thereby intimates a responsibility for providing security for individuals based on membership in the community of humankind that is distinctive from the (Hobbesian) responsibility to provide national security and the (Grotian) responsibility to provide national *and* international security through sovereign statehood and international society. Perhaps that is why Kant's international thought is seen as particularly cogent for understanding the ethics of security in our interconnected and globalized world.

Kant develops his argument under the rubric of *cosmopolitan right* or *jus cosmopoliticum*: a 'universal right of mankind' that acknowledges the legitimate claim of all men and women, regardless of their citizenship, to protection by public authorities.[44] The idea of 'cosmopolitan right' implies what is in contemporary world affairs referred to as 'human security'.[45] Kant sees sovereignty and international society as 'necessarily culminat[ing]' in this final and highest form of public right so that human rights are no longer only natural rights, but are now also positive legal rights that are to be upheld by states and by international society. Moreover, he emphasizes the 'interconnectedness' of these juridical arrangements so that the failure of any one of them to express the fundamental principles of rightful human conduct will undermine the others 'and the whole system would at last fall to pieces'.[46] This notion that the world is a constitutional 'whole' – a juridical community of both states and individuals – is a badge of Kantian international thought.

According to that cosmopolitan reasoning, if anyone in the world is juridically unsafe, nobody is safe. If the suffering of people in particular states were tolerated by international society it would threaten the entire edifice of international peace because of the interconnectedness of the parts that form the whole. Thus, the juridical elements of international society cannot be justified in isolation. Public right cannot exist in parts. It can only exist as a whole. Indeed, national security, international security, and human security are all parts of the same unified juridical arrangement; and if anybody in the world is juridically unsafe, nobody is juridically safe, because the world of states would be tolerating barbarians in its midst. This kind of argument seems to have contemporary relevance for judging sovereign states that are unable or unwilling to provide domestic security for their people. The suffering that goes with domestic insecurity cannot be tolerated by civilized men and women, or by civilized governments, who are duty-bound to uphold the *jus cosmopoliticum*. Systematic human rights violations, genocide, civil war, terrorism, and other barbarous activities that take place within states cannot be condoned and cannot go unpunished if security in fuller human meaning is to prevail on earth – that is, if the entire population of the world is to be juridically safe.

This Kantian approach to human security can be contrasted with Hobbesian and Grotian thinking about security. For Hobbes, states that exist and survive without providing for the safety of the people cannot be justified as 'states' properly so-called: they would be states of nature rather than orders of civil law. Their rulers and officials will have forsaken their duty by failing or neglecting to uphold the supreme law. Indeed, on Hobbes' view a failed state is no state at all: the term 'failed state' is merely another name for the state of nature. In such places it is up to the people to sort themselves out politically by instituting an authoritative and capable government; and, should they prove themselves incapable of doing so, they leave themselves open to conquest and subordination to an alien authority. For in Hobbes' way of thinking, no power can be responsible for providing security in foreign places without also taking sovereignty into its own hands, because sovereignty without security is worthless and security without sovereignty is nonsensical.

But today some states, perhaps many states, have a problem, sometimes a severe problem, of pervasive domestic insecurity. That is a problem for the Grotians more so than it is for Hobbesians. Certain sovereign states have failed, and in some cases failed very badly, in their supreme duty to provide safety for their people. However, they have not failed to protect them from foreigners; they have failed to provide them with safety from domestic menaces and predators. Sovereignty and security have become separated in the domestic sphere of these 'failed states' or 'collapsed states' or 'quasi-states'.[47] These states are conspicuous for being secure internationally: they benefit from the generally observed norms of equal sovereignty, non-intervention, and territorial integrity. But the people who reside in these places are at profound risk domestically. They are in danger, not from other states, but from their own government or fellow citizens, so much so that their condition turns Hobbes on his head.

Kantian thought on 'international right' goes some way in anticipating the practices and values of post-colonial and post-1945 international society; it is Grotian in its high regard for the freedom and equal rights of sovereign states and it is consistent with the many provisions of the UN Charter, including the rights of non-intervention and self-defence. However, Kantian thought provides no easy answers for existence of quasi-states or for their remedy. It affords no right of conquest: to do so would admit a crime against the international right of states to continue to exist despite being defeated in war. Moreover, we live in a world in which the practices of imperialism are said to have been swept away by decolonization: the rights of conquest, colonialism, and – presumably – state partition have been abolished.[48] Ours is a world of states in which sovereignty is generally recognized and the norm of non-intervention is usually observed, regardless of the domestic conditions of states. However, the normative change that accompanied the emergence of post-colonial international society has had some very significant consequences for the safety of the people. For it signifies that sovereign states can rightfully exist and be recognized even if their governments refuse or fail to provide for the safety of their people. Such states possess sovereignty but only of a negative kind: freedom from foreign intervention and invasion based on the right of non-intervention.

But the dilemmas posed by these states have served to resurrect the discourse, if not the practices, of empire. Indeed, Western members of international society flirt with ideas of trusteeship, even though they shy away from that term – as in the case of the United Nations and NATO administration and military occupation of Kosovo. Trusteeship, an idea very closely tied to the age of empire, takes the rights and responsibilities of state sovereignty out of the hands of the local people and places it in the hands of foreigners. For it assumes that some people are not ready, for whatever reason, to arrange their own security and thus must have outsiders arrange it for them. Towards the end of the imperial era, such arrangements were supervised by international organizations, such as the League Mandates System and the UN Trusteeship Council. Thus, Article 22 of the League of Nations covenant declares that 'those colonies and territories ... which are inhabited by peoples not yet able to stand by themselves under the strenuous conditions of the modern world ... form a sacred trust of civilization'. The 'tutelage' of such peoples was 'entrusted' to certain 'advanced nations' and 'exercised by them as Mandatories on behalf of the League'.[49]

But in a universal society of sovereign states the resurrection of trusteeship or some other form of internationally supervised tutelage is a controversial move that requires moral reasons of a fundamental kind to justify it.[50] Kant does not hold firmly to the doctrine of negative sovereignty in which the domestic sphere of independent states is off-limits to international society. On the contrary, he conceives of sovereign states as constituted by persons who are at one and the same time citizens and human beings. In other words, the society of states is a community of both states and citizens. Kant also makes provision for cosmopolitan right as well as international right, and he understands cosmopolitan right as acknowledging the principle of freedom not only of states but of individual human beings. In that regard, he anticipates the expansion of international humanitarian law which has been such a striking feature of international society since the end of the Second World War. But cosmopolitan right goes well beyond existing human rights law, as well as the normative framework of state sovereignty, in emphasizing the international duty of states to safeguard the liberty and lives of all people.

Beyond Hobbes but not as far as Kant

The doctrine articulated by Kant is certainly gaining ground among many intellectuals and academics and among some politicians at the present time. Whether contemporary international society is actually moving in a solidarist direction of *jus comopoliticum* is an empirical question that shall be left for others to answer. Whether it ought to be moving in that direction is the fundamental question that I shall address in these concluding reflections. This question, it must be stressed, is the occasion for a very important academic as well as political debate, the significance of which rivals the debate about nuclear weapons during the Cold War. The academic contribution to such debates, as I understand it, is to try to sort out the main normative positions, not with the aim of prescribing action but, rather, with a view to understanding the situation in as complete a manner as possible.

The Hobbesian voice in this debate assumes that people, either as individuals or as groups, are responsible for looking after themselves, not only personally, but also socially and politically; and they are understood to be capable of looking after themselves even if they have not done so thus far. Rulers and subjects are obliged to obey the supreme law that is the safety of the people. But there is no such political obligation in Hobbes' international state of nature. He recognizes a right of war and a right of conquest in the relations of states. He also recognizes a right of intervention and a right of colonization, at least so far as it is ultimately justified by the security of the intervening and colonizing state. Moreover, Hobbes does not recognize any bona fide international rights in which state jurisdictions are respected under international law. He allows no conception of negative sovereignty that is expressed in the right of non-intervention and he makes no provision for placing the right of war in the hands of an international society, which is, after all, something which is entirely alien to his conceptions of things. In sum, then, when it comes to questions of security Hobbes is the political theorist of self-reliance par excellence. His people are strong, wilful, and able to look after themselves.

The Kantian voice in this debate assumes that people, either as individuals or as groups, are responsible not only for looking after themselves, but also for respecting the liberty of other people and their humanity. Indeed, citizens of particular sovereign states are no less bound to the *jus cosmopoliticum* than any other group of people. They are all, each one and the same, responsible members of something called humanity. Thus, Kant allows for wars of right conduct in the name of justice in addition to wars of self-defence. His wars are emphatically just wars as opposed to wars of interest. He recognizes a right of intervention in states that fail to uphold the standards of human community and he sides with a doctrine of humanitarian war upheld by republican states. For he envisages a time in the future when the universal presence of such states will effectively put an end to war and the suffering and insecurity visited by war.

There is an intermediate voice, what we might term 'Grotian', but which is better understood as that of post-1945 and post-colonial international society. This voice issues a decisive rejection of the extensive liberty and rights that Hobbes places in the hands of sovereign rulers; and it rejects no less decisively the expansive notion of 'human' responsibility that Kant places in the hands of all human beings and right-minded republics. The kind of normative reasoning I have in mind has a name: it is the doctrine of international pluralism based on sovereign state jurisdictions.[51] And it is that middle of the road position that I shall defend against both Hobbes and Kant. This pluralist middle road repudiates the armed invasion of sovereign states except for self-defence or to uphold international peace and security. It also repudiates the proposition that any country should hold foreign territories as dependencies and their people as colonial subjects, or worse, colonial wards.

On a classical liberal view, negative sovereignty has important value as a basis of political freedom – i.e. it presupposes an internationally safeguarded territorial sphere inside of which people are free to get on with the business of building their own state if they have the political virtues to do so. Hobbes could not conceive of this kind of constitutional freedom outside the framework of the sovereign state. He would probably see negative sovereignty as just so many words and so much breath of diplomatists nodding and winking as they utter them. But against Hobbes' deep scepticism, the history of the past half-century suggests that international society can create juridical spheres that are normatively safeguarded from foreign military power, providing that the protected state is not in violation of international law. Such insulation from foreign military power is not insignificant in ethical terms, the most compelling argument for which is probably the claim of freedom it proposes and defends. And it is precisely this claim of freedom that augurs against the view that a people's success or failure in state building should determine the right of outsiders to interfere by the threat or use of armed force or other compulsive means in their domestic affairs.

This same claim of freedom underwrites an objection against any Kantian demand that international society engage in an enterprise of threatening or using armed force to institute civil conditions in states which to date have failed to institute them by themselves. If people in some countries presently lack those virtues, even those mired in civil war, they should not be penalized by being turned into wards of international society under the tutelage of foreign powers or international organizations. This objection does not arise out of an indifference to human suffering or a lack of respect for human rights. It is an objection that proceeds from the proposition that important values are at stake, namely political freedom expressed as a right of sovereign statehood and the global good of international peace and security.

Military intervention in a sovereign state to give security to its population is a distinctive form of benevolence that has paternalist overtones. Paternalism is a policy of protecting people from themselves by interfering with their self-authored and self-directed action. International paternalism is fundamentally opposed to the notion of independent states and free people,[52] and it is fundamentally contrary to the society of sovereign states that has been in existence since the middle of the twentieth century. Of course, Kant would not see the doctrine of humanitarian war instigated by Western democracies to rescue failed states in their neighbourhood as paternalist; instead, he would see it as upholding the universal community of humankind, which in our world is expressed in terms of universal human rights. However, and perhaps paradoxically, he also views paternal government as 'the greatest conceivable despotism' because it treats adult and sane human beings 'as immature children' who cannot be entrusted with responsibility for their own lives. A paternal government 'suspends' their freedom and obliges them 'to behave purely passively', as if they had no will of their own.[53]

Many contemporary advocates of humanitarian war seek refuge in the international law of human rights and the purportedly superior political virtues of democracy. By contrast, the Grotian position that I wish to defend understands international human rights as an undertaking by sovereign governments to uphold such rights in their own jurisdictions, but not as an undertaking to confer on a foreign power or international organization any liberty or responsibility to force such humanitarian action by armed intervention. It understands democracy in the same self-determining way: not as something to be granted by generous foreigners – the possibility of which is open to serious doubt – but as an expression of the political will of the people and government of an independent country. Sovereignty places the security of people in their own hands, and in that way it can be understood as, fundamentally, a liberal and democratic institution.

Notes

1 This essay develops some thoughts on security that were presented originally in Jackson (2000), Chapters 8, 11. I am grateful to William Bain for his advice and help in bringing it to a conclusion. Jennifer Jackson Preece provided helpful comments on an earlier draft.
2 Morwood (1995), p. 124. *The Compact Edition of the Oxford English Dictionary* (1971), pp. 2704–5.
3 Bull (1995), p. 18.
4 See, for example, Hobbes (1998), pp. 144–6.
5 Several of the essays in this volume proceed from the reality that the relation that is normally drawn between sovereignty and security is often not borne out in practice. See, for example, the contributions by K. J. Holsti (pp. 41–4) and A. Roberts (pp. 181–3). Others explore arrangements that might be instituted in response to such failures, for example, W. Bain's chapter on security and trusteeship (pp. 197–9], and J. Jackson Preece's chapter on security and multi-culturalism (pp. 149–52).
6 Hobbes (1998), p. 143.
7 Hobbes (1998), p. 143.
8 Bull (2000), p. 198.
9 Hobbes (1998), p. 143.
10 Holsti notes in the following chapter that some forms of contemporary war are distinctive for reversing this reasoning in so far as the apparatus of the state is mobilized to prey on the citizens it is meant to protect. Jackson Preece explores a similar dilemma (Chapter 8), namely that which arises when the uniformity of community collides with a kind of diversity that is seen as a threat to life in community.
11 Hobbes (1998), pp. 143–4.
12 Hobbes (1998), p. 27.
13 Hobbes (1998), p. 73.
14 Hobbes (1998), pp. 78–85.
15 Hobbes (1998), pp. 78–9.
16 Hobbes (1998), p. 143.
17 Hobbes (1998), pp. 78–80.
18 Weber (1947), p. 156.
19 Oakeshott (1975), p. 322.
20 Hobbes (1998), p. 166.
21 See Cooper (2002).
22 Hobbes (1960), pp. 237–46.
23 See Hansard Society (1953).
24 Jackson and Rosberg (1982).
25 Hobbes (1960), p. 120.
26 Hobbes (1960), p. 83.
27 Hobbes (1960), p. 83.
28 Bull (2000), p. 197.
29 Hobbes (1960), pp. 84, 232. Michael Oakeshott (1983) expresses Hobbes' view as follows: 'Most of the so-called international law is composed of instrumental rules for the accommodation of divergent interests' (p. 163).
30 Hobbes (1998), p. 51; see also Hobbes (1960), p. 103.
31 Grotius as quoted by Wight (1991), p. 39. The term 'Grotian' is used here to refer to a contemporary school of international relations of that name, and not necessarily to the thought of Hugo Grotius. See Grotius (1925). For excellent commentaries on Grotius' international thought see Bull *et al.* (1990).
32 The best statement of this argument remains Bull (1977).

33 The quotations in this paragraph are from *The Oxford English Dictionary*, http://dictionary.oed.com, date accessed: 25 September 2005.
34 See Bain (2003a).
35 *NATO Handbook* (1995), p. 232.
36 Kant (1991), pp. 104–5.
37 Only a brief summary of Kant's argument is possible.
38 The villains are Grotius, Pufendorf and Vattel. See Kant (1991a), p. 103.
39 Kant (1991a), p. 126.
40 Kant (1952), p. 452.
41 Kant (1991b), p. 171.
42 Kant (1991b), p. 171.
43 Kant (1991b), p. 165.
44 Kant (1952), p. 434.
45 Jackson (2000), Chapter 8.
46 Kant (1952), p. 435.
47 See Jackson (1990).
48 This is a pre-emptive norm of international society: the 'territorial integrity norm'. However, there are always exceptions to confound theory: in this case the post-Cold War partitions of the Soviet Union, Yugoslavia, and Ethiopia are particularly noteworthy. For two thorough discussions see Zacher (2001), pp. 215–50; and Fabry (2002), pp. 145–74.
49 See Miller (1928), p. 737.
50 The dilemmas that go with resurrecting trusteeship are explored in the contribution to this volume by W. Bain (pp. 202–4).
51 I use the word pluralism in its historical meaning in political and legal philosophy and not in its current meaning in social science.
52 See Mill (1963), pp. 368–84; and Walzer (1992), Chapter 6. Negative sovereignty is not paternalist: it is a sovereign right of all states, powerful and weak, large and small.
53 Kant (1970), pp. 87–92.

3 Reversing Rousseau
The medieval and modern in contemporary wars

K. J. Holsti

[In war] one kills in order to win; no man is so ferocious that he tries to win in order to kill.*

Jean Jacques Rousseau

I offer my apologies to the memory of Attila and his conquerors, but the art of arranging how men are to live in peace is even more complex than that of massacring them.**

Georges Cleménceau

These two statements offer important insights into the nature of war as it has developed in recent years. Our popular images of war as armed contest between organized military forces representing states – a Clausewitzian conception of war – are increasingly at odds with current practices. An observer of wars a century ago could look dispassionately at the clash of arms between trained soldiers and conclude that ethical issues were not seriously engaged because war was an inherent right of sovereigns and, in any case, the main victims were the warriors who were trained to accept death as part of their *métier*. Security referred primarily to the safety of the state and its territories. In contrast, today the main objects of attack are not foreign territories, access to strategic points, or the establishment of colonies, but innocent civilians. The abuses of war are no longer confined to sacking a few cities and pillage. They include ethnic cleansing, massacres of village and town populations, organized rape, environmental destruction to induce mass starvation, and systematic economic predation.

I make the following propositions in the analysis that follows. First, Rousseau was wrong. Contemporary wars are being fought in order to kill rather than to achieve known political aims, and their frequency is increasing. Second, Rousseau presents an Enlightenment image of war, personified in the writings of Clausewitz, where the purpose of armed combat is to win. In many recent wars, winning has not been a purpose; on the contrary, the purpose has been to prolong the war as long as possible in order to attain other, mostly non-political goals. Third, the great French politician and peacemaker of 1919, though at the time considered by many a cynical exponent of *Realpolitik*, understood that the art of making peace is extremely difficult. His description fits perfectly with the problem of ending typical contemporary wars. When a major purpose of war is to kill, and when winning is no longer the primary objective of violence, why make peace? I also consider another portrait of contemporary war, one occasioned by the 'revolution in military affairs'. This type of war seeks to return to a highly disciplined type of armed conflict where many of the rules of war and humanitarian law are observed – a resurrection of Rousseau, but one that is far from perfect. The chapter concludes with some observations about the ethical quandaries in the international management of contemporary wars. Is there a developing norm of community responsibility to end many contemporary wars? If so, does this indicate the emergence of a human solidarity that challenges the norm which promotes coexistence in the society of states, the obligation not to interfere in the internal affairs of states? I conclude by suggesting that the antinomy between solidarist and pluralist conceptions of world order is characterized incorrectly.

Kill in order to win: the classical model of war

The image of war that permeates the literature of international relations derives from the classical wars of the eighteenth and nineteenth centuries. Rousseau's epigram reflects the Enlightenment era practices of war where it was still primarily a state-organized and controlled gentleman's activity, imbued with notions of honour and loyalty, which adhered to the distinctions between the state and armed forces, between combatants and civilians, and between belligerents and neutrals. Following Clausewitz, war was an instrument of statecraft, undertaken to defend or pursue political interests that were known, articulated, and mostly limited. The purposes of war were to gain monopolies over trade, to challenge successions, to gain territory (and thereby sources of revenue) and strategic outposts, and to maintain or restore regional and European balances of power. Michael Howard provides a concise characterization of war as Rousseau and Clausewitz understood it:

> The prime characteristic of the military is not that they use violence, or even that they use violence legitimized by virtue of their function as instruments of the state. It is that they use that violence with great *deliberation*. Such violence, purposeful, deliberate, and legitimized is normally known as *force*, and the use of *force* between states is what we mean by war. War consists of such deliberate, controlled, and purposeful acts of force combined and harmonized to attain what are ultimately political objectives.[1]

In this conception of war, killing is an instrumental and unavoidable cost when two or more states cannot resolve their conflicting interests through diplomacy or other forms of statecraft.

Wars of this kind are inherently limited because political purposes are also limited. Once attained, there is no further justification or need for violence. As Howard emphasizes, these kinds of war are also controlled. States control them by three means: first, they control the time when peace is transformed into war (via declarations of war). Second, they control the main lines of strategy. Third, they control the termination of war; that is, they define what it means to win.

State controls are not the only instruments of constraint. In addition, war has a distinct culture reflecting the norms of the warrior. These are in turn artefacts of more general cultures and conceptions of morality. In the medieval era, there was the Christian code of chivalry. In feudal Japan, it was Bushido, or the 'way of the warrior', which laid down strict rules of combat and etiquette that prevailed in both peace and war. During the Enlightenment era, the officer corps of the European powers emerged primarily from the nobility and the actual conduct of war reflected their particular value systems. Michael Ignatieff suggests that 'warrior's honour' was both a code of belonging and an ethic of responsibility. Warriors typically distinguish between combatants and non-combatants, legitimate and illegitimate targets, moral and immoral weaponry, and between civilized and barbarous treatment of prisoners and wounded. Armies train soldiers to kill, 'but they also teach restraint and discipline; they channel aggression into ritual. War is redeemed only by moral rules.'[2] These types of restraints on war transcend culture, location, and history.

Other constraints derive from the peculiarities of the use of force in different eras. During Rousseau's time, wars were in part restrained by financial limits. Professional military forces cost a great deal. They were the largest single investment of the state, and therefore not a resource to be squandered in great pitched battles and wars of annihilation. The military etiquette of the era reflected the need for parsimony: the boundaries defining when it was honourable to surrender, for example, were set pretty low so that it was not necessary to fight to the last man. In addition, manpower, economic, and agricultural constraints limited the size of armies and navies.[3]

Finally, restraint in eighteenth and nineteenth century European war derived in part from historical memory, in this case, the memories of the uncontrolled mayhem of the Thirty Years War (1618–48). This war earned a well-deserved reputation for how wars should not be fought. Nascent states lost control of officers in the field who pursued their own agendas. Political purposes became blurred, often losing priority to the personal ambitions of officers and their mercenaries. Armies marauded, raped, pillaged, and massacred their way across Central Europe. Defections and desertions were commonplace. In many respects, the three classical eighteenth century distinctions between state and armed forces, combatants and non-combatants, and neutrals and belligerents were devices instituted to remedy the ills and political risks that appeared in the Thirty Years

War.[4] And all of these restraints helped to fashion what Paul Kennedy and George Andreopoulos call 'discriminate warfare'.[5]

Most important, at the time Rousseau (and Clausewitz) wrote, war was becoming increasingly institutionalized in regularized practices, norms, rules, and etiquette. The latter three components must be more than rhetorical. Practice must match the norms, most of the time. Their origins were no doubt the lessons of the Thirty Years War and the unwritten codes of honour of the nobility. These spread through imitation so that by the end of the eighteenth century they were fairly standard throughout Europe, including Russia.

Throughout the nineteenth century and continuing until today, numerous efforts have been made to codify and extend the largely customary *jus in bello* in positive treaties and conventions. They started with the eighteenth century rules of neutrality and after a hiatus of almost 100 years with no significant further developments, they blossomed in the latter half of the nineteenth century. Major signposts along the way include the 1863 United States General Order No. 100 (the Lieber Code), the 1864 Geneva Convention for protection of the sick and wounded, the 1868 St Petersburg Convention prohibiting the use of certain kinds of missiles,[6] the 1899 and 1907 Hague Conventions, the 1922 Hague Aerial Bombardment Rules, the 1948 Genocide Convention, and the 1949 and 1977 Geneva Protocols. Taken together, these instruments seek to limit and restrain the use of force by (1) identifying legitimate and illegitimate targets, (2) specifying rules of conduct with regard to prisoners, civilians, and wounded, (3) outlawing the use of certain weapons, (4) prohibiting the deliberate killing of distinct civilian groups, and (5) defining the legal status of belligerents, that is, identifying parties to be bound by the laws of war.

In the eighteenth and early nineteenth centuries, analysts and practitioners constructed the use of force as an instrument of statecraft. War was in its ideal form an activity of the state, by the state, and for the state; and while the ways in which wars were fought could be limited, the right to use force, even for conquest, was not limited in any formal way. However, in the past hundred years the use of armed force as an instrument of statecraft has been transformed from a right deriving from sovereignty to a crime. It has been delegitimized. The steps along the way are familiar and need no recounting here, though they are signified in the Hague Conventions, the League of Nations Covenant, the Kellogg–Briand Pact (1928), the Stimson Doctrine (1931), the Montevideo Convention (1933), the United Nations Charter, the Nuremberg and Tokyo war crimes trials, the Helsinki Final Act (1976), the Pact of Paris (1990), and the charters and founding documents in numerous regional organizations. Under present restrictions, states can use force legitimately only in two circumstances: for individual or collective self-defence, or in fulfilling obligations under Chapter VII of the United Nations Charter after the Security Council has previously determined that there has been a threat to the peace, a breach of the peace, or an act of aggression.

If one were to read the thousands of pages of text outlining prohibitions and obligations in the conduct of war (*jus in bello*), along with the texts that delegitimize the use of force in international relations (*jus ad bellum*), one might be led to believe that we have seen progressive movement in moral sensibility and in the control of state violence. This view might be further substantiated by the statistics that reveal a dramatic decline in the incidence of interstate war since 1945.[7] But if we loosen our definition of war to include all forms of organized violence, particularly wars conducted within states and by private groups, then we might well have a serious case of what Stephen Krasner has called 'organized hypocrisy'.[8] We have the rules of war and they have been articulated into increasingly greater detail covering broader fields of military activity; but we also have an increasing gap between the rules and common practices. In fact, as I argue in the next section, we are seeing the deinstitutionalization of war. The practices of war today are in fact regressing even from eighteenth century standards, and increasingly resemble those of the Thirty Years War and the Hundred Years War. In other words, we are seeing a reversal of Rousseau.

Contemporary wars: winning in order to kill

Some analysts have observed that rules restraining the conduct of war have often been breached. There has never been a perfect fit between norms and actions. Even in Enlightenment 'discriminate' warfare, massacres, plunder, rape, and breakdown of discipline occurred.[9] However, most of these events were relatively infrequent, or were justified by various notions of military necessity (e.g. sacking a town in order to provoke other towns to surrender without resistance). These analysts have also noted that observance of the rules of war tend to be culture-specific. They apply in wars between states in the European society of states, but they do not apply in the use of force elsewhere. Wars between cultures has been termed *bellum romanum*, defined by Michael Howard as warfare 'in which no holds were barred [note the past tense] and all those designated as enemy, whether bearing arms or not, would be indiscriminately slaughtered'.[10] Georges Clemenceau referred to the famous wars of atrocity of Attila and Genghis Khan, but he might just as well have looked at the history of European and American use of armed force against those whom they constructed as 'savages', 'barbarians', and 'pagans'.

Many of these events were warfare in the sense that they were organized and directed by state or colonial authorities, but they differed from Rousseau's (and Clausewitz's) conception of war precisely because one of their main features was to win in order to kill. The objective of organized force was to kill as many of the adversary as possible, regardless of whether or not there was a political reason to do so. The list of such organized massacres is lengthy and makes depressing reading. Its highlights include the mass killing and enslavement of the Indians in Mexico and Peru by the conquistadores, the American colonists' wars of extermination against the Pequots, and later the Republic's massacre and ethnic cleansing of the Seminoles and other tribes. The American 'pacification' of the Philippines (1899–1901) was in fact a massacre of rural peasants that involved the burning of whole villages. The victims, which number more than 100,000, were mostly women and children.[11] In Vietnam the massacre of innocent civilians, prisoners, and other non-combatants became almost routine. In Argentina government authorities offered bounties to private citizens who hunted aboriginals in Patagonia. The fate was the same for the native inhabitants of Tasmania, who were eventually wiped out. Dozens of wars of resistance against colonialism were put down in the same spirit: the purpose of combat was to kill the maximum number of adversaries. The physical make-up of the body counts was immaterial. Women and children counted the same as men. Indeed, Martin van Creveld describes the typical campaign against the resisters of colonial administration not as war, but as a safari: '[European troops] slaughtered the natives like beasts, scarcely stopping to distinguish between chiefs, warrior, women, and children.'[12]

Hitler's orders during the Second World War were of the same kind, although on a more massive scale. The whole idea of an order based on race required the killing of all those 'beyond the pale'. The purpose of military conquest was not just to obtain *lebensraum* or to construct a 'New Order' for Europe, it was also to secure the conditions for killing or enslaving those who were caught in the ambit of the *Wehrmacht*. Hitler set up bureaucratic organizations whose main purpose was to kill civilians rapidly through gassing or shooting, or more slowly through slave labour and starvation. He organized *Einsatzgruppen*, concentration camps, crematoria, and special units within the armed forces – the Gestapo and the SS – all for the purpose of killing civilians and prisoners of war. Camps for Soviet prisoners, in particular, were mighty killing machines that disposed of over three million victims. None of this is intelligible in any common understanding of the 'necessity of war'.

Hitler was explicit in his reversal of Rousseau. He made it clear that in the war against the Soviet Union there was to be no application of the laws of war (*keine Kamaraden*). He proclaimed to his generals that this was a new kind of war, *a war of extermination* in which there will be no place for chivalry.[13] Hitler explained this kind of war by saying: 'This struggle is one of ideologies and racial differences and will have to be conducted with unprecedented, merciless and unrelenting harshness.'[14] Military victory was not just a stage in achieving a political project to obtain living space or expand the German empire, but a necessary prelude to getting on with the task of killing vast swathes of populations in the occupied territories.

As the incidence of interstate wars has declined in the last six decades, the incidence of wars within states and private violence – sometimes termed 'wars of national debilitation'[15] – has increased dramatically. Many of their characteristics deviate from the Rousseau–Clausewitz concept of 'discriminate' war. The state no longer controls many military operations; rather, they are conducted by all types of 'militias', gangs of thugs, professional racketeers, drug runners, and hopped up, testosterone-toxic children brandishing guns they can barely hold. Their purposes, as we will see, have little to do with a Clausewitzian notion of politics. Civilians are not *hors de combat*. They become – as in Bosnia and many other places – the deliberate targets of military activity; indeed, the adversary forces almost ignore each other so that they can retrain their weapons against civilian populations.[16] The list of atrocities committed against civilians in these wars is extensive. In Bosnia and several places in Africa (e.g. Darfur), state-sponsored rape became not only an adjunct of war, but also a serious and profitable business activity that involves buying and selling women as sex slaves. In Liberia, Charles Taylor's militias employed 'conspicuous atrocities' as part of their military strategy.[17] Planned and organized famines are also part of these wars of national debilitation (these were also a practice of Western colonial armies). Here, the main victims are the young and the elderly.

Then we move on to the genocides and politicides, truly the transcendence of 'politics' as we understand the term. These are the ultimate reversals, not only of Rousseau, but also of Hobbes. The great Leviathan is instituted by contract to keep men (literally in Hobbes) from each other's throats.[18] The whole purpose of government is to provide security to individuals. But one of the great shames of the past century has been the deliberate use of force and terror by government to destroy their own populations. The threat to individual security in many countries comes not from foreign armies, neighbours, or members of other ethnic, religious, or language communities, but from the state itself. Since 1945 more people have been killed by their own governments than by foreign armies.[19] Like Hitler, the great tyrants of this and the twentieth century have planned, organized, and exhorted people to kill. If the military is used, its purpose is to win in order to kill. Mao's 'Great Leap Forward' and 'Great Proletarian Cultural Revolution' were as much killing exercises as public policy. Macel Nguema turned upon his people, as did Idi Amin and Pol Pot. In Rwanda, the government created a new military organization for the specific task of preparing for and implementing a genocide in which the *gendarmerie*, civil administrators, party cadres, and employees of parastatals all played a part. The government also created the *Interahamwe*, an ideologically motivated militia force composed mostly of unemployed youth.

Nothing in the ensuing carnage even begins to resemble classical war. There was no conception of victory, no declaration of war, no peace, no diplomacy, nothing resembling 'statecraft', and no restrictions on killing. The sole purpose of all the mobilization, bureaucracy, and establishment of new organizations is to kill.[20] Indeed, no classical political philosopher promoted the idea of the state as a tormentor of its population. Nothing in Hobbes' concept of the state of nature or the social contract serves as a prototype or justification for the great government-inspired and organized murder of its own people. It has been the state, not ancient 'ethnic hatreds' that causes most pogroms, ethnic cleansing measures, expulsions, and ethnocides. These were all wars, but not against other states.[21]

In contrast: Rousseau and Clausewitz on winning wars

Rousseau could express his optimistic view of human nature (although elsewhere he was more pessimistic) because military activity in his era balanced means and ends. Killing, as he suggests, is a necessary cost of achieving known political objectives. To win is to achieve an end of the state through the application of force, thereby compelling an adversary to stop using force. Clausewitz popularized this view by emphasizing that war is a continuation of politics by other means. He implied that force is not the *first* choice in the defence or pursuit of known objectives, but is probably the last choice when others have failed. It is a *continuation* and not the initiation of politics.

The purpose of military action is to bend the will of the adversary at the least possible cost. It is definitely not to kill or to annihilate in an unrestrained fashion and without known and carefully delimited purposes. In the field, winning wars in Rousseau's era was quaint and even novel by today's standards. There was usually a major military engagement, defined by one or both parties as a watershed, which basically defined the winner and the loser (Blenheim, Saratoga, Waterloo, and the like). Surrender was followed by a formal ceremony, in which the losing general presented his sword to the winner. This symbolized the end of armed resistance and the acceptance of a return to negotiations to define the new state of peace. Often military officials themselves would negotiate a preliminary peace on the spot, which was subsequently followed by a formal peace conference to define in detail the new legal situation. This typically involved the sale, partition, and acquisition of territory, the payment of indemnities, the establishment of new regimes for the use of waterways, and the guarantee of shipping rights and the like. Quite frequently the peace established – as both Utrecht and Vienna attest – a new balance of power for the 'repose' of Europe. In short, winning was a means of adjusting the legal and territorial situation within the European society of states. It was neither a means of replacing that society, destroying its members, nor freeing resources for massive killing.

Reversing Rousseau and Clausewitz: winning as punishment

The portrait of winning sketched above may be understated. After all, in the eighteenth century three great powers carved up Poland into non-existence and by any measure some peace treaties were draconian for the losers. However, most arrangements of peace were organically connected to the purposes of the war that, as I have suggested, were fairly concrete and limited. Their purpose was to rearrange, not to revolutionize. In 1815, France lost territory, but only that which it had gained through the armed conquests of the previous twenty-four years. Even the peace treaties between Russia and the Ottoman Empire, though little more than temporary truces, disclose a limited character. The legitimacy and existence of the parties was not in question.

The peace arrangements of 1919 broke dramatically with the earlier practices of the European society of states. Punishment and guilt replaced rearrangement. The Versailles *diktat*, breaking with European traditions of negotiating the end of war and contradicting Woodrow Wilson's earlier promise of a 'peace without victory', was not a negotiated peace. It was a set of arrangements, based on the assumption of German war guilt, negotiated among the victors and imposed on the Germans on a take-it-or-resume-the-war basis. Germany had been a leading member of the European society of states, a participant in the Concert of Europe, and also a member of the European club of royalty. However, in 1919 the victors downsized it territorially, sunk its navy, stripped it of its colonies (taken over by the victors), and banned it from the League of Nations until 1926. They imposed economically ruinous reparations and limited the *Reichswehr* to 100,000 men, a fraction of the military forces of the victors. All of this was justified as punishment for Germany's sin of starting the war.[22] Of course, we are still paying for the follies of 1919, which fundamentally changed the concept of winning a war. War was no longer an instrument for defending or advancing national interests, but an opportunity for punishing and ostracizing the losers.

The next step was the doctrine of unconditional surrender. Given the atrocities committed by both the Germans and Japanese prior to and during the Second World War, one can at least understand the theme of punishment as the basis for peace. But it went even further than the punitive peace of 1919, for it symbolized the changing purpose of war, away from 'a continuation of politics by other means', to a policy of obliterating the adversary as an independent state, occupying it, and reconfiguring it in the victors' self-image. The old idea that politics would resume after concluding a negotiated peace was now dead. In its stead was the idea of the puppet or ward, an occupied territory that lost its legal status as sovereign state, to be restored only when the victors decided it would be in their interest. The concept of 'win' in total war is as extreme as the conduct of the war itself. There are no politics in peacemaking, only total surrender. The loser has no bargaining capacity, only a hope of charity or mercy granted by the victors. These are the practices of the life and death of states and societies, not the continuation of politics 'by other means'.

Of course not all modern wars have ended in this fashion. The Soviet–Finnish Treaty of Paris (1947), while draconian, was at least negotiated. On the whole, the Allies dealt with defeated Italy in a reasonably lenient fashion. The treaty ending the Vietnam War, if only a fake, was at least negotiated. If we ever have a Russian–Japanese peace treaty, it will have to be negotiated. The terms ending the 1991 Gulf War were limited to the withdrawal of Iraq from Kuwait and the promise to destroy all weapons of mass destruction. Following the relevant resolutions of the Security Council, the United States did not march into Baghdad to oust Saddam Hussein but limited itself to the main task which was the liberation of Kuwait, that is, undoing an initial aggression. The Kosovo war in 1999 ended in a similar fashion. The terms of the agreement basically restored the *status quo ante*, except that the Yugoslav government had to withdraw its official presence from the province. Other cases of more traditional war-ending practices can be cited, but we must note the fundamental transformation of peacemaking modalities in the two great world wars of the twentieth century.

Reversing Rousseau and Clausewitz: from win to no-win in war

We see Rousseau and Clausewitz reversed in yet another way. The concept of winning, in war as in sports and competitions, implies an end state. To win a war is to end the war. This may seem obvious, but in the context of many contemporary wars it is only partly the case. One purpose of many of these wars is to prolong the killing. War becomes an end in itself. This is very much in contrast to contemporary Western images of war that tend to portray it as a disease, a breakdown of rationality, a pathology, a result of poor communication, or lack of mutual understanding. On this view, the quicker a war can end, the better. Even Clemenceau, who understood how difficult it is to fashion a lasting peace, could not imagine that some parties involved in war do not, ultimately, want to end that state of affairs. Alas, we have great deal of evidence that many of the contemporary purveyors of war have more to gain by perpetuating the killing than by ending it. We get a clue to the problem when, as I have noted elsewhere, the average inter- and intra-state war since 1945 has lasted more than twenty-five years.[23] This compares to 3.7 years for European wars between 1715 and 1814. This is apparently not just a case of peace being elusive, that it is difficult to find the right compromise solutions through negotiations, it is rather a case in which one or more parties to the war do not want to end it *under any circumstances or set of proposals.*

The Clausewitzian concept of war, shared by Rousseau and others of his era, sees war as ultimately having a political purpose, usually defined in terms of the national interest. But many contemporary wars lack political purpose, hence rendering problematic any notion of 'winning'. There are no ideological goals to pursue, no sovereignty to establish, no prestige or status to earn, and no noteworthy political rewards – even capturing state power. War is no longer a continuation of politics by other means; it is an end in itself. Martin van Creveld offered this insight long before the study of 'ethnic' wars recently became fashionable:

> to say that war is an 'instrument' serving the 'policy' of the community that 'wages' it is to stretch all three terms to the point of meaningless-ness. Where the distinction between ends and means breaks down, even the idea of war fought 'for' something is only barely applicable. The difficulty consists precisely in that a war of this type does not con-stitute a continuation of policy by other means. Instead, it would be more correct to say ... that it merges with policy, becomes policy, is policy.[24]

Many of the typical post-1945 wars involve groups, clans, factions, and parties that seem to have clearly articulated political objectives. These range from secession (Tamil Tigers), through self-protection and resis-tance (various armed groups in southern Sudan), to attempts to capture the state apparatus (Charles Taylor in Liberia). But often as these wars drag on, purposes become lost in the mist of infrequent battles, weak cap-abilities, factionalism, and the prospects for personal enrichment. The purpose of Renamo was not to capture the state but to destroy it. Nihilism replaced political purpose. Even in terms of military planning, as Donald Snow reminds us, there is also 'an apparent absence of clear military objectives that can be translated into coherent strategies and tactics'.[25]

Although some dispute this view,[26] the duration and futility of so many of the wars of national debilitation suggest that political and ideological motivation are at best weak; and even if existent, they are frequently replaced by personal or factional aims. The sad truth is that in many of these conflicts, the protagonists profit from the state of war. War termina-tion and peace have little appeal, even where ostensible political gains can be made through them. For too many of them, peace would involve incur-ring substantial personal costs and lost opportunities. Let us, then, review some of situations where the purpose of war is not to win in the political sense, but to continue the fight.

First, with the proliferation of 'militias' and other organized fighting groups often lacking central control, the opportunities for graft, extor-tion, drug running, and other forms of criminal activity are immense. To these activities, according to Duyvesteyn, we should add pillage, blackmail, trade in stolen goods, forced labour, theft of humanitarian aid, and the (unlawful) extraction of natural resources.[27] All of these forms of black economy have been seen in ex-Yugoslavia, Liberia, Sierra Leone, Sudan,

Somalia, the Congo, and elsewhere. In these places the dividing line between combat and criminality is increasingly blurred at all levels. At the top, 'leaders' like Charles Taylor in Liberia and Mohammed Aidid in Somalia are in effect 'roving bandits'.[28] In ex-Yugoslavia middle-level groups such as Zeljko Raznatovic's ('Arkan') famous 'Tigers' roamed the countryside killing adversaries while engaging in looting, extortion, and a variety of other 'black' activities, including the development of a drug-trafficking ring along what is called the 'Balkan Route'.[29] At the lowest levels, child soldiers man roadblocks in order to extort whatever they can from passing traffic. These kids profit much more from illicit activities than from working on their parents' farms or wandering unemployed in city streets. In some cases, such activities are necessary for survival because phantom governments and local warlords have no resources with which to pay the troops.

A second reason these wars are transformed into no-win contests is because of factionalism, lack of central control, and the development of highly localized power centres. In these circumstances there can be no overall strategy or political purpose because rebels, or in some cases 'government' forces, are so deeply divided, perhaps over tactical and ideological issues but more often over dividing spoils of war, that they are incapable of prosecuting a war in the traditional sense. Paralysis prevails in places like Mobutu's Zaire or Kabila's Congo. There is no possibility of victory or winning; mere survival is the basest of aims, which, as suggested above, depends primarily on various forms of plunder and extortion. And in such conditions there is every incentive for various factions to transform themselves from politically motivated groups into local warlords.

A third possibility, perhaps best represented until recently by the Palestinians, some groups within the Irish Republican Army (IRA), and the National Union for the Total Independence of Angola (UNITA), is that political power can be maintained best by the continuation of conflict. Here, peace is construed as a threat to power. Armed conflict, even though at low levels, guarantees political continuity and preserves what in effect has become a way of life, which may include handsome profits generated through illegal activities. It is then not terribly difficult to understand how civic conflicts in places like Angola, Sudan, and the Congo can continue for more than twenty-five years, despite innumerable domestic and international efforts to arrange peace. War pays. It pays both psychologically, in terms of maintaining power, and economically, for example, by the sale of captured resources and diamonds.

Fourth, wars may drag on because no one has the authority to stop them. There is no control over the dozens of militias, irregular forces, and paramilitary groups that sprout in the vortex of social breakdown. In the Yugoslav case, the United Nations Commission of Experts identified eighty-three paramilitary groups that operated in the war.[30] Government authorities franchised most of these groups, specifically so that state authorities could escape moral accountability associated with regular troops.[31] Elsewhere, these groups take on a life of their own as their personal and economic pursuits prevail over larger collective purposes.

Finally, there is the presence of non-governmental organizations (NGOs), which, to most people, epitomize the impulse of humanitarian sentiment that transcends national borders. These groups are taken as evidence of a nascent global moral community and of humanitarian politics that is uncorrupted by narrowly defined national interests. Yet, whether dealing with civilian casualties, providing food for famine-stricken victims of war, or rehabilitating child soldiers, outside humanitarian intervention may actually prolong war. Michael Ignatieff, in an examination of the humanitarian activities of the Red Cross in these wars, puts it thus:

> The ICRC's devoted delegates struggle to enable the population to survive the unendurable, but lurking in the back of every delegate's mind is the possibility that in patching up the wounded, housing the homeless, and comforting the widows and orphans, they are simply prolonging the conflict, giving a society the capacity to keep on destroying itself.... It is a universal feature of postmodern war for combatants to appeal to outside intervention to stop the conflict; when, invariably, outside intervention fails to stop hostilities, the combatants use this as an alibi to keep on fighting ... the failure of interventionists is taken as a moral excuse to keep on waging war. At the same time, the humanitarian interveners themselves become dependent on the hostilities they are trying to contain or stop.... To put it bluntly, war has been good for [humanitarian] business ... and there seems no easy way out of the vicious cycle of intervention prolonging the agonies it was supposed to stop.[32]

There is the further consideration that the activities of NGOs may provide a reason for outside powers *not* to intervene. The ineffective, convoluted, and bureaucratized intervention of the United Nations in the Bosnian war probably prolonged that conflict while providing the United States and some European allies cover for becoming more involved. The Dayton Peace Accord was achieved only after the United States and its allies applied strong coercive measures beyond those envisaged in United Nations resolutions. Similarly, the puny United Nations observation force in Rwanda in 1994 also provided a pretext for France and the United States to remain uninvolved even when daily warnings of an impending genocide were reaching the United Nations and members states' foreign ministries.

I have listed separately these factors that help explain the persistence and duration of wars of national debilitation, but on the ground they are usually tied up together in a way that makes them inseparable. As such, they help us understand why winning a war is often no longer the purpose of armed combat. Rousseau and Clausewitz had a view of war that emphasized its rational, political purposes. But many of the wars we have seen since 1945 do not fit the Enlightenment model. If they once had known political ends, they often disappear or wash out so that war becomes an end in itself. The purpose of combat slowly transforms into other agendas, including revenge, personal profit, sustaining a way of life, criminality, and the like.

Making peace in no-win wars

Clemenceau noted the difficulties of making peace, even in an era when military forces were under strict government control, when armed forces did not directly target civilians, and when the purpose of employing armed force was to win – that is, to attain some known political objective. Further weight is added to his observation when it is considered that the peace of which he was one of the main architects was in hindsight a diplomatic disaster. Under the circumstances of many contemporary wars, particularly in wars where victory is not a main purpose, the task of arranging peace is a precarious enterprise that is frequently met with failure. Armed conflicts continue to ebb and flow in Sri Lanka, Burma, the Congo, Sierra Leone, Liberia, Somalia, Sudan, Kashmir, Tajikistan, Nagorno-Karabakh, Palestine, Northern Ireland, Bougainville, Afghanistan, Aceh, Haiti, and other places. Some of these contests have dragged on for more than thirty years despite the implementation of a broad range of conflict resolution procedures. This is not the place to examine the vast literature on conflict resolution, peacekeeping, and peacemaking; however, it is worth noting that they are all premised on a Clausewitzian conception of armed conflict. They usually assume central control over armed forces, clear lines of command and communication, known political ends, and articulated sets of interests that can be negotiated, redefined, and scaled down through processes of negotiation, reconciliation, and learning. Of course, there have been notable successes in some of these efforts – one thinks of Northern Ireland as a potential candidate for the success list – but the ratio of successes to failures or non-successes (continuing efforts) is not impressive.

The problem with standard peacekeeping and peacemaking approaches is that they do not fashion reconciliation strategies in terms of conditions on the ground. Achieving peace is no longer a matter of locating the minimal conditions of two sides to a conflict and then negotiating some sort of compromise. Can peace be realized when the power (one hesitates to use the term authority) of the adversaries is so decentralized or non-existent? We live in an era where the typical war evokes memory of Hedley Bull's famous term, the 'new mediaevalism'.[33] It is a return to the war of private actors, including bandits, criminals, militias and paramilitaries acting mostly on their own initiative, tax collectors and extortionists, children, local warlords, NGOs, and mercenaries. One can read Fernand Braudel's description of the Hundred Years War (1337–1453) and find in it amazing similarities to many of the current wars of national debilitation:

> The Hundred Years' War was nothing like modern conflicts. . . . It would be more appropriate to call it a 'hundred years of hostilities'. . . . The battles – sociological and anarchical as much as political – were intermittent, punctuated by truces and negotiations. On average, there was perhaps one year of actual fighting in five. But the countryside was laid waste, either by pillaging troops, who invariably lived off the land, or by scorched earth tactics.[34]

Braudel could very well be describing UNITA, Renamo, and any other number of parties to contemporary conflicts in the Sudan, the Congo, and several other places. Bull's term thus seems appropriate.

How does one deal with such conflicts? A growing literature on war termination is developing. During the Cold War analysts focused on 'conflict resolution', which usually raised only one question: how to terminate hostilities between the armed forces of adversarial governments. Now the problem is how to move beyond the end of fighting to explore the modalities of fashioning enduring peace settlements. This is no easy task, since one of the characteristic features of 'wars of national debilitation' is that they rarely seem to end. Ceasefires may end the killing for a while, and peace agreements may bring some stability, but there is a high probability that all these arrangements will unravel.[35] In fact, the mortality rate of peace agreements in these wars is unusually high. Within five years about 40 per cent of the peace agreements have been systematically violated and fighting resumed. These wars typically do not so much end as move underground, only to resurface later. Burma (since 1962), Sri Lanka (since 1983), Kashmir (since 1948), Sudan (since 1955, with a respite between 1975 and 1983), Angola (since 1974), Palestine (since 1964), and Afghanistan (since 1979), have been at war, off and on, for decades. There have been many peace treaties in these wars but no peace. Few predict that NATO forces will be able to leave Bosnia, Kosovo, or Afghanistan in the foreseeable future. Interestingly, it is precisely where more traditional forms of interstate warfare have taken place, as between Iran and Iraq, Ethiopia and Somalia over the Ogaden, and Ethiopia and Eritrea, that relatively stable peace arrangements have been achieved. For the remainder, peace is still an elusive enigma as peacemakers must confront loose controls over combatants, weak or non-existent local power centres, the structures of black economies, the economic incentives that sustain the fighting, and the provision of outside assistance (e.g. the large funding the Tamil Tigers mobilize from Tamils living in other areas of the world). Terminating more traditional wars seems easy in comparison.

Human security in wars of national debilitation

We need little reminder that if there are people in these wars who profit from the continuation of violence, the vast majority of people in a society are direct victims. The figures are well known. In the First World War approximately 5 per cent of the casualties were civilians. In the Second World War that figure increased dramatically to 50 per cent. But in most post-1945 wars the figure climbs to 90 per cent, the majority of whom are women and children. They, rather than the combatants, are the main object of military attack, extortion, ethnic cleansing, rape, and murder. They are the victims primarily of government forces, and, secondarily, of their adversaries, whether secessionist movements, local warlords, roving bandits, or ideological factions. And in some instances, as in Bosnia, Croatia, Kosovo, and Rwanda, they are the victims of their neighbours and even of their friends. Security does not exist where the Leviathan is collapsing or where ethnic communities are mobilized to war against each other. Michael Ignatieff nicely captures the situation:

> No one in [the Yugoslav] villages could be sure who would protect them. If they were Serbs and someone attacked them and they went to the Croatian police, would the Croats protect them? If they were Croats in a Serbian village, could they be protected against a night-time attack from a Serbian paramilitary team, usually led by a former policeman? This is how ethnic cleansing began to acquire its logic. If you can't trust your neighbours, drive them out. If you can't live among them, live only among your own. This alone appeared to offer people security. This alone gave respite from the fear which leaped from house to house.[36]

In these circumstances potential victims have few choices. They can resist and join the fight if they have the means, they can sit tight and hope for the best, or they can flee. Most choose the latter. Today, there are approximately fifty million people who are internally displaced or who have become refugees as a result of war. Unfortunately, though, that figure is unlikely to decline any time soon. There remain too many areas of the world – tough neighbourhoods – where the Hobbesian version of the state of nature prevails. Rousseau and Clausewitz would have been appalled at the extent to which the critical distinction between combatants and civilians has broken down.

Resurrecting Rousseau and Clausewitz: the 'revolution in military affairs'

While most armed conflicts in the world today share more similarities with medieval war than with classical eighteenth and nineteenth century European wars, there is another notable trend of which we must take note: the 'Revolution in Military Affairs' (RMA). The RMA refers to the application of the most advanced technology, particularly information technology, nanotechnology, and precision guidance technology, to warfare in order to reduce the 'fog' and 'friction' of war. It is also provides a way of sanitizing war by directing firepower exclusively to military targets in a bid to avoid or to minimize civilian casualties. Thus, the RMA signals a return to eighteenth and nineteenth century concepts of targeting, and equally important, to a Clausewitzian notion of the use of force for known and limited political purposes. This was the pattern in the Gulf, Kosovo, and Iraq ('shock and awe') wars. The RMA is also consistent with the classical 'just war' principles of proportionality and discrimination.

The RMA suits a hegemonic world power particularly well. I will not go into the arcane areas of information or cyber war, terrorism, and other methods the weak can employ against the strong, but only emphasize that developing technology at least holds the potential for a return to a kind of war that is conducted between armed forces. Of course this is not a picture without blemishes. In 1991 some coalition missiles hit civilian concentrations in Baghdad and destroyed infrastructure that had serious consequences on civilian health and welfare. In the Kosovo war allied bombs killed more than 1,000 Yugoslav civilians as well as destroying the Chinese embassy in Belgrade. In Afghanistan approximately 3,000 civilians died as a result of American bombing. And in Iraq (2003) the invasion phase of the conflict killed perhaps 20,000 fleeing soldiers and innocent civilians. Many of the dead were victims of mistakes that resulted from the inevitable technological failures and human errors that are a part of any human enterprise. Still, one would rather be a civilian in Baghdad in 1991 or 2003, Belgrade in 1999, or Kabul in 2001, than one in the Dresden or Tokyo of 1945, or the Congo or Sudan today.

The significance of the RMA is the subject of considerable debate: will it increase or decrease the likelihood of war? What happens when others begin to catch up with the American technological lead? What are the vulnerabilities of 'high-tech' weapons systems, particularly to 'cyber war'?[37] This is not the place to enter the fray. Let me simply reiterate the point that the most modern technology can help to make the actual conduct of war more consistent with the laws of war. It can ameliorate the situation of 'organized hypocrisy', where the laws of war develop further and pile up on each other, only to be ignored and systematically violated by combatants. It may help restore the ideas and sentiments underlying Rousseau and Clausewitz, where killing has a known political purpose (presumably an ethically justifiable one), and where winning is defined as achieving that ethically justified goal.

But no matter how promising these technological developments might be, those who wage modern warfare with such sophisticated weapons have not become immune to committing atrocities, massacring civilians, using direct or outsourced torture, and, in other ways, targeting and abusing non-combatants. The American military in the 2001 Afghanistan and 2003 Iraq campaigns have provided plenty of evidence to those who underline the continued culpability of Western democracies in systematically violating the laws of war.[38]

Normative implications

The description and analysis above raise at least two important theoretical issues. First, even if the descriptions are in part ideal types not entirely representative of *all* practices, the question arises whether the types of armed conflicts predominant in the contemporary world are indeed wars in an institutional sense. Are we labouring with an outdated vocabulary of war? Second, what do the descriptive patterns tell us about pluralist and solidarist ethical positions on questions of international peace and security?

John Mueller has argued that the types of armed conflicts characteristic of the post-Cold War era are not really wars in the classical sense.[39] They do not have political purposes, fought by governments with the objective of 'winning'. They are primarily predatory activities closer to organized criminality. They are 'fought' presently by criminals and youth who neither recognize nor are aware of the laws of war. Few have formal military training. It is not so much that Rousseau has been reversed, but that we are seeing a relatively *new* form of organized violence more akin to thuggery than war. '[W]ar has ceased to exist to a considerable extent, and much of what today we call war should more aptly be characterized as crime or banditry.'[40] It is at best 'residual warfare', which exists where there is a vacuum or collapse of state authority, and where criminal control over valuable natural resources provides the main source of personal and group enrichment.[41] This is not the world of Clausewitz, but of a moral order considerably below that of the Mafia. Thugs, robbers, rapists, and torturers may dress in battle fatigues to offer a simulacrum of the 'warrior', but beneath the clothing are hardened criminals, many released from jail during armed raids. They may occasionally preach ethnic virtue, but the real name of the game for them is predation. We thus use the term 'war' very loosely in describing this category of armed activity; and, therefore, it might be more appropriate to employ another term, so that the discourse of 'humanitarian intervention' is not conducted in the idiom of classical war, whether interstate or civil.

The United Nations Charter and other international conventions that deal with questions of intervention and human rights are largely silent on the problem of 'residual' wars, 'wars of national debilitation', and politicides. Most of these wars are not necessarily or even frequently a threat to 'international peace and security'. Although they attract mercenaries, NGOs, foreign corporations, and arms dealers as casts of characters that often sustain the predation, their sources are predominantly local and regional. The question then arises whether the international community has a responsibility to put an end to the killing and looting when the armed conflict is no threat to international peace and security as understood in the UN Charter. Many governments contributing troops to protect civilians in 'residual wars' have shown little willingness to sustain the sacrifices required to achieve a lasting peace. The Americans withdrew from Somalia after suffering less than 100 casualties; the Belgians withdrew from Rwanda (urging others to follow their lead in abandoning the victims) after ten of their soldiers were butchered by Hutu killers; Spanish troops were withdrawn from front-line operations after seventeen had been killed in Bosnia. It should come as no surprise, then, that troops contributions in the Congo and Darfur have been minimal.

While brigands, pirates, thieves, and other types of criminals have always been associated with wars, they were usually adjuncts to armed combat between organized armed forces fighting traditional interstate or civil wars. Now they have become key actors. That they disclose slight resemblance to traditional armies raises two important questions: (1) does the international community have a responsibility to deal collectively with their depredations; and (2) how to do it at a tolerable cost? A number of subsidiary questions also arise. We have had to confront one of them recently: should members of a terrorist group, trained to kill civilians in faraway countries, be accorded the same rights as prisoners of war? Many people have difficulty in accepting the view that trained terrorists are somehow different from soldiers; that they do reveals the extent to which we continue to think conceptually in the categories of classical war. We need to resolve this intellectual issue because so long as we insist on naming these conflicts as 'wars', the legal and moral rules we apply to classical or Clausewitzian wars will apply to them as well. This may be inappropriate.

If we have what is essentially a *new* phenomenon, with historically distinct aetiologies, then our proposed solutions to the problem (assuming that there are some) might also be inappropriate. Most international norms pertaining to questions of war were designed to deal with Clausewitzian and classical civil wars. We have not yet developed norms that might be more appropriate for dealing with organized criminality. In particular, the neutrality norm that permeates peacekeeping operations, which assumes the moral equivalence of the belligerent parties, needs to be subjected to scrutiny. But in Liberia, Angola, Sierra Leone, Somalia, and elsewhere, there is often a clear distinction between predators and their victims, which suggests that if a legitimating body such as the Security Council determines that collective intervention is appropriate, then it should also be ready to use armed force against the perpetrators. Paradoxically, then, peacemaking and peacekeeping may require a normative reorientation that recognizes or even emphasizes guilt.

For those who invoke an international 'duty beyond borders'[42] to assist
the victims of these wars, the norms associated with state sovereignty, such
as the non-intervention principle, cannot be invoked to override collective
(international) responsibility. But are the solidarist ethic of collective
responsibility and the pluralist ethic of state freedom necessarily incommensurable?[43] The report of the International Commission on Intervention and State Sovereignty (2001), parts of which are incorporated into
the Secretary-General's 2005 proposals for UN reform, does not go so far
as to advocate a *right* to intervene to protect victims of predation. Instead,
it argues instead that the international community has a *responsibility* to act
collectively, first through early warning and traditional diplomatic means,
and, second, through the use of force. Fulfilling that responsibility, the
report argues, is not inconsistent with pluralist norms of state sovereignty.[44] The rationale for this position is that an inherent component of
state sovereignty is a responsibility to protect citizens; and when a state
fails to do so, either on account of incapacity or indifference, or because
the state itself has become a threat to the security of its citizens, it is in violation of its own sovereign responsibilities. Framed in this way, the non-
intervention principle is transformed into something less than an
insurmountable obstacle.[45] Collective armed intervention does not violate
sovereignty, but is a last-ditch effort to *restore* the normative basis of sovereignty. Thus, the international community has a responsibility to resuscitate weak, collapsing, and failed states, and to restore them to some
minimal level of sovereign responsibility.

   If we take the Commission's and Secretary-General's analyses as indicative of the current state of thinking about the problem of 'residual' wars,
then the solidarist position seems to be gaining ground. The military
operations by *ad hoc* coalitions to protect populations at risk, as in Kosovo,
or to liberate populations from tyrannical rule, as in Afghanistan and Iraq,
are further evidence of a developing ethic of legitimizing the use of force
for the collective purposes of the international community. In such operations we see the culmination of a great transformation in the normative
underpinnings of the use of force in international relations (*jus ad bellum*)
in the past century. Armed force is no longer an inherent right deriving
from sovereignty, but can be used – or even threatened to be used – only
for self-defence or for purposes defined by the international community
through decision bodies such as the Security Council. The Gulf War in
1991 was truly a collective enterprise. However, the war in Kosovo was
more contentious because it was undertaken without Security Council
authorization; yet as a normative, as opposed to a legal, project it won considerable international support. Similarly, there was little international
criticism against the Economic Community of West African States
(ECOWAS) for its intervention in Liberia or Sierra Leone, or for the
United Nations-authorized operations in Sierra Leone and the Congo. In
contrast, there has been considerable soul-searching and self-criticism for

not having intervened in Rwandan genocide in 1994. All of this constitutes an increasing body of evidence to support the proposition that the 'safety of the people' is an international responsibility; and to the extent that the report of the Commission and the Secretary-General's reform proposals reflect current practice, there is an emerging ethic of human solidarity.

However, both the report and current practice also support the pluralist position, which sees norms of state sovereignty as promoting a condition of peaceful coexistence. The report clearly states – and the Secretary-General concurs – that sovereignty is the clearest expression of a community's will to live separately and that the ultimate purpose for exercising the responsibility to aid human beings under threat *is to restore the viability of the state.*[46] The purpose of armed intervention is not to compromise sovereignty, but to strengthen it. The document is thus at once both an expression of solidarist and pluralist ethics.

Current official (as distinct from some academic) thinking does not move 'beyond' the state, but seeks to find ways to protect innocent civilians when the state fails to do so or is itself the main threat. The issue, then, is not states versus some other form of political organization; it is rather one of dealing with weak, collapsed, or failed states and the armed conflicts they generate. We are confronted with a new kind of problem, the aetiology of which is reasonably well understood, if contested.[47] What to do about it remains a highly political question, in part dictated by the circumstances on the ground. A strict construction of the non-intervention principle, which some would argue is emblematic of the pluralist conception of international life, might lead to the conclusion that nothing should be done about 'residual' wars unless they are or become a genuine threat to international peace and security. But if the whole purpose of armed intervention is to restore and resuscitate the state, as current practice suggests, then, paradoxically, it requires the violation of the non-intervention principle in order to sustain some states. In other words, pluralist ends justify anti-pluralist means.

If we grant this much, then the antinomy between solidarist and pluralist ethics as they relate to security seems rather artificial. Collective armed intervention to protect people from various forms of predation is an expression of human solidarity.[48] But the purpose of intervention does not end with protection, for that would imply a form of perpetual international tutelage over people at risk. Pluralists can rejoice that, after all the exhausting work of intervention, peace-keeping, and peace-building, black holes of state authority might be transformed into functioning sovereignties encompassing distinct national (and moral) communities. Few argue against the proposition that, ultimately, the security of people depends upon the state; and, in that sense, sovereignty and security must go together. Providing security is the primary responsibility of the state; but when it fails to meet that responsibility, or when it becomes the main threat to the security of individuals and groups, then the international community has a responsibility to set matters right. So in confronting the perpetrators of 'residual' wars or 'wars of national debilitation' it must be willing to use force in a manner quite distinct from the ethics of traditional peacekeeping operations. Wars that reverse Rousseau provide plenty of justification for such a response.

Notes

* Vaughn (1915), p. 313.
** Holsti (1991), p. 175.
1 Howard (1979), p. 3.
2 Ignatieff (1998), pp. 117, 157.
3 Rothenberg (1994), p. 87.
4 Holsti (1991), pp. 63–70.
5 Kennedy and Andreopoulos (1994), p. 215.
6 The Convention also included the classical, Clausewitzian definition of war: 'The only legitimate object which States should endeavour to accomplish during war is to weaken the military forces of the enemy.'
7 See Mueller (1989); Saurin (1995), p. 247; and Holsti (1996).
8 Krasner (1999).
9 Rothenberg (1994), p. 87.
10 Quoted in Ignatieff (1998), p. 148.
11 Drinnon (1997).
12 Van Creveld (1991), p. 41.
13 Cf. Parker (1994), p. 56.
14 Bullock (1971), p. 374.
15 Gelb (1994), pp. 2–6.
16 Bojicic and Kaldor (1997), p. 160.
17 De Waal (1997), p. 315.
18 See R. Jackson's contribution to this volume (Chapter 2) for an extended discussion of the Hobbesian approach to security.
19 Rummel (1994).
20 Shaw (2003).
21 Holsti (2000), pp. 143–69.
22 The allies did not invent the peace-as-punishment practice. Germany itself imposed a draconian peace on the Bolshevik regime in 1918. However, at least that peace was negotiated.
23 Holsti (1990), pp. 705–17.
24 Van Creveld (1991), pp. 142–3.
25 Snow (1996), pp. 1–2.
26 See, for example, Duyvesteyn (2000).
27 Duyvesteyn (2000), p. 12.
28 Duyvesteyn (2000), p. 20.
29 Bassiouni (1997), p. 42. For a vivid description of 'one day in the life of Yugoslav paramilitaries', see Ron (2000), pp. 609–49. Peter Andreas offers an excellent analysis of the role of criminal activity in the Bosnian war. He adds the point, however, that without such activity, the Serbian faction probably would have overwhelmed the Muslims. In other words, criminality may have saved the Bosnian state. See Andreas (2004), pp. 29–52.
30 Bojicic and Kaldor (1997), p. 30.
31 Ignatieff (1998), p. 133.
32 Ignatieff (1998), pp. 158–9.

33 Bull (1977), pp. 264–76.
34 Braudel (1988), pp. 159–60.
35 See Wallensteen and Sollenberg (1997), pp. 339–58; Heraclides (1997), pp. 678–707; and Licklider (1998), pp. 121–32.
36 Ignatieff (1993), p. 18.
37 See Owens (1998), pp. 63–70.
38 See Jones (2004).
39 Mueller (2001).
40 Mueller (2001), p. 15.
41 Mueller (2001), p. 19.
42 See Hoffmann (1981); and Wheeler (2000).
43 For an elaboration of this claim of state freedom, see R. Jackson's contribution to this volume, (Chapter 2). J. Jackson Preece discusses a similar notion of freedom, albeit one which pertains to diversity within community as opposed to between states. See Chapter 8.
44 International Commission on Intervention and State Sovereignty (ICISS) (2001).
45 For further discussion of the 'responsibility to protect' see Sir A. Roberts, Chapter 9.
46 ICISS (2001), p. 7.
47 See Buzan (1991), Chapter 2; Holsti (2000); and Ballentine and Sherman (2003).
48 One of the difficulties of the solidarist position remains, however, that 'If the "international community" is responsible, then no one really is': (ICISS, 2001, p. 220). A notion of global responsibility says little about who should act, when, and how. Numerous studies demonstrate that a sense of social responsibility is seldom distinct from self-interest. Collective armed intervention is no exception.

4   Guardians of the practitioner's virtue

Diplomats at the warrior's den[1]

Sasson Sofer

In the intercourse between nations we are apt to rely too much on the instrumental part ... men are not tied together by paper and seals.[2]

Edmund Burke

In war the result is never final.[3]

Carl von Clausewitz

The clash between warriors and diplomats is an inherent pattern of modern history. The *fortuna* of great men rests on conquests, rapid decisions, and *celeritas* in execution. The diplomat's creed is that of obedience; he seeks to cope, not to conquer. De Callières has rightly observed that there is no such thing as a 'diplomatic triumph'.

The confrontation between Metternich and Castlereagh on one side and Napoleon on the other is a striking example of two different understandings of peace and security – indeed, of international reality itself. In the summer of 1813 Metternich was patiently solidifying the coalition against Napoleon. After he concluded, with Russia and Prussia, the Treaty of Reichenbach, he left immediately for Dresden to meet the Emperor of France.[4] This famous interview of 26 June 1813 lasted nine hours. Napoleon greeted Metternich: 'So you want war? Well you shall have it'. Later, he added: 'That I should dishonour myself? Never! I know how to die; but never shall I cede one inch of territory'. But when Metternich ridiculed the effectiveness of Napoleon's troops, he exploded, 'You are not a soldier. You know nothing of what goes on in a soldier's mind. I grew up upon the field of battle, and a man such as I am cares little for the life of a million men'. Metternich reacted calmly: 'If only the words that you have just uttered could echo from one end of France to the other!' It remained to Talleyrand to bring France back to the negotiating table and provide peace to Europe and his country.[5]

Castlereagh was most effective in shaping the Second Peace of Paris. The terms of peace were utterly incomprehensible to Napoleon. 'After a triumph beyond all expectations; – what sort of peace is it that England has signed? Castlereagh had the continent at his disposal. What great advantage ... the peace he has made is the sort of peace he would have made if he has been beaten'.[6] But Castlereagh had placed the ultimate interests of Europe above the immediate advantage of England. His main thesis, writes Harold Nicolson, was 'security but not revenge'.[7]

'Peace with honour' is demanded from the diplomat; warriors may, not once, proclaim their readiness to defend their country's honour even if the national interest would suffer thereby. After he had lost the battle of the Marne in 1914, the younger Moltke declared:

> the highest art of diplomacy in my opinion does not consist in pre-serving the peace under all circumstances but in shaping the political situation of the state continually in such a manner that it is in a position to enter the war under favourable circumstances.[8]

The contempt for civilians, and in particular for diplomats, could not have been more conspicuously demonstrated than by the case of Prussia. Here the struggle for supremacy between diplomats and soldiers continued endlessly in the century that began in 1815. From the foolery of Field Marshal Blücher to the half-imbecility of Wilhelm II, who once declared that 'politics must keep its mouth shut during the war until strategy allows it to talk again'.[9] Even Bismarck, 'the greatest of all junkers', did not escape the wrath of the military. At the height of his achievements in the years between 1866 and 1870, he fought bitterly with the military leadership over war politics. Only rarely could the standpoint of the Wilhelmstrasse be heard and made acceptable. The First World War completed the breakdown of the German foreign office.[10] The 'frocks' were despised on the other side of the hill as well. Sir Henry Wilson said after the San Remo conference of 1920 that 'We soldiers' considered them 'all rotters. Nothing is decided'.[11]

The relationships between diplomats and sovereigns are usually turbu-lent more than harmonious. Referring to Talleyrand, Metternich, Cavour, and Bismarck – the great diplomats of the nineteenth century – A. J. P. Taylor writes that they were dependent most of their careers on the less talented, suspicious, and slow-witted monarchs.[12] Machiavelli had offered a possible remedy to such deficiencies. At the end of chapter 23 of *The Prince* he states: 'The prince's wisdom does not come from having good policies recommended to him; on the contrary, good policy, whoever sug-gests it, comes from the wisdom of the prince'.[13]

Diplomacy proved to be more effective than other means in the arsenal of nineteenth century statesmanship.[14] The European Concert rested on a mechanism of mutual consultation and accommodation. These essential requirements were defined by Metternich: 'All I ask is a moral understand-ing between the five great powers. I ask that they take no important step, without a previous joint understanding'.[15] The same is true of Bismarck. He was, perhaps, deceptive in his personality and policy but not in his statesmanship. After 1871 he compelled the European powers to follow a peaceful course; 'seeking security for Germany, he gave it to every state in Europe'.[16]

The merits of diplomacy

Military victory cannot serve solely as the foundation of an enduring peace. A peace by agreement is a peace that may be more lasting. Diplomats understand that there is no absolute security. All credible security arrangements of modern times, those fashioned by a prudent schemer like Cardinal Richelieu, or liberal democrats like Wilson and Roosevelt, were intended to serve a certain collective good. Writing from the standpoint of the professional diplomat, Abba Eban concludes that 'he is obliged more than any of his colleagues to perceive the limitations of national positions and to seek legitimacy for national policies in terms of a broader ideal'.[17] De Callières is equally trustful of diplomatic merits as compared to military power:

> It is therefore easy to conclude, that a small number of ministries, well chosen, and disposed in the several states of Europe, are capable of rendering to the Prince, or state which employs them very great services; who with a small expense do frequently as much service as standing armies would be able to do.[18]

De Callières' judgement is most apparent when we compare the achievements of Richelieu and Mazarin to those of Louis XIV. Richelieu based his crafty containment of the Habsburgs on the concept of balance of power and on a plan of collective security system founded on trust and the dependence of one state upon the other. In the last and most devastating of Europe's religious wars, the differences between Protestants and Catholics were among the last of his considerations.[19] Dating roughly from the death of Mazarin in 1661 and the assumption of government by Louis XIV, France's power was drained in countless wars. France was ultimately defeated, despite having the grandest army in Europe. In 1684 the philosopher Leibniz published an anonymous satire on Louis, *Mars Christianissimus* ('The Most Christian King'). He advised Louis to seek glory outside Europe by conquering Egypt and by protecting the continent against the infidel Turks.[20] Three centuries later, in a different clash of faiths, Averell Harriman advised in July 1951 that, 'military strength alone cannot win this basically ideologist struggle. The only solid foundation on which to build security is economic development ... a free and expanding economy'.[21]

The essence of diplomacy has not changed. Its first function is the 'minimization of friction'. 'The essential to good diplomacy', Nicholson wrote, 'is precision'. It is the task of the diplomat to clarify the situation in order to define international reality in exact terms, and by so doing to save his country's policy from 'the horrors of vagueness'.[22] These prelimi-nary acts serve diplomacy's ultimate purpose: 'it seeks, by the use of reason, conciliation and the exchange of interests, to prevent major con-flicts arising between sovereign states'.[23] Such treaties and concords must be solidified by a broader legitimacy or a 'diplomatic culture' which nour-ishes the bonds of international society. The great alliances in history were balanced between the mundane and higher values; security has a real and tangible existence, but it also rests on shared rules and norms.

When Nelson called 'a man-o-war the best negotiation in Europe', he was only partially right.[24] The Hobbesian nature of security tends to mini-mize the role of diplomacy. Staunch realists see diplomacy as only a neces-sary element of power politics. Among the salvos that John Mearsheimer directed against multipolar structures is the revelation that 'coalition strength would depend heavily on the vagaries of diplomacy'.[25] On the contrary, diplomacy succeeds by being precise; strategic deterrence, vagueness, or ambiguity should be employed only as a resort deemed necessary for the sake of agreement. James Eayrs rightly shows contempt to the entire paraphernalia of strategic signalling: 'Tacit negotiation is negotiation without negotiators, foreign policy without foreign offices, diplomacy without diplomatists'.[26] It is an absolute discharge of the 'indi-rect approach' – deploy all weapons, conceal no danger, and remain at the mercy of your adversary's 'rational choice'.

We should also regard apprehensively the method of coercive diplo-macy. The risks of misperception and escalation outweigh its presumed economy.[27] Despite the claim that coercive diplomacy implies apparent gains, it remains a risky procedure. Success necessitates the most subtle and crafty diplomatic measures, qualities that are rarely encountered. Apart from the risk of misunderstanding and escalation, coercive diplo-macy ultimately depends on military performance, which is out of the reach of diplomats, and sometimes of elected governments.

Referring to the style of old diplomacy, A. J. P. Taylor observed that 'many diplomatists were ambitious, some vain or stupid, but they had something like a common aim – to preserve the peace of Europe without endangering the interests or security of their countries'.[28] Diplomats were not necessarily morally superior, but they did act in a different social milieu. *Dignitas* defined things to be done or not done. It was a delicate and subtle play where you could convince your adversary of his limits, or even of what were his best interests.

One may assume that professional diplomats regard a broader defini-tion of security as a mixed blessing. The diversion of attention towards human security, 'such chronic threats as hunger, disease and repression', and the definition of human rights as a justification for war is by itself a noble goal.[29] It could also very well be a digression from the main task of preserving peace; it makes diplomatic deliberations much more compli-cated. The ethical dilemma of using force to secure peace is no less acute in a post-heroic age. To achieve the 'certainty of zero casualties' by sacri-ficing the life of innocent civilians and by destroying infrastructures makes war a ritual of self-inflicted wounds.[30] The diplomat's natural inclination is towards collective security, understood as an arrangement which accom-modates the interests of all parties and which rests on reciprocity. The ethics of collective security flows from considerations of moral duty as well as self-interest. It is based on the assumption that states form an inter-national society with defined rights and duties.[31]

Diplomacy and security are inherently connected. Martin Wight has succinctly defined this association: 'it is the task of diplomacy to circum-vent the occasions of war'.[32] The diplomat's obligation is to evade a polit-ical void, and to maintain the diplomatic efforts until an agreement is reached. The employment of diplomacy as a last resort is usually detri-mental to international security.

The diplomat's understanding of international security is presumably the most coherent and objective among practitioners. In comparison to politicians and national leaders, diplomats are less influenced by domestic considerations. Security is a state responsibility, and the diplomat serves, in this regard, the ultimate duty of rulers, which is to ensure the safety of the people. The sovereign, not the diplomat, faces the dilemma of using force in order to secure peace. Diplomats assist by using their craft to fashion frameworks of security and concords beyond the nation state. When diplomats step into the world of utopia, or serve autocratic schemes, they put at risk their moral duty and the *raison d'être* of their profession.

The diplomat's task becomes complicated by the expanded scope and responsibilities of international security. Holsti firmly attests to the fact that the arrangement of peace is daunting at best when the sides to a war are not states but quasi-states, social and religious movements, tribes and ethnic minorities.[33] In such chaotic situations it is much more difficult to set the right preferences and find the proper remedies. Diplomacy has to adapt itself to the new legal and normative foundations of international politics as it was able to do so during all periods of modern history.

The practitioner's virtue

The duty of a diplomat, at all times, was first and foremost to further the interest of his own country. The diplomat, however, is unique among civil servants in the inherent connection between his ethics and professional competence. The ideal diplomat follows almost a stoic path – prudence, civility, a moderate and balanced temperament, accommodation, and dis-pensation of the state of nature and the 'posture of gladiators'.[34] Absolute victories and unconditional surrenders hardly need diplomacy.[35]

The convergence of such traits and faculties, necessary for the fulfil-ment of the diplomatic task, makes for moral behaviour. It should be remembered, though, that diplomacy is neither an intellectual endeavour nor a moralistic occupation. It is, rather, the product of what Robert Jackson defines as 'situational ethics'.[36] It is exemplified by Bismarck as 'the capacity of always choosing at each instant, in constantly changing situations, the least harmful, the most useful'.[37]

As a civil servant, the diplomat is existentially entrapped in a dilemma of moral dualism: he must obey the expedient, and when the situation demands, the morally dubious instructions of his government. At the same time his absolute duty is to secure peace.[38] In this way his loyalty to principles is forfeited by his practical and formal duties.

The diplomat is constrained by the ethics of prudent statecraft. Deceit and duplicity contradict the essence of diplomacy, and its ultimate aim to negotiate a lasting peace between rival parties. It would be pretentious to claim that diplomats are either the advocates of a certain moral doctrine, or of being the promoters of a true justice. Gordon Craig and Alexander George argue that 'moralities often are more concerned with the symbolic aspects of foreign policy than its actual substance'.[39] But, as the trustees of a civilized dialogue among nations, many diplomats adhere to principles that are at the core of international ethics – prudence, sound judgement, and responsibility. It is in line with Oakeshott's understanding of morality as 'the art of mutual accommodation'; Aristotle, Aquinas, and Burke did not separate prudence from morality.[40]

A moral dualism may arise when a sovereign and his diplomats support different policies. The diplomat is cornered, in this case, by a contradiction of obligation and interest. Both must justify their act and account for their deeds. To what extent are diplomats responsible for their sovereign's acts? Tallyrand, in a flagrant historical example, would have answered in the affirmative. He continued to serve France's interests, and its national salvation, in a condition of total collapse that was not of his making.

In an essay on 'Morality and Foreign Policy', written in the mid-1980s, George Kennan drastically limited the moral responsibility of the professional diplomat. A decade later, Kennan was highly apologetic about his writings on morality and diplomacy.[41] His starting point was that of Alexander Hamilton: 'the rule of morality is not precisely the same between nations as between individuals'. Kennan enumerates several reasons to validate this dichotomy – first, the conduct of diplomacy is the responsibility of governments and, second, its primary obligation is to the national interest, not to the 'moral impulses' of society. Those interests are military security, the integrity of political life, and the well-being of its citizens. Finally, Kennan writes that 'there are no internationally accepted standards of morality to which the U.S. government could appeal if it wished to act in the name of moral principles'.[42] He also regarded interventions on moral principles as defensible only when they indeed served national interests.[43]

However, Hare and Joynt have concluded that in fact Kennan does believe in the applicability of some moral principles to international relations. They argue that American ideals are a source of hope and inspiration to the world, and go on to say that he believed that American diplomacy can be successful only by adopting strong moral standards.[44] Kennan had serious reservations about his country's questionable means of gathering military intelligence and about the practices of covert operations.[45] As ambassador to Moscow he regarded such measures as an abuse of the diplomatic code. In his memoirs he complained that 'I could not get over my concern at the recklessness – the willingness to subordinate every thing to military considerations – that appeared to inspire official Washington'.[46] Kennan's ideal was a precise balance between the military and the political.

Whatever are the reservations of the diplomat about his country's policy, he has no choice but to faithfully execute his government's orders. The position of an accredited envoy provides a shield of prerogatives and privileges; it does not change the fact that he is mercilessly dependent upon his master's whims. These, together with historical forces, tend to place in question the obedience of the civil servant. Brian Cubban has thus summarized the duty of the professional:

> As a civil servant you are on the side of power. Your loyalty to ministers is absolute. You are there for that purpose. If you feel that the system is being abused, you must look, and be able to look, to your professional head, the head of the civil service, to take a professional view and if necessary put the point to the Prime Minister knowing that in extremis the head of the civil service can resign. If you are still desperately upset, you may feel, as a citizen, that you must leave, but as a civil servant your only duty is to the government of the day.[47]

One may add that effective diplomacy rests on the assumption that the diplomat is speaking for the 'supreme source of power' in his country and would be backed by its authority in anything he undertook to say in its name. By his self-discipline the diplomat is cornered into the following moral dilemma: his responsibility endures even when it is evident that governments tend not to trust the advice of diplomats when matters of high importance are pending.[48]

What moral responsibility does the diplomat hold for his government's actions? Not much, if we accept Nicolson's separation between foreign policy and diplomacy. 'Diplomacy', he writes, 'is not an end but a means; not a purpose but a method'.[49] Ends and purposes are decided by governments. Writing in the same vein, John Vasquez separates 'substantive policy' from foreign policy behaviour: 'practices are subordinated to policies and can serve a number of different policies; whereas policies are never subordinated to practices'.[50] The separation between policy and practice, substance and method, is at best morally troubling. There is no absolute escape from it because it defines the terms of reference of the diplomatic profession. The subordination of practices to different policies with no reference to international norms, turn diplomacy into a mere instrumental tool. Jackson's judgement on this case is sound: 'the practical discourse of politicians and diplomats is clearly normative and not merely instrumental. Its main basis of justification is the state and the society of states'.[51]

De Callières writes that 'we must not form to ourselves ideas of Plato's Republic in the choice of persons who are designed for these kinds of employment'.[52] If we understand correctly de Callières advice, then it is a rejection of messianic, utopian, and absolutist ideas in diplomacy. There can be no productive diplomacy with an exclusive definition of ends. Indeed, there is an inherent tension between the art of the possible and the desire for the *summum bonnum*.

The diplomat is required to judge whether the end justifies the means. He should neither err on the side of power nor on the side of morality.[53] The diplomat may heed Aristotle's principle to 'lean against' one's dispositions as a result of early training.[54] It is difficult, though necessary, to act according to Hoffmann's criterion: 'a man who employs the principle of political prudence in such a way that they can co-exist with morals'.[55] This substance of this view is expressed succinctly by Robert Jackson: 'The ethics of statecraft is, above all else, a situational ethics the core of which is the norm of prudence'.[56]

The diplomat's ethics is that of responsibility, and not that of conviction. Ethics is a form of judgement and of knowledge. The diplomat operates with the concrete, not the abstract. He must judge what is advantageous or disadvantageous, but he also must calculate what is right and what is wrong.[57] Prudence calls for the attempt to reconcile the desirable with the possible. Thus, the Aristotelian categories of understanding, good sense, deliberation, and experience are in order. Diplomats must acknowledge the historical evidence. By observing an ethics of responsibility they are destined to be forsaken in the clash between statesmen and captains of war.

Diplomacy is a unique case where morality results from both its practice and purpose. Diplomats are the guardians of the practitioners' virtues that stem from necessity. The *dignitas* of his method and the nobility of his ultimate goal, peace, combine to make the good diplomat tread along a stoic path: toleration, suspended judgement, self-limitation, advocating on the basis of legitimate claims and honesty, labouring for concord and the harmony of interests, and advancing towards the collective good by prudence and moderation. The fact that diplomacy began to be portrayed as unnecessary or out of place after the First World War, cannot only be attributed to the changes in the structure and norms of international politics; it was the result also of the decline of public virtues.[58]

Pluralism and diplomacy are the essence of international society. Diplomacy flourished in the city-states of ancient Greece, the Italian kingdoms during the late Renaissance, and in Europe after Westphalia. During all these periods political entities were separate, in a situation of a potential conflict, but also where norms and standards of civilization were common to all participants. Diplomacy will thrive as long as states will remain the salient form of international society. The essence of pluralism is the foundation of a concord that recognizes the existence of separate political entities that have a stake in promoting and preserving the institutions and norms of international society.

In this pluralist image of diplomacy the diplomat is a man of *societas*. Martin Wight considered the Concert of Europe as the most Grotian period for the very reason that mutual confidence was founded on a balance of power negotiated on equal terms between sovereign great powers.[59] Indeed, Wight rejected Kantian solidarism and Wilsonian 'open diplomacy' as anti-diplomacy and as 'a stance of moral isolationism'.[60]

The diplomat's fate is bound up with the acceptance of prudent and civil political norms and rules of behaviour. The diplomat is a symbol of international society. Between solidarist utopias and the realists' 'posture of gladiators', the diplomat is inclined towards a pluralist conception of international politics. The absence of diplomacy would represent a radical change in the world order. Martin Wight writes that 'if there is [an] international society ... then there is an order of some kind to be maintained, or even developed'.[61] In the midst of the road of our pilgrimage to the *civitas maxima* stands international society.

Notes

1 Copyright 2005 from 'Guardians of the Practioner's Virtue: Diplomats at the Warrior's Den' by Sasson Sofer. Reproduced by permission of Taylor & Francis Group, LCC., http://www.taylorandfrancis.com.
2 Quoted in Wight (1966), p. 97.
3 Quoted in von Clausewitz (1984), p. 80.
4 Nicolson (1970), pp. 38–43.
5 Nicolson (1970), pp. 152–7.
6 Nicolson (1970), p. 237.
7 Nicolson (1970), pp. 236–7.
8 Vagts (1956), p. 3.
9 Halborn (1968), pp. 123, 129.
10 Vagts (1956), p. 79.
11 Vagts (1956), p. 8; see also, Mowat (1935), pp. 23, 103; and Dayan (1981), pp. 140, 280–1.
12 Taylor (1967a), p. 23.
13 Machiavelli (1977), p. 68.
14 See also, Liddel Hart (1941), pp. 202–3: 'If you concentrate exclusively on victory with no thought for the after-effect ... it is almost certain that the peace will be a bad one, containing the germs of another war'.
15 Taylor (1967a), p. 24.

16 Taylor (1967a), p. 89.
17 Eban (1977), p. 591.
18 de Callières (1983), p. 73.
19 Holsti (1991), pp. 30–2; and Kissinger (1994), pp. 56–67.
20 Ross (1984), pp. 10–11.
21 Rovere and Am Schlesinger (1951), p. 250.
22 Nicolson (1967), pp. 207–8; and Bull (1977), p. 182.
23 Nicolson (1970), p. 164.
24 Eayrs (1971), p. 72.
25 See Steiner (2000).
26 Eayrs (1971), p. 72.
27 Craig and George (1983), pp. 189–203.
28 Taylor (1971), p. xxiii.
29 See Buzan *et al.* (1998); Rothschild (1995), 53–98; Baldwin (1997), 5–26; Ullman (1983); and Dalby (2000).
30 It is worth noting that the Revolution in Military Affairs (RMA), which provides the means by which to both discriminate between combatants and non-combatants, and to systematically destroy civilian infrastructure, provides no relief from profoundly political dilemmas such as the need to avoid casualties. For a discussion of the RMA and contemporary war, see Holsti in this volume (Chapter 3).
31 Hendrickson (1993), pp. 1–15.
32 Wight (1986), pp. 137–8.
33 See Holsti's contribution to this volume (Chapter 3).
34 The stoa articulated both a cosmopolitan and ethical doctrine. The true stoic acts were according to reason and law (*officium medium*), not according to absolute duty (*officium perfectum*). A virtuous man is a person who may define the best path of action in a given situation. The stoics advocated the virtues of scepticism, moderation, and justice. Of more importance, the stoics played an important role in defining and articulating the *ius gentium* and the *ius naturale*, the founding stones of the Grotian approach.
35 Oren (1984), pp. 11–12.
36 See Jackson (2000), Chapter 6.
37 Taylor (1955), p. 115.
38 Nicolson (1954), p. 68.
39 Craig and George (1983), p. 272.
40 Jackson (2000), pp. 77–96, 130–55. Jackson defines international ethics as a special moral sphere; diplomatic practice falls naturally to the category of virtues, 'disclosed in performance'. See also, Gerth and Wright (1974), pp. 70, 249, 267–301.
41 Kennan (1993), pp. 208–10; and Kennan (1996), pp. 269–82.
42 Kennan (1996), pp. 269–71.
43 Kennan (1996), pp. 273, 282; and Hare and Joynt (1982), p. 43. It seems, according to Kennan, that 'morality is too high, too abstract and too rigid a standard for foreign politics'.
44 Hare and Joynt (1982), pp. 42–9.
45 Kennan (1972), p. 135; and Kennan (1996), pp. 277–9.
46 Kennan (1972), pp. 137, 141.
47 Cubban (1993), p. 10.
48 See Dunn (1996), pp. 9–12; on the ambivalence of heads of state in this regard see Churchill (1948), pp. 210–13; see also, de Callières (1983), p. 111.
49 Nicolson (1970), p. 164.
50 Vasquez (1993), p. 91.
51 Jackson (2000), p. 377.

52 De Callières (1983), p. 84; see also Der Derian (1987), pp. 134–67; and Craig and George (1983), pp. 269–78.
53 See also Welch (1994), pp. 23–37.
54 See Hare and Joynt (1982), p. 7.
55 Hoffmann (1981), p. 28.
56 Jackson (2000), pp. 19–21, 41, 153.
57 See Harbour (1999), pp. 1–8; Olafson (1973); Valls (2000), pp. 3–11; and Coll (1991), pp. 33–51.
58 See also Bull (1977), pp. 178–9.
59 Wight (1991), pp. 180, 184.
60 Wight (1991), pp. 154–6. Wight adds that, 'it is natural therefore that the primary instinct of the Kantian is to sweep away the whole of the traditional diplomatic system, to step out of it, as out of rags, and clothe himself in beliefs and ideology alone.'
61 Wight (1966), p. 102.

5 Great powers and international security[1]

Cathal J. Nolan

The core organizing principles – sovereignty, formal equality, independence, and non-intervention in each other's internal affairs – which still govern the international society of states, were laid out in the several treaties bundled together as the 'Peace of Westphalia' in 1648.[2] Even so, some states have always been more equal than others. Among the nearly 200 states extant in the early twenty-first century, the majority are at most regional powers and most are quite minor countries. Historically, small states seldom exercised major influence on world affairs, and often were not even free to choose their own historical path. On occasions when small states were influential in international relations, they were so usually in a negative sense: they rose in importance if they were objects of aggression or competition among the Great Powers, or pawns in regional constructions of the balance of power assembled by the Great Powers.[3] Many small states are historically interesting and important in their own right, and today some play important roles in issues of regional consequence. Yet, despite gales of political correctness which insist that the stories of all nations are of equal moral weight, the truth remains that they are not: the axis around which world history and international relations turns is the concentrated resources and determinative behavior of the Great Powers, whether acting severally or together. For the same reason, the main ethical considerations pertaining to issues of international security also have been, and largely though not exclusively remain, the province of the greatest and most powerful states.

Why do relations of power, especially relations among the Great Powers, still dominate the crucial ethical considerations of international security? Because raw power as a motive and moving force in the affairs of states and nations retains pervasive importance, and thus must remain central to the elaboration of international security arrangements. Even with the end of the Cold War and the apparent triumph of liberal-internationalist ideas about security, partially in fact and globally in rhetoric and in international law, the reality abides of conflict-ridden struggles of power among discrete political communities (states). It is the standards set by, and the actual behavior of, the most expansive and powerful of these political communities, the Great Powers, which are of most significance in determining the larger patterns of international relations. Among the international community of states at the start of the twenty-first century it is still the most powerful states, rather than the 'clash of civilizations' from which they arise and to which they give whole or partial political expression, and the wars and other sustained conflicts in which they become involved, that are the prime movers of world events and the course of world history. Even a small action taken by the leader of a Great Power often has a far more important impact on world affairs than most signal decisions taken by leaders of small powers. That means that even lesser – whether in character or in talent – individuals in charge of the affairs of Great Powers have a broad influence on world history and politics owing to the indisputable public consequences of their moral choices, actions, or omissions as leaders. Most often, this influence is far weightier than that of even a moral or intellectual titan, should the latter be consigned by chance to lead a Lilliputian land. There may be a twenty-first century Napoleon somewhere biding his time and awaiting his moment of destiny; or a Bismarck, Stalin, Churchill, or Lincoln. But if such persons are New Zealanders, or Fijian, or Cameroonian, or Canadian, their impact will be trivial and their lives will likely pass unmarked in international history. In contrast, leaders of Great Powers, even those who might be generally judged as mediocrities, must be assessed and dealt with in the daily affairs of all other states. They must be coddled, or opposed, or appeased, as circumstances and prudence demand, because they play key roles in shaping the evolution or breakdown of international security.

Power and obligation

Before considering the obligations of contemporary Great Powers it is useful to remember which powers have been Great Powers, and why. It is also helpful to review the broad history of their relations, with a focus on their deepest ethical obligations on matters of war and peace. The term 'Great Powers' was first used in a treaty only in 1815, at the Congress of Vienna. It was elevated to common usage after 1833 through the influential works of the great Prussian historian, Leopold von Ranke. For centuries before that, however, the term 'Great Powers' was understood to mean those states whose economic, military, diplomatic, and other capabilities made their interests, ideologies, and policies of inescapable concern to all states and other members of international society.[4] Moreover, it was well understood that it was the Great Powers which sustained or challenged international norms and which set and, either jointly or unilaterally, enforced the rules of any given historical international order. Modern communications technology (the telegraph and steamship in the mid-nineteenth century), imperial expansion, and the growth of world commerce rapidly completed the construction of a single world political system that had been underway since the start of the sixteenth century. Until then, the prestige of being one of the Great Powers adhered almost exclusively to the larger empires of Europe: Austria (Austria–Hungary after 1867), France, England (Great Britain after 1707), Prussia (Germany after 1870), and Russia, as well as to the Ottoman Empire from *c*.1453 to 1856. Membership in the Great Powers club was legally extended beyond Europe and the Near East with the rise to the first-rank of power of the United States, which was signaled by the Union victory in the American Civil War (1861–65). That shift in status, and therefore also in global responsibility, was recognized everywhere in the world by 1870, except paradoxically in the United States itself, where Great Power recognition and responsibility was not overtly sought by most until 1898.[5] Indeed, the heavy obligations which attended America's preponderant power were not accepted beyond a small elite, led principally by Theodore Roosevelt, until 1917; and even then, it was accepted all too briefly, and soon abandoned.

The first non-Western power other than the Ottoman Empire accorded Great Power status was Imperial Japan. Tokyo gained its place at the conference table with surprising but impressive victories in two Asian wars, the First Sino-Japanese War (1894–95) and the Russo-Japanese War (1904–05). In the second contest it fought to a stalemate an established Great Power – which should remind us that a primary means of gaining Great Power status is victory in a significant war.[6] Over the course of the twentieth century several states fell from the rankings, and one ancient empire finally regained world respect after two centuries of chaotic decline and national humiliation. Italy was revealed by the world wars to have been at best a pseudo-Great Power, a pretender which acted and was treated like a Great Power from *c*.1900 to 1943, only to end in disastrous imperial over-extension, defeat, division, and occupation by contending armies of real Great Powers. The Ottoman Empire was stripped of its non-Turkish provinces and expelled from the Great Power club upon its defeat in 1918, a calamity so serious it provoked a secular and political revolution which led to renunciation of the caliphate a few years later and modern Turkey's abandonment of any imperial pretensions. Germany and Japan were temporarily barred from readmittance to the club by gross misbehavior that brought about the Second World War. In both cases, total defeat and occupation in 1945 brought home a new, subservient status. Japan recovered only a measure of its pre-war status by the mid-1980s. Germany remained physically divided until 1990, and upon its territorial and economic reunification affirmed that it sought only status as a 'normal' country, and that it shunned any form of *Weltpolitik*.

China spent the first half of the twentieth century broken and split, a battlefield of other powers' armies. It sought to regain its ancient place as one of the world's leading states and civilizations in the second half of the century. Its progressive recovery of Great Power status accelerated with its intervention in Korea in 1950, where Mao Zedong spent a million Chinese lives to fight the United States to a standstill, mainly in order to display national power. Once again, in Vietnam after 1959, China strenuously supported a proxy war that blocked US military power from a region Beijing deemed vital to its own security and ideological interests. Acceptance of China as a recovered Great Power came after 1979, as it made sustainable gains in economic development and some political modernization as it finally shook off the deleterious legacy of Mao's erratic, ill-conceived, and idiosyncratic dictatorship. Still, even China was overmatched by the two superpowers during the Cold War, just as all states remain overmatched by the United States in the post-Cold War era. It is likely that into the first several decades of the twenty-first century, and perhaps longer, the Great Powers will remain familiar: China, Japan, Russia and the United States. To that obvious list one must add India as a rising Great Power, albeit one badly hobbled by internal dissension, vestiges of outdated economic policies, and intensely hostile relationships with its neighbors and main nuclear rivals. While time may well amend that list, it is as plausible as any other that might be assembled at this historical juncture of great uncertainty and transition.[7]

Assessing and ranking raw material power is not enough. This fact is recognized in the special obligations Great Powers are asked to assume, including disproportionate financial and material contributions to the United Nations and to peacekeeping operations, and for which most nowadays are provided special legal rights (the veto in the Security Council, and weighted voting in international financial institutions). This special role is also recognized in hypocritical form, as revealed by the Great Powers themselves in assertions of an animating, moral mission even when they have been engaged in the most egregious acts of aggression and self-aggrandizement.[8] Moreover, even the Great Powers must make grand plans and pursue strategic interests within a larger international society which reflects wider economic, political, military, and moral realities, and which upholds certain legal and diplomatic norms. A full understanding of world affairs – which is much more than just relations among states and nations – is incomplete without proper awareness of the moral character and sophisticated nature of this 'international society,' its successes and failures, and its prospects for containing conflict and encouraging international security cooperation. One must also appreciate that even today, there is no greater engine of social, economic, political, or technological change than war, or, to put it more accurately, the ever-present threat of war even in times of peace. Modern war and the modern state, as well as the international society of states and its laws, all evolved together, each deeply influencing the other. World wars – wars which drew most of the Great Powers into determined conflict with one another – only compounded these manifold effects.[9] For this reason, international society has always regarded – and in the twentieth century formally proclaimed – that self-restraint from the unilateral and unprovoked use of force is the primary moral obligation of states. In addition, it has long been understood that it is especially important for, and a special obligation of, the Great Powers to abstain from unilateral force, since these states are most capable of severely damaging defections from international civil behavior.[10]

Until the end of the eighteenth century, this key moral obligation of Great Powers was embraced – as well as constrained – by the concept of the balance of power. In its classical form, the primary interest protected by the balance of power was the most basic right of international society: the right of all recognized members of that society to continued existence. This right was supposed to be enjoyed by small powers alongside the great. And in the immediate wake of the Westphalian settlement, until the mid-eighteenth century, it mostly was. The balance of power thus was originally conceived and applied in Europe as a conservative instrument of international security, intended to maintain the political and territorial status quo against violent, unilateral change (though not against any change, or change by Great Power consensus). The primary value it projected was the independent existence of states as the cornerstone of international law and order. The balance of power was not directly concerned with advancing toward a more perfect peace or implementing social justice: peace could and often did give way to war if deterrence of aggression failed; or if 'compellence' became necessary to re-establish an equilibrium in the states system. Concern for national or ethnic justice – what would come to be called in the twentieth century the right of self-determination – was submerged beneath deep anxiety about maintaining a viable international order, undisturbed by internal revolts or external breakdown of the several multinational empires which were then its leading members. Regard for individual justice, for what in the mid-twentieth century was identified, proclaimed, and then codified in international law as universal human rights, was not then evident at even a rudimentary level.

By the end of the eighteenth century, moreover, several of the Great Powers had forgotten the Westphalian underpinning, the original ethical content, of the balance of power.[11] New, more modern leaders whom Voltaire styled 'enlightened despots' – leaders such as Frederick the Great and Catherine I – threw restraint aside and instead pursued a wolf-like diplomacy wherein the balance of power was cynically invoked as a cover for naked imperial expansion at the cost of the rights, interests, and even the existence of smaller powers. This trend toward the destruction of international society in favor of *Machtpolitik* famously culminated in three Great Power partitions of Poland. The brutal extinction of one of Europe's oldest and largest states between 1772 and 1793, in the name of the balance of power, destroyed faith in the eighteenth century balance system as a natural, benevolent mechanism which worked to preserve the rights and independence of all sovereign states. Instead, the balance of power system was exposed as having deteriorated into, at best, a device for preserving equilibrium among mutually rapacious Great Powers (all of whom also, and as a direct result of the partitions, increasingly feared the others); and at worst, a shared excuse for territorial aggrandizement.[12] Moreover, among liberals everywhere but Britain, the rape of Poland obscured moral distinctions between the ill-behaved – but still relatively restrained – conservative monarchies of Europe, and the much greater threat to peaceable international relations then rising in the form of aggressive, militarized French nationalism, which subsequently fed into the fathomless personal ambition of Napoleon Bonaparte.[13]

But for all that decay and legal and political confusion, the moral content of the classical balance of power system among the Great Powers of Europe should not be overlooked. At its best it sought not a mere equilibrium among the Great Powers, but also a just equilibrium, a balance not only of power but also of international rights and duties and good faith among nations. That kind of balance, the original conception and also the general practice until the mid-eighteenth century, was supposed to allow all members of international society to participate in a peaceably evolving, increasingly law-governed international order. Furthermore, out of the calamitous breakdown of international order from 1792 to 1815, as so often happens in international relations, came a real advance. At Vienna, in 1815, the Great Powers strove to recover the original moral content of the old balance of power idea, and then to formalize and even institutionalize it as a foundation for future peace. This more sophisticated, more conscious and less smug concept of Great Power responsibility – known as the Concert of Europe – was a direct response to the extraordinary chaos and disruption of normal relations attendant on the Napoleonic Wars.[14] It also built upon the positive experience of Great Power cooperation in the Grand Alliance whose members had finally set aside several bitter quarrels and combined to defeat Napoleon and France.

The Congress of Vienna, and the concert system to which it led, was a true turning point. We now may see that it was the first of four great efforts in modern international history at sustaining Great Power cooperation in times of peace, at achieving better governance of international relations by ongoing consultation, and decision making by consensus based upon agreed, general principles of international justice. In each of the first three attempts, in 1815, 1919–20, and again in 1944–45, victorious alliances comprised of otherwise strikingly different and often hostile Great Powers sought to extend wartime habits of cooperation into the post-war period. They did so not merely to shape and control the geopolitics of the post-war world, though that motive was certainly present. They did so also in order to construct a more regular and lawful international society. Each time this was attempted, the Great Powers failed to sustain their effort, falling out over territorial or ideological differences, or falling prey to the bitter revanchism of some other Great Power left outside the consensus by defeat, or for ideological reasons still unreconciled to the idea of condominium.

Even the Concert of Europe, by far the most successful of these attempts at peacetime collusion – and the first true effort at international governance through collective provision of international security – was an *ad hoc* arrangement. It quickly departed from its original conceit as a system of regular congresses of the major powers, where ongoing consultation and negotiation might avoid or resolve future conflicts.[15] And yet, in each case, even a failed effort at peacetime cooperation significantly advanced the cause of international organization and the scope and authority of international law, and progressively moved the ratchet of reform a notch or two forward. I submit that we are living through the fourth major experiment in Great Power cooperation, one that is irregular but sustained, and hence more reminiscent of the Concert system than of any other historical era. It has been underway, I would suggest, since *c.*1985, when the Soviet Union signaled its desire for assistance in extricating itself from an imperial misadventure in Afghanistan and from the burden of its empire in Eastern Europe. Around that same time, China made known its intent to return to full membership in the community of nations, starting with an embrace of the world economy. It also signaled that it would behave with greater restraint and wider responsibility within the United Nations and on selected regional issues. These powers joined the United States, France, Britain, Germany, and Japan in rudimentary and experimental, but still promisingly cooperative, forms of world governance.

Each of these periods has lessons to teach about Great Power obligations and the possibilities of sustained cooperation. The Concert of Europe began as a simple attempt peaceably to resolve the odds and ends of wartime issues. But out of that process, for the first time in international history, the Great Powers agreed to meet regularly to consult on matters of common security concern – to 'act in concert' so that their foreign policies mutually reinforced a common interest in peace. In short, they agreed to cooperate to manage the balance of power re-established by force of arms at Leipzig in 1813 and confirmed in 1815 at Waterloo. How? By establishing a condominium over smaller powers on matters deemed to concern the international security of the whole society of states. At times this arrangement was abused, as when Alexander I of Russia and the 'Holy Alliance' crushed liberal revolts in Italy, Poland, and Spain. But overall the system worked: it actually helped keep the peace in Europe for another four decades. Insofar as it worked (and other factors also helped prevent war during this period, notably the generational and fiscal exhaustion of most European states), it did so because the Great Powers reaffirmed a central ethical understanding that the balance of power was an instrument to protect the rights of all states, and was not again to be used as cover for mutual aggression wherein the powerful did as they wished and the weak suffered what they must. It worked because they also agreed that notable territorial changes in Europe (independence for Greece in 1829 and for Belgium in 1831) must be made by a consensus among all five members of the condominium, and should be accompanied by compensation to the rest if one of the five gained a significant advantage. Despite glaring imperfections, real progress was made toward acceptance of an overt Great Power obligation to underwrite and reinforce international order, above all through restraint of themselves and each other.[16]

The breakdown of this ethical consensus, of mutual caution and self-restraint, came with defection by Russia, always the most difficult of the five major powers in the Concert system. At mid-century St Petersburg renewed its old expansionist drive into the Balkans and Central Asia at Ottoman expense, but this time unilaterally, leading directly to the Crimean War (1853–56). But the decisive defection from cooperation was Prussia's, some ten years later. 'The great questions of the time are not decided by speeches and majority decisions,' Bismarck said, 'but by iron and blood.'[17] With this contemptuous return to the ethics of *Machtpolitik*, Berlin moved to establish continental hegemony, first by guile, but ultimately by force of arms. Prussia used the *Zollverein* (customs union) to cement the smaller north German states to itself, and to build an industrial infrastructure upon which its later military successes rested. Bismarck then reorganized the army and bureaucracy and led Prussia into a series of short, successful wars against Denmark (1864), Austria in the Seven Weeks War (1866), and most damagingly, France in the Franco-Prussian War (1870) – a contest provoked by his personal, cynical manipulation of diplomatic correspondence.[18] It is true that, as A. J. P. Taylor later wrote of this policy, soon dubbed *Realpolitik* by its admirers: 'Bismarck fought "necessary wars" and killed thousands; the idealists of the 20th century [fought] "just wars" and kill[ed] millions.'[19] Even so, the deepest roots of the first of the total wars of the twentieth century, the Great War of 1914–18, clearly drew nourishment from the disturbed soil plowed by Bismarck's 'blood and iron' foreign policy; by his contempt for fairness and balance in Great Power relations; and by his insistence that Germany's security must be absolute, even if this threatened the security of every other power in Europe.

Under Bismarck, in 1871 Prussia achieved a rarified position atop the greasy pole of international politics, as the unifier of Germany and European hegemon, a pinnacle of power not reached since France last perched there in the final years of Bonaparte. While Berlin's military unilateralism against Denmark and Austria in order to unite Germany may be defended, its permanent alienation of France with a harsh *diktat* and annexation of Alsace-Lorraine was inexcusable. To paraphrase Talleyrand, 'it was worse than a crime, it was a blunder.'[20] For this act signaled that

Germany henceforth would seek unique advantage, that its demand for a 'place in the sun' could be satisfied only at the expense of displacing several other major powers, and thus that Berlin held in contempt the old moral consensus about a just equilibrium among the Great Powers. This moral, and not just geopolitical, shift is best illustrated in Bismarck's famous admonition that his diplomacy aimed to ensure that Germany was always 'one of the three in an unstable system of five Great Powers.' But why was that system now permanently unstable, after 1870, when it had proven remarkably stable from 1815–53? Because Bismarck's unilateralism had fundamentally destabilized it, a fact concealed from view only by continual adept piloting by Bismarck.[21]

This great disturbance of the established order did not stop at Germany's nor Europe's edge. The geopolitical earthquake in Europe set off by Prussia caused tsunamis of change as far away as Africa and Asia. Bismarck's diplomacy squeezed most remaining moderation from international relations, and once more set the powers at odds, and at each other's throats. The idea of compensation, too, was gravely distorted (as another Prussian, Frederick the Great, had distorted it over Silesia a century before). Now, territorial compensation became the new cover for Great Power aggrandizement, as hapless peoples and territories outside Europe were caught between the driving hammer of one Great Power's imperial ambition and the anvil of another's resistance. The penetration of China accelerated and threatened further violence, as the Great Powers carved from it vast spheres of influence and imposed ever more unequal treaties on Beijing, Tokyo, and throughout Southeast Asia.[22] Simultaneously, the 'scramble for Africa' began. In just twenty-five years, and in an unseemly and dangerous competition for territorial concessions, the Great Powers made cavalier colonial swaps and traded *de jure* acceptance of each other's claims and seizures. On the whole, Bismarck thought this acquisition of colonies foolish, even though he claimed several for Germany, but he also thought it useful to keep France and Britain distracted from Central European affairs and incapable of forming an anti-German alliance. 'We Germans fear God,' he told the Reichstag in 1888, 'but nothing else in the world.' That pleased bombastic nationalists, but it was not a prescription for a sustainable European or world order, and even Bismarck knew it. In his last years as Chancellor he accurately foresaw that the young Kaiser, Wilhelm II, would prove impetuous and dangerously adventurist. Sure enough, after the old man's resignation in 1890, much that had been achieved for Germany through *Realpolitik* was unsteadily gambled away in a new and dangerous *Weltpolitik* by an unstable ruler and the Prussian military class which upheld him. In other words, the Bismarckian system was so structurally wobbly that it could not and did not survive the removal of Bismarck's steadying hand from the tiller.

Obligation forsaken

Three times in the course of the succeeding century – in the First and Second World Wars and the Cold War – one or more of the Great Powers defected from their primary obligation to sustain general peace, which resulted in 200 million violent deaths and decades of distorted development and international confrontation. The deepest origins of the Great War remain controversial, but it is clear that its main antecedents were shifts in relative power and serious unresolved disputes among the Great Powers, and to a reduced extent also among several lesser powers, with roots deep in the nineteenth century.[23] Even deeper causes were volcanic social and economic tensions in Europe, and the widespread reality of political reaction, beneath which moved a magma of frustrated national ambitions, ethnic and minority resentments, and religious and social hatreds, all surging toward eruption under a cap of frustrated promises of political liberalism and industrialized prosperity. Once the drift to war began, statesmen and generals found it could not be easily channeled or arrested: too many Europeans wanted war, for one reason or another – though probably none wanted the holocaust they actually got. The Great War broke open three multinational empires (the Austrian, Ottoman, and Russian), spilling their diverse peoples into new and untidy states in the Balkans, and Central and Eastern Europe, and shifting into a new pattern of state creation: in the nineteenth century new states were forged by wars of unification, but after the First World War they would emerge mainly from violent division of older, larger states and empires. The war also left a global legacy of bitterness which would take a second world war to quell, and introduced the twentieth century to mass death which later decades would consummate in the pitiless institutionalization and rational calculation of slave labor and death camp systems in Germany, Russia, China, and several other countries.

The Great War was so destructive of international society that it may be seriously argued that most of the subsequent evils of the twentieth century are directly traceable to that catastrophe: the ascent to power of the Bolsheviks and of that monstrous state, the Soviet Union; and the rise of warlords like Mussolini, who tipped Italy into fascism, defeat, and occupation, and Adolf Hitler, who emerged from the trenches in 1918 fanatically determined to mobilize Germany for victory and the 'big revenge.' Without the First World War it is difficult to imagine the rise to power of fascist and totalitarian thought, thugs, and politics in dozens of countries; the later devastation of whole nations and regional economies; the collapse into anarchy of entire societies; and the nearly 200 million violent deaths and mammoth disruption of the normal lives of hundreds of millions more innocent people that marked the twentieth century. All that resulted from the failure of Great Power responsibility before and during 1914. There followed a precipitous decline in the accepted norms of world order, and lasting damage to the idea of civilization itself. That failure was hardly made up for in the 1920s by erecting a screen of internationalist rhetoric, behind which the Great Powers divided and agreed upon precisely nothing. It was symptomatic of this collective failure of the Great Powers in the interwar period that at no time were all of them members of the League of Nations – that institutionalized chimera of state responsibility which all the major powers sooner or later shunned and eventually abandoned.[24]

True, the League of Nations was a real advance for the idea of permanent conferencing, and for peaceful resolution of interstate disputes. Many of its organs dealing with labor, health, and other regulatory issues were of lasting benefit to all humanity. Yet, at no point did it achieve even the preliminary condition – universal membership – for collective security, its proclaimed international security doctrine; and never did it approach an international ethical consensus such as had sustained the far less formal but far more effective Concert of Europe.

Most security measures the League undertook represented a narrow view of security and too often seemed designed to prevent not the next, but the previous war. Fact-finding missions, good offices, 'cooling-off' periods, and arbitration all seemed to be aimed at preventing accidental war, a goal which spoke to the widespread (but misplaced) belief that the First World War had been a great accident, planned by no one, whereby the powers had 'stumbled into war' due to their secret alliances and overly-complex mobilization plans. Similarly, the League's sponsorship of disarmament conferences left public opinion in the democratic states utterly unprepared to face the crisis of the 1930s. In that decade several Great Powers simultaneously set out to rearm as part of deliberate plans for aggression, which meant that deterrence rather than disarmament was the policy called for by the facts, which from 1931 hardly needed finding out. This was not acceptance of international responsibility; it was an abdication of the obligation to prepare for war in order to preserve the peace. Thus, the League was not employed in any significant way to affect the outcomes of the Japanese conquest of Manchuria, the Italian invasion of Ethiopia, or the intervention by Italy, Germany, and the Soviet Union in the Spanish Civil War. It never enjoyed the confidence of the fascist leaders, who despised it, and quickly lost the support of the Soviets and the West (a by-product of the latter's failure to use it properly). In that sense, the ethical concept of the League of Nations – the idea that the Great Powers, supported by the smaller powers, shared a general obligation to maintain international peace and security – did not fail: it was never tried.

The Second World War was so vast, so truly global in its conduct and effects, that it is next to impossible to summarize its legacy for international affairs. In addition to sixty million dead – a raw fact which of itself was corrosive of international order and of civilized politics for several generations – in parts of the world the fighting simply continued. Civil wars broke out or resumed in China, French Indochina, Greece, Indonesia, Palestine, and Yugoslavia. Fighting also continued in Ukraine and elsewhere within the Soviet Union, as the Red Army was forced to fight to re-establish Stalin's writ where bitter, anti-Soviet populations feared it should run again. Hundreds of the world's greatest cities lay in utter ruin, their populations scattered and forlorn, and many of its greatest architectural and artistic treasures were forever lost to bombs or fire. The world economy was shattered, and had to be rebuilt and reoriented to civilian production if millions more were not to starve, or perish from cold, disease, or despair. Property damage was far greater than in the First World War: transportation systems – railways, ports, roads, canals and dykes, and thousands of bridges, in dozens of countries – lay in ruin. Some thirty million persons were forcibly displaced by massive 'ethnic cleansing' in Eastern and Central Europe. Millions more were forced from their homes in Asia, Africa, and the Middle East. The political systems and post-war character of entire societies and economies were decided not by choice, or reason, or national will, but by whichever army – Soviet or Western – occupied their territory. Contrary to Great Power agreement and the hopes of tens of millions, Korea was divided, Austria was divided, Germany was divided, and Europe was divided, which cleaved the world into hostile armed camps that dominated the long, chill peace of the Cold War.

The opportunity for Great Power cooperation at that moment of vast destruction was huge: never before had so many nations – there were forty states in the United Nations Alliance – expended so much blood and treasure in a common cause. For the second time in a single generation, modern war's marriage to industrialization was made clear, and revealed as no longer tolerable. The moment was ripe for establishing a new world order, and in fact most nations recognized that and wished to seize the hour. The chance was squandered, we know now, mainly because of the coarse ideological inability of the Soviet *nomenklatura* to imagine a cooperative, pluralistic world order in which Russia might live peaceably with other states. Instead of what just a few years later Nikita Khrushchev would call 'peaceful coexistence' with the West, or what Mikhail Gorbachev forty years on would call 'new thinking', the world was treated to paranoid insistence that the only way to secure Russia's frontiers was for Moscow to have troops on both sides of every border.[25]

Forsaking a new security ethic, the Great (and small) Power coalition which had won the Second World War fell out over division of the territorial and geopolitical spoils, and over reconstruction, reparations, and ideology. No general peace conference was ever held. The skeletal structures of the League of Nations were salvaged and redressed as the United Nations Organization. But when the proposed solutions of United Nations security and Bretton Woods economic cooperation broke down, the world divided. The United States found itself in effective mastery of the Western hemisphere, Western Europe, Japan, and the Pacific – in what has been aptly called an 'empire by invitation.'[26] Washington quickly set about the reconstruction of the war-torn regions in a mostly benign manner, financing, defending, and rooting democratic capitalism in Austria, Italy, Japan, and West Germany, as well as releasing the Philippines to its own people, even while its role in Latin America was far less happy or progressive. In contrast, the Soviet Union malignantly bestrode Eurasia for the next four decades, brooding over a vast empire which began to decay the moment it was acquired. Yet, beneath the rigid surface terrain of dominance by the 'superpowers', deeper currents of erosion were at work throughout the Cold War. For also shattered was the idea that in matters of international security small states should defer to the Great Powers. Replacing it was a radical assertion not just of a right of peoples and nations to self-determination, first proclaimed during the Great War, but a right of all states to equal representation in the determinative councils of world affairs.

In the Far East, the disruption of the *ancien régime* was so immediate and so extensive that returning European imperial powers, such as the British under Lord Mountbatten in Burma and the French in southern Indochina, felt compelled to use surrendered Japanese troops to quell local unrest and restore public order. But in India, Africa, the Middle East, and other colonies which remained loyal to empire, demands for outright independence were made that no longer could be ignored. This was the greatest – and wholly unintended – consequence of the failure of the Great Powers in the 1930s and of the Second World War: it reversed a European imperial expansion underway for over 400 years, which at its apex encompassed most of the globe.[27] After the Second World War the imperial powers tried to return to their possessions, but within twenty years several (Britain, Belgium, and Holland) withdrew to their national homelands. It took bitter, anti-colonial wars to drive the same lesson home in Paris and Lisbon, and a long, losing cold war to teach it to the imperialists in Moscow. But by the end of the century it was clear that old agreements on who should run the world – that governance was the exclusive province of the Great Powers – was at an end, even in the absence of viable institutions to do the job erected on the basis of radical state equality, which was everywhere asserted as the new governing norm.

A higher realism

What may we glean from that historical record? First, we may conclude that the ethical underpinnings of international security exist in fact and not just aspiration, and that they are far more than a trivial influence in the affairs of states. The states have both been changed by the course of international history, and they have learned from it. Today, what might be called 'Westphalian fundamentalism' (in the form of claims to a radical right of non-intervention in one's 'internal affairs') is seldom invoked, and even then is seldom respected.[28] Most leaders understand that their states exist within an international society in which shared norms import- antly shape the rules and character of interstate relations. This fact influ- ences the diplomacy of even the Great Powers. Furthermore, it is now clear that during the twentieth century there were three major efforts in which creative diplomacy importantly advanced the conceit of an inter- national society of states, and a basic, shared ethic of security which has its deepest roots in the experience of the Concert of Europe and the classical nineteenth century balance of power system.

Following each of the World Wars, and again after the Cold War, major structural and legal reform was undertaken which made explicit in inter- national law – law built into the new and universal international organi- zations, the League of Nations and the United Nations – liberal- internationalist principles as the governing norms of international society. Following each of those global contests the victors – and the United States in particular – deliberately and effectively imposed their core values on modern international relations. The clear trajectory of this liberal reform movement was obscured, but not blocked, by the length and multiple diversions of the Cold War. But since the more fundamental change was advancing beneath the surface of superpower relations, it emerged instantly and in powerful form as soon as the Cold War concluded. We saw it in the Charter of Paris adopted by the CSCE nations, in the invocation of Article 51 of the UN Charter to liberate Kuwait, and in various 1990s sanctions regimes imposed against Iraq, Serbia, and Haiti. The key mechanism producing this reform was what I have elsewhere called the 'ratchet of hypocrisy,' by which ethical principles entered the permanent dialogue among states initially for largely self-serving reasons, but in the process became entrenched as international governing norms.[29]

After each world war, and after the Cold War, it was principally the United States that sought to establish a sustainable peace based on a modi- fied balance of power, in which equilibrium was to be reinforced by collective deterrence of aggression by all the Great Powers. At Paris and again at Yalta and San Francisco, and following the collapse of the Soviet empire, it was mainly US representatives who framed the path to world peace in terms of traditional liberal assumptions about the causes of war, which, in the main, involved the creation of representative institutions in the defeated nations and the eradication of barriers to mutual prosperity through free trade.[30] Each time, the proposed new world order was to take into account the right to self-determination, democratic ideals, and several modes of conflict resolution. All of this was to be undergirded by the 'Open Door' (free trade) in commercial relations, thought to guaran- tee rising prosperity for participating nations. This grand experiment failed after 1920 because, having initiated it, the United States itself with- drew from the collective responsibility it had called for from all Great

Powers. It failed in 1945, despite America's recommitment to the project, because the Soviet Union was incapable of accepting a constructive role or cooperative international obligations, and instead sought the false grail of absolute security for itself in Eastern Europe. It then actively undermined international cooperation and collective governance through sustained campaigns of subversion and aggression by proxy.

It is not yet clear if the renewal of this experiment, called forth by the Gulf War coalition in 1990–91, has already failed. It may be quietly taking root in historic, transformative changes in patterns of Great Power cooperation which are less spectacular, or disguised as regional settlements. In any event, the current distribution of real power in the world means that the society of states remains locked in a pattern set by the ebb and flow of US leadership. It thus generally tacks in the direction of modifying international relations with liberal-internationalist mores. Impressively, at the start of the twenty-first century most of the world's advanced, prosperous, and stable societies embraced a security doctrine that assumed mediation through international organizations, as well as the broad idea of collective governance of world affairs based upon increasingly shared values and interdependent commerce. Indeed, some states that originally bitterly resisted this approach now endorse it even more enthusiastically than does the United States, at least in their rhetoric.[31] This underlying shift in the norms of international society is partial but real, even if also obscured in academic literature by simplistic pronouncements of 'unipolar moments' and insistent calls for managing 'US hegemony.'[32]

The story of the new international security ethic largely began, but it has not ended with, the United States. By the start of the twenty-first century new norms had entered the bone and sinew of international law and organization, and had begun to take on a muscular life of their own – such as in sanctions enforcement against Iraq, in nation-building efforts (however inept or ineffective) in Afghanistan and several other 'failed states,' and in collective 'interventions' in Kuwait, Haiti, Bosnia, Kosovo, and East Timor. This led analysts, leaders, and the informed public to engage in a wide-ranging debate on the ethical content of foreign policy. Consciously or not, such discussions center mainly on various proposals for a compromise between long-term acceptance of democratic values globally, and both the moral and practical complexities raised by the need for instrumental security, which is still achievable mainly through a deterrence posture that underwrites the global balance of power. By now, there has evolved a rough consensus around a modified liberal-internationalist view, a more prudent Wilsonianism, which sees long-term national and international security as best achieved by progress toward a confederation of interdependent, free societies. In this view, concern for the promotion of democratic values and moral norms in international relations, prudently and cautiously pursued, does not run contrary to respect for the requirements of the balance of power. Instead, the balance of power is sustained, rather than challenged, by a conscious if cautious goal of developing an expanding community of democratic nations, which should over time exhibit mutually reinforcing self-restraint because of their shared political values and interdependent economies. This 'higher realism,' as Arthur Link once called it,[33] is already a partial fact: the society of states has already incorporated a passive form of liberal-internationalism into its governing law and its international organizations, without threatening the distinctive tolerance of the states system which is captured in the moral and political concept of sovereignty.[34] As a result, slow progress may be made in the further construction of laws and institutions, and the spread of moral norms, that over time stand to civilize the means by which sovereign states engage in and resolve their most serious conflicts.

Conclusions

At the start of the twenty-first century an unspoken consensus exists among the Great Powers as to their basic international obligations. The main principles of this consensus are, in order of importance: (1) to maintain a sound political and social order within their own national borders, which given their vast size comprise much of the world; (2) to uphold political order in their regions, by military intervention if necessary, or what in the past was called their 'spheres of influence' or even 'backyards'; (3) to cooperate in upholding an international security order which respects the sovereign rights of all members, but increasingly accepts a limited right of international investigation and even collective intervention to abate the human consequences of failed states, and to block aggression by states which threaten to use weapons of mass destruction; (4) to themselves respect and to advance the main corpus of international law (that is, binding obligations among full members of the society of states); (5) to promote free commerce as both a practical good and as conducive to mutual prosperity and to long-term international peace; (6) to provide humanitarian relief in times of overwhelming national disaster or in places where 'failed states' or genocidal regimes give rise to grave humanitarian crises; and (7) to cooperate on devising solutions to resonant global issues which remain beyond resolution by any single state or region.

It may surprise some readers that maintaining a reasonable, just domestic political and social order should rank at the top of the list of Great Power obligations. Yet, the evidence strongly suggests that sustaining internal stability is both a feat that rests ultimately on advancing more than just political, social, and economic relations internally, and is the single greatest contribution any state, especially a Great Power, may make to international security. After all, the two states which have done more than any others to advance a new international ethic of cooperative security, the United States and Great Britain, are historically (certainly over the past 135 years) the most internally stable and successful of the Great Powers. Over the course of the twentieth century, they applied lessons of their domestic political experience to problems of international governance with increasing insistence and, finally, also with some success.[35] That is why, for all its appalling bloodletting and destruction, the twentieth century still ranks among the most creative eras in human history in terms of international institution building, the progressive definition and codification of international law, and the expansion of mutually beneficial norms of economic and public welfare cooperation.

During the twentieth century these two states converted other Great Powers to their view of the necessary supports of sustainable peace in an era of industrial warfare.[36] Most spectacular in this regard is Germany, for eighty-five years the most dangerous, volatile, and violently revisionist of all the Great Powers. But today Germany is stable and prosperous, and despite the sometimes petty character of its foreign policy, it radiates a democratic ethic throughout Central Europe, reaching even into western Russia. Can there be any doubt that the import of greater internal social and political justice, in the form of free markets and democracy, and guaranteed in its incubation period by Anglo-American military power, is what stabilized Germany? Is there really much doubt that these same devices now promise to do the same thing for Central and Eastern Europe, now that those territories have been liberated from the dead hand of Soviet political and economic failure? As for Japan, after 1945 it was compelled to leave behind a brutal militarist and imperialist past to embrace instead the economic and security ethic of its sole occupier. This gave newly cooperative expression to its enormous national abilities. That more than any other factor has permitted stability and, more recently, also democracy to diffuse widely into Northeast Asia, as South Korea, Taiwan, and finally China itself looks to Japan with less fear and for a regional model to emulate in order to escape their own troubled pasts.

Many questions about Great Power governance persist. The departure of the United States from a traditional stabilizing role, with its policy of 'regime change' and occupation of Iraq from 2003, is likely only momentary in the longer term. A policy of 'liberate and leave,' whether ultimately successful or not, may disrupt the Middle East in locally profound ways and somewhat adjust Europe's relations with Washington, but it is unlikely to shift the largest patterns of international diplomatic and political interaction. These have been set by the great wars, both hot and cold, of the previous century which saw the triumph of the liberal-democratic states in battle, and of their norms and grand strategic vision in diplomacy, centered on the leadership and sustained by the military and economic power of the United States. All the disagreements, some of which are quite serious, about proper tactics that occurred along the way should not obscure the core facts of fundamental democratic success and reform of international relations. Thus, the two key questions about Great Power behavior that are most important at this moment in world history do not directly concern the behavior of the United States or the fate of minor countries of the Middle East.

The first key issue is Russia, the great disruptor of international security during the second half of the twentieth century.[37] Post-Cold War Russia remains an internally unstable and a deeply unjust society, with only pockets of substantial improvement in the lives of its citizens since the extinction of the Soviet Union in 1991. Rather than converting to a market society which could absorb its Soviet-era underemployed, and promise over time to raise to affluence most of its citizens, since 1990 Russia's political system instead deformed into a rank kleptocracy in which the worst of the old Soviet order – the *nomenklatura* and security services – allied with traditional criminals to pick the bones of a dead economic system. The palpable dissatisfaction of the Russian people with this corrupt transfer of assets and denial of future opportunities is dangerous to all of Russia's neighbors. This can be seen in rising nostalgia for Soviet imperialism which attended and partly drove a brutal war in Chechnya and the rise to power of President Putin. It is not yet clear whether this is a sign that imperial disintegration has further to go, or that Russians intend to stop it with cold steel and hard-hearted policies. Already, there are indications that Russian leaders who are formally and rhetorically democratic intend to play the old Soviet-era game of stirring racism and xenophobia among the population. And they have carried this beyond Russia's borders, renewing intervention in the domestic political affairs of several states of the 'near abroad.' In the longer term, Russia's corrupt and increasingly autocratic domestic politics preclude its participation in any cooperative security system constructed by other states in Europe.

In the face of such facts, what can the outside world do? Virtually nothing, except defend peripheral new democracies such as Poland, Georgia, and Ukraine from illicit Russian political interference. All have a stake in the success of reform in Russia: the world cannot afford to have so vast a region remain so ill-governed, xenophobic, poor, disrespected, and resentful. But other than providing technical assistance and moral encouragement at the margins of Russian reform, there is almost nothing non-Russians can do to help. Russians must cultivate their own orchard, or see it wither: it is the primary obligation of Russia to put its own house in order so that its chronic problems do not spill over into wider international affairs.

The other great security question at the start of the new millennium is: what will be the future direction taken by China? Eighty years of extraordinary turmoil and chaos marked China, from the Boxer Rebellion of 1900 to the purge of the Gang of Four and the launch of fundamental economic reform by Deng Xiaoping. The internal instability of that giant, natural leader of Asia was the fundamental cause of decades of insecurity, famine, and war in the whole Northeast Asian region. China's inability to govern itself during the first half of the century invited repeated foreign intervention, then drew the Japanese into the quagmire of the 'China War.' That was followed by a horrendous civil war among the Chinese, and then a quarter century of gross domestic as well as international irresponsibility under Mao. Finally, however, China regained its footing and resumed a trajectory toward normality and prosperity, around 1980. Within just five years it was behaving more predictably and more responsible (internationally) as well. The most important contribution to human welfare made by modern China to date is to clothe, house, feed, protect, and govern better its vast population. As much as we might like Beijing to play a more positive role in non-proliferation or in peacekeeping operations, and to engage other facets of collective world governance, the greatest contribution it could make to world security would be to complete a transition to new, more stable internal politics. The current system in China is only superficially orderly and solid; but everyone suspects that in fact it sits atop a pressure cooker of seething ethnic, regional, and class resentments.

Whether China's governing elites can adapt their political theory and institutions as quickly and successfully as they have their economic policies is of cardinal concern to all humanity. Some signs are hopeful, others raise deep concerns. Whatever the outcome, there can be no doubt of its importance: should China struggle through to emerge as a prosperous, broadly democratic (or at least, politically more modern and representative) Great Power over the next two or three decades, the whole superstructure of security in Asia, and the world, would be enormously strengthened. With rising affluence and growing domestic experience of peaceful conflict resolution, a strong China would likely – though not certainly – learn to cooperate closely with Japan and other regional democracies. Together, these states might anchor a regional security system wherein an ethic of cooperation steadily replaces centuries of xenophobia, instability, and war. Perhaps that is an illusory hope. But it is well to consider that failure to achieve that transition would instead encourage the usual suspect policies of terminally illegitimate regimes: resort to more repression and aggressive nationalism as a means of deflecting outward the building pressures for internal political and social reform.

Notes

1 *Power and Responsibility in World Affairs*, Cathal J. Nolan, ed. Copyright 2003. Reproduced with permission of the Greenwood Publishing Group, Inc., Westport, CT.

2 A set of discrete 'Treaties of Westphalia' (Münster and Osnabrück) were negotiated by Catholic and Protestant kings and prices, assembled in separate cities of the state of Westphalia, formally ended the Thirty Years War (1618–48), the Eighty Years War (1567–1648), and a number of lesser, parallel conflicts. Taken together as the 'Peace of Westphalia,' these major treaties codified key

rules of a still emerging nation-state system, shifting real power from the 'horizontal' universalist claims of popes and emperors to 'vertical' structures of the nation states. The process would take another 100 years to complete even in Western Europe, and 200 more to spread globally, but 1648 still serves as a useful marker of this fundamental change in the trajectory of world history in favor of the dominance of the modern state and states system.

3 See Pastor (1999); Chase et al. (1999); and S. Cornell (2000).

4 The Great Powers by consensus, and by period: (1) seventeenth century – Austria, France, the Holy Roman Empire, the Netherlands, the Ottoman Empire, Spain, Sweden; (2) eighteenth century – Austria, England, France, the Ottoman Empire, Prussia, Russia; (3) 1815–1918 – Austria, Britain, France, the Ottoman Empire, Prussia (German Empire 1871–1918), Russia, the United States (by 1865, though some would dispute this claim), Japan (1895), and some thought also Italy, as a member of the Central Alliance before the First World War; (4) 1919–45 – Britain, France, Germany, Italy, Japan, the Soviet Union, and the United States; (5) 1945–91 – Britain, China, France, Germany (c.1955), Japan (c.1964), but all clearly overmatched by the two superpowers, the Soviet Union and the United States, with the United States alone left standing as the pre-eminent Great Power, even as a global 'hegemon,' after 1991. After the United States, it is unclear which states should rank among the Great Powers in the post-Cold War period, and in what order. But most would agree that standing above the ranks of middle and small powers still, by one criterion or another, are Britain, China, France, Germany, India, Japan, Russia, and the United States.

5 In 1867 Russia sold Alaska to the United States, mainly to avoid a conflict over exploitation of its gold fields, such as had earlier helped lead Mexico into war with the United States over California. In 1868 the French abandoned their imperial project in Mexico. In 1870 Great Britain signed the Treaty of Washington, resolving all of its outstanding differences with the United States. In each case, an underlying motivation was to avoid entanglement with the manifest capabilities of a dynamic new Great Power, clearly revealed by 1865 by its victory in the Civil War and thereafter unchallenged master of a vast, continental empire.

6 See Barnhart (1995).

7 A classic and still widely used exposition of power analysis is Morgenthau (1985). Also a classic, of a different sort, is Beloff (1979, 1959).

8 All great empires, civilizations, and nations have expressed a sense of historic mission which at least their elites felt called upon to perform. Chinese emperors sought Signification of conquered provinces, while Rome argued that its own expansion brought the *Pax Romana* to barbarian nations. Muslims spoke of the *Dar al-Islam*, or 'Area of the Faithful' (Submission), by which they meant all lands occupied or ruled by Muslims. This they distinguished from the *Dar al-Harb*, or 'Area of War,' comprising all countries not yet conquered by Muslims (but which implied that, in the fullness of time, they would be). Many Spanish and Portuguese empire builders sincerely believed that they were doing God's work in conquering the New World. In the nineteenth century, France proclaimed that it had a *mission civilisatrice*, and some in Britain shouldered the 'white man's burden.' Meanwhile, Americans pursued their 'manifest destiny,' and Russia advanced pan-Slavism even where other Slavs asked them not to. In the twentieth century, Japan coined the mock-imperial slogans of 'Asia for Asians' and the 'Greater East Asia Co-Prosperity Sphere,' the Nazis ranted that the Third Reich served the higher morality of race superiority, and Soviet leaders boasted that in subverting neighboring states they were doing the great work of dialectical history. At the start of the twenty-first century, a resurgent

China insisted upon reunification of its ancient empire – including several areas, such as Tibet, occupied by non-Han peoples – on the principle of 'One China, One Culture.' For a specific case, see Nolan (1991), pp. 509–31.

9 See Cimbala (1996); Gilpin (1981); Hamish and Errington (1993); and Kennedy (1989).

10 That was the real significance of the Kellogg–Briand Pact of 1928 (officially, the 'General Treaty for the Renunciation of War'), duly agreed by some sixty-five states, including later aggressors such as Italy and Japan. This 'Pact of Paris' was touted by more naive liberal-internationalists as an advance for moral consciousness among states, but criticized by most realists as a prime example of legalistic and moralistic folly in statecraft and diplomacy. Neither view seems entirely merited. It was later cited in the Nuremberg and Tokyo war crimes trials to support charges of 'crimes against peace,' and thus became a generally recognized component of customary international law. Portions of its text were also adapted as Article 9 of the post-Second World War Japanese 'peace constitution.'

11 The moral content of the balance of power should not be overlooked or underestimated. As the classical school of Grotian international relations theory notes, and great statesmen have always understood, at its best the balance of power seeks not mere equilibrium, but also a just equilibrium and a peaceably evolving international order. Nor is it invariably opposed to liberal-internationalist conceptions of world order, as cruder liberals sometimes aver. Rather, it is both capable of underwriting and reinforcing a liberal-international order and, indeed, remains essential to that prospect. Without a modicum of national political justice, ethnic and other challenges arise which may overwhelm a given balance; but without practical attention to the balance of power, idealistic policies which aim to enhance international justice may instead lead to chaos, upon which even greater injustices are usually in close attendance.

12 By the 1770s Russia saw Poland as a satellite state and undermined any effort to reform or strengthen it. But while it wanted to dominate Poland, it was forced to accept partition by two neighboring powers. Prussia also coveted Polish territory, which lay between its central and eastern provinces. Austria insisted on territorial compensation to preserve its relative position in Eastern Europe. Thus, the three partitions of Poland: (1) in 1772 portions of Poland were annexed by Austria, Prussia, and Russia, with Poland losing one quarter of its territory and five million subjects; (2) in 1793 Austria was excluded from a round of annexation by Prussia and Russia, with the latter acquiring the lion's share of territory; and (3) in 1795 the rump of Poland was extinguished, divided among the three eastern powers.

13 For example, Thomas Jefferson – blinded by distance and political romanticism – penned naive praise for Robespierre and The Terror, gravely underestimated the threat and near-limitless ambition of Napoleon, and over-indulged a personal Anglophobia that was deeply contrary to his nation's interests in seeing revolutionary France, if not the ideals of the French Revolution, contained.

14 It is a rather obvious, but also necessary, point to make that the idea of 'Great Power responsibility' does not presuppose that Great Powers always or even mostly act responsibly. But on occasion they have done so and, further, such occasions have witnessed the most significant advances in the evolution of international society. It is true that, too often, talk of Great Power responsibility evokes a deep cynicism that dismisses the idea as deception or some other sort of window dressing. But such cynicism has no proper place among the historically well informed.

15 The practice of diplomacy by regular congress (or conference) lasted only from 1815 to 1822. In that brief 'congress system' the Great Powers which defeated Napoleon (Austria, Britain, Prussia, and Russia) were joined by France under its restored king. Five congresses were held: Vienna, 1814-15; Aix-la-Chapelle, 1818; Troppau, 1820; Laibach, 1821; and Verona, 1822. France used these gatherings to return to international good graces, especially with the three conservative monarchies. Britain attended only as an observer from Troppau on, and left the system at Verona. Austria, Prussia, and Russia met again in St Petersburg in 1825, but the congress system was then abandoned in favor of the much looser Concert of Europe, which included Britain. The postwar periods which followed the First and Second World Wars were far less successful in managing Great Powers relations and the balance of power, but they went further than the congress system by ushering in a system of permanent conferencing in the form of the League of Nations and the United Nations Organization.

16 *Inter alia*, see Bridge and Bullen (1980); and Wilmot (1992).

17 Quoted in Thomson (1990), p. 308.

18 On July 13, 1870, the King of Prussia (later Kaiser of Germany) Wilhelm I sent a telegram to Bismarck from the spa at Ems, concerning a meeting with the French ambassador. Bismarck altered this 'Ems telegram' to make it appear as if France had made excessive demands and the king had treated its ambassador with disrespect. Then he released it to the press. French public opinion rose to the bait, and within a week forced the declaration of war by Napoleon III which Bismarck wanted. That launched the Franco-Prussian War, which overthrew the Second Empire and led to European dominance by Germany.

19 Taylor (1967), p. 94.

20 Quoted in Bartlett (1919).

21 For a more positive view of Bismarck's statecraft see Planze (1993), pp. 39–56.

22 The 'unequal treaties' were a series of one-sided agreements with foreign powers in which Japan and China were compelled to open to Western trade, diplomacy, and even military missions. China was forced to accept a permanent foreign presence in its coastal cities (treaty ports), onerous terms of trade, and extraterritorial capitulations to foreign citizens and governments. The main treaties with China were Nanjing (1842), Tientsin (1858), and Shimonoseki (1895). A spate of lesser treaties were signed in 1860, modeled on Nanjing, wherein China was forced to legalize the opium trade, open dozens of additional treaty ports, clear the Yangtze to foreign vessels and trade, permit Christian missionaries access to the rural interior, and accept resident ambassadors from the major European powers. The main treaty with Japan was the Treaty of Kangawa (1854) with the United States, soon imitated by agreements with the other Great Powers. Unlike China, Japan emerged from foreign domination fairly quickly, then joined in imposition of additional unequal treaties on China. The egregiously imperialist 'Twenty-one Demands' made by Japan on China in 1915 were not only well within the unequal treaty tradition, they were far more extreme than anything other foreign powers had ever attempted. This disruption of the largest nation in Asia continued into the middle of the twentieth century. Full external tariff control only returned to China in the late 1930s. Some extraterritorial provisions were not renounced by Britain or the US until 1943, and then only on behalf of their alliance with China against Japan during the Second World War.

23 These included: (1) the slow fading of Ottoman power, which left a power vacuum in the Balkans and opened contentious territorial issues; (2) a corresponding decline of Austrian power, which Vienna was desperate to arrest, compounded by the archaic and unsustainable character of Vienna's multina-

tional empire in an emergent era of insistent nationalism; (3) internal weakness and fear – and thus aggressiveness and sensitivity to slights against 'national honor' – within the Russian Empire, recently exacerbated by the Russian Revolution (1905) and the humiliating loss of the Russo-Japanese War (1904–05); (4) the bitter legacy of Germany's territorial acquisitions following the Franco-Prussian War, and subsequent French revanchism; (5) the dangerous *Weltpolitik* pursued by Germany after 1890, and the unsettling belief of its civilian and military leaders that a window of opportunity existed to use German power for aggrandizement, but that it would close by *c.*1920; (6) Britain's reluctance to adjust to a relative decline in its status vis-à-vis Germany; (7) the existence of broad alliances or near-alliances which helped spread the war beyond the Balkans; (8) abrasive colonial rivalries; and (9) a series of key crises and war scares which raised international tensions from *c.*1900-14, worsened animosities and inflamed conflicts.

24 The United States never overcame its isolationism and stayed outside the League through its entire existence. Germany was admitted in 1925 at Locarno and given a permanent seat on the Council, but Hitler withdrew German membership in 1933. Japan withdrew in March 1933, in protest over the League's expressed interest in Tokyo's aggressive mischief in Manchuria. The Soviet Union joined in 1934, but it was expelled in 1940 for its unprovoked attack on Finland. Italy withdrew in 1937, over League sanctions introduced over the Abyssinian War. The League was formally dissolved in 1946, but the UN carried forward most of its basic structures.

25 See the compelling case for primary Soviet responsibility for the Cold War made by Gaddis (1997).

26 See Lundestad (1990), and (1998).

27 Mao Zedong in China and, separately, Hô Chí Minh concerning Vietnam, stated that Japan's initial defeat of the colonial powers during the Second World War greatly advanced the cause of revolution in their respective countries.

28 In fact, there is an ongoing debate throughout the history of international society about which grounds may warrant and justify forcible intervention in another state's internal affairs. For example, Grotius, Wolff, and John Stuart Mill all speculated on the circumstance that may call for intervention. These circumstances are always situated historically, but they were never wholly absent from international history or international society.

29 Nolan (1993a), pp. 223-39.

30 On this point, see Nolan (1993b).

31 For example, even democratic states such as Great Britain and Canada bitterly resisted American insistence on building respect for human rights as a state obligation into the Charter of the United Nations. On this point, see Nolan (1993b), pp. 181–206.

32 See the articles by Ikenberry, Ajami, and Maynes (2001); and Nye (1996), pp. 63–76.

33 Link (1993), pp. 95–108.

34 A masterful defense of the approach of the society of states approach to understanding international relations is Jackson (2000).

35 See Young (1997).

36 France remains a prickly pear of a nation state, but despite its odd forays into neo-colonialism and reflexive indulgence of the rhetoric of *raison d'état*, it too is today deeply committed to the liberal-internationalist approach to international security. For instance, see Keiger (2001).

37 See Kennedy-Pipe (2001); and Ulam (1974).

6 Security and self-determination

James Mayall

Self-determination and security are two of the most potent and contested concepts in modern social and political thought. Their potency – to which the frequent references elsewhere in this book to the political thought of Thomas Hobbes and Immanuel Kant bear witness – stems ultimately from their association with two of the deepest taproots in the human psyche: fear and desire, in particular fear of danger and desire for freedom. The contest arises because these are not terms that can be given a positive or unambiguous definition. For the same reason, the relationship between them will shift, depending on how they are perceived and analysed.

Consider, for example, the two most familiar accounts of this relationship. Most realists would agree that the first responsibility of any government is to guarantee the continued independence of the country over which they preside, and hence to provide for the physical security of the population. They do not often consider the identity of states – or indeed the democratic or human rights of the people – as important in themselves, although these days they would probably concede that they are factors to be entered into the calculus of relative power.

Similarly, they are likely to accept the interdependence imposed by the modern world economy, without abandoning the assumption that the underlying purpose of economic exchange is to deprive competitors of advantage. Where once Mercantilists were obsessed with plundering a fixed store of wealth, whether locked up in precious metals or exotic spices, modern realists remain determined to capture market share and to fight off predators. The success of this strategy will depend crucially on the accuracy of the calculation of the forces arranged against them. Consequently, the security of both state and people will also depend on this calculation. On this view, the national interest, as interpreted by state authorities, still determines the course of world politics, for better or worse.

Liberal internationalists see the matter differently. The formula advanced by Wilsonian liberals after 1918 inverted the realist analysis, although their conception of political identity was only slightly less superficial. They believed that the only proper guarantee of security was a democratic constitution, under which the rights of the people to govern themselves would be explicitly recognized. If pressed on who these people were, they would most probably have answered the nations. These were the self-evident collective groups that possessed the right of self-determination on grounds identified by J. S. Mill half a century earlier.[1] In other words, security would flow naturally from the mutual recognition of identity; that is, from the acknowledgement that in collective life, as in personal life, the only constraint placed on liberty was that it should not be at the expense of others.

Notoriously, this vision turned out to be fatally flawed when implemented in practice. But it remained both attractive and influential, despite being largely discredited by the experience of the interwar years. This was partly because it was closely linked to the principle of non-discrimination in liberal economic thought. The economic institutions established after 1945 – the IMF and GATT in particular – paid lip service to the primacy of national security. Currency convertibility in the first case, and trade liberalization in the second, were conditioned by the maintenance of balance of payments equilibrium and full employment. If these conditions were not met as a result of circumstances beyond the control of governments, then it was accepted that questions of national security take precedence.

Nonetheless, the underlying philosophy of these institutions held that an open economy which recognized the autonomy of both individuals and corporations provided a better guarantee of security than a Mercantilist closure of international borders and the almost inevitable involvement in an arms race that would accompany a rise in political tensions. This philosophy has enjoyed a revival since the end of the Cold War, as liberal enthusiasts reinforce the democratic peace argument with the idea of a deregulated world economy, policed by the World Trade Organization.

This juxtaposition of the most familiar rival positions suggests two preliminary conclusions. The first is that no final resolution of the relation between self-determination and security is available, even in principle. Those who deploy these concepts in political argument generally believe that they have a clear meaning and an unequivocal and mutually reinforcing relationship. They do not.

For Mazzini in the nineteenth century, as for Jawaharlal Nehru in the twentieth, insecurity flowed from a denial of identity. The solution lay in slaying the imperial dragon. Self-determination would be achieved through unification in the one case, independence in the other. It was self-evident, they believed, that Italy should belong to Italians just as India should belong to Indians. But who were to count as Italians and Indians? And where were the boundaries to be drawn, within which Italians and Indians could feel both safe and secure?

The answers to these questions were not at all self-evident. The resentment that some Italians felt when lands occupied by Italian speakers were left outside the new nation state acted like a permanent itch on the national psyche. How it was to be treated became an issue in Italian domestic politics and bequeathed to the world the concept of irredentism, which provided a direct nationalist challenge to the traditional concept of international order. The fact that some Italians were 'unredeemed' under the new political dispensation did not mean the Italian state was willing to surrender the German-speaking province of South Tyrol to Austria. Its disaffection was a constant, if for the most part latent, threat to territorial integrity until an autonomy agreement – originally negotiated between the two countries in 1946 – was finally implemented in 1992.[2]

The diversity of India rendered a linguistic or ethnic criterion of nationality implausible. But Nehru's commitment to secularism and to the anti-colonial conception of self-determination was underpinned by a powerful belief in India as an integrated and unique civilization.[3] In 1947, the Indian National Congress, which he led, reluctantly accepted partition and the creation of Pakistan under the two nation theory; however, any subsequent challenge to the idea of a united India was ruthlessly suppressed. Independent states such as Hyderabad and Goa, which were deemed to be historical and geographical anomalies, were incorporated by police action, while the Naga and Mizo rebellions on the northeast frontier were put down and their leaders imprisoned until such time as they were willing to be co-opted into the Indian system. However, it is the contested state of Kashmir, over which India and Pakistan fought two wars and now confront one another with nuclear armouries, which most vividly illustrates the way in which a conflict over self-determination can undermine rather than reinforce both national and international security.[4]

The second conclusion to be drawn from juxtaposing the realist and liberal positions is that they are not so diametrically opposed as they may appear at first sight. Indeed, it is what they hold in common – most notably the assumption of the self-evident and non-problematic nature of the state – that opens up a space within which compromises can be reached, and the everyday business of international relations conducted, in a reasonably orderly manner. In other words, it is because realists and liberals contest the relationship of security and self-determination on the basis of shared assumptions about political authority and the sovereignty of national governments that they need the institutions of international society, including international law and diplomatic practice, through which to conduct the argument.

I shall return to the consequences of this argument in the final section of this chapter. Here, I want to stress the limitations of the approach from an ethical point of view. We can learn from it why certain positions have been adopted. For example, we can understand why it was agreed, in the interests of security, to interpret the right of self-determination as a right to independence from European imperial powers based on the principle of *uti possidetis*. But, by itself, this story will explain neither why it is so difficult to move beyond this interpretation, nor the nature of the dilemmas to which it repeatedly gives rise. To answer these questions, it may be helpful to look in more detail at the concepts themselves, and their psychological origins.

Security: the emotional power of the status quo

Security is a relative concept, but not entirely so. Reflect for a moment on what we intuitively recognize as insecurity. At one level, this intuition is unlikely to be universal. We know that human beings are highly adaptive; and, presumably, that is why they have survived so successfully. They can – and do – live in all sorts of environments, many of them inhospitable. Indeed, there is a widespread assumption that emotional security, defined in terms of maintaining the bond between a child and its natural parents (particularly its mother) is more important than material affluence or physical comfort for its subsequent development into a person capable of autonomous action and, therefore, of self-determination in the common sense meaning of the term.

It is on account of this belief that, in industrial countries, the authorities are reluctant to remove children from their parents, even those that come from the most dysfunctional families. Small children – as all parents know – are tyrannical traditionalists: they like an established routine. If they are unfortunate enough to grow up in an unstable, unenlightened, or chaotic household, this environment will constitute the familiar status quo. It is, after all, the only world the child knows. It may stimulate them to escape, as it did Gavino Ledda, the author of the powerful autobiography *Padre Padrone*. This book, which was subsequently made into a brilliant film, tells the story of a sensitive but brutalized little boy who eventually leaves rural Sardinia to find education and the possibility of self-determination.[5] But like many others before and after, the emotional power of what many of us would think of as a world of chronic insecurity, proved irresistible. He went back.

In discussions about human security it is sometimes argued that there is an absolute level of destitution – the point where relative deprivation turns into starvation – which defines the real meaning of insecurity. This is no doubt true. When we think of the frequency with which this situation arises, it opens up a grim prospect indeed. It also raises one of the most fundamental ethical dilemmas of our time: since starvation is avoidable, should those who, in theory at least, could do something about it, intervene irrespective of the political situation and even, if necessary, in opposition to the wishes of the local government? However, in this limiting case, the victim has lost all capacity for autonomous action and, therefore, for self-defence, so the problem is not one of a trade-off between self-determination and security. Rather it is a problem for third parties who are called on to offer disinterested relief, and whose own basic security is not threatened.[6]

A more useful measure of the limits of relativism in relation to security is suggested by what, it seems to me, is likely to prove a virtually universal reaction to natural disaster. 'A bad earthquake', Charles Darwin wrote after his experience in Chile in 1835, 'at once destroys the oldest associations; the world, the very emblem of all that is solid, had moved beneath our feet like a crust over fluid; one second of time had created in the mind a strange idea of insecurity, which hours of reflection would not have produced.'[7]

We know that human beings can live with the prospect of imminent natural catastrophe, as they do every day along the San Andreas fault or on the slopes of Vesuvius. In such circumstances the near certain knowledge that the past is likely to repeat itself becomes a constitutive part of their identity. In the wake of the tsunami that devastated the Indonesian province of Aceh at the end of 2004, and wrecked havoc on a smaller scale in Sri Lanka, Thailand, and India, the tourists are likely to stay away for a time; but even without the substantial international help that the disaster elicited, the local population have little choice but to rebuild their homes and their lives. What else can they do? Again, we find that the status quo holds trumps. We may reasonably hazard that people who find themselves in these kinds of circumstances cope with their situation partly with the help of a strong version of the denial that we all practice when confronting the dangers of everyday life, and partly by persuading themselves that the odds against renewed disaster are long. To be sure, they are shorter than against the earth being hit by an asteroid, but not so short as to make abject surrender to the forces of nature a rational strategy.

Nonetheless, if we are proofed against over-investment in fears, whose object we have not experienced, Darwin's account of an earthquake he *did* experience has the ring of authenticity. Perhaps the imagery with which he described the event was coloured by his training as a natural scientist and by the intellectual preconceptions of his country and social class. But it is difficult to believe that, in any important sense, his reaction to the earthquake was culture specific. It is more plausible to assume that the process of living through a natural catastrophe will have traumatic effects on anyone who experiences it, although the ways in which they deal with the trauma may indeed differ with cultural background. If this argument is accepted in relation to typhoons, earthquakes, or floods – catastrophes that are typically classified as 'acts of God' – it seems reasonable to assume that experience of man-made catastrophes, be they war, terrorism, genocide and ethnic cleansing, or hyper-inflation, will have broadly similar consequences.

The main difference is that governments cannot ultimately be held responsible for 'acts of God', even given the formidable predictive powers of modern science, whereas in the modern nation state they are held responsible for inflicting war on the population (particularly if they lose) or for committing acts of economic folly. This was not always so: for much of recorded history war was accepted, along with pestilence, famine, and death, as one of the four horsemen of the Apocalypse. When they might choose to ride was as unpredictable, but also as unavoidable, as changes in the weather. This is no longer the general assumption because the modern state, unlike its predecessors, allegedly rests on popular sovereignty – that is, on the self-determination of the people. It is *their* welfare, *their* homeland, and *their* identity – attributes that are more often than not conflated – that have to be protected from external attack and internal decay.

Self-determination and the power of denial

For those on the liberal side of the debate that I sketched at the start of this chapter, security – particularly military security – is seen as a realist preoccupation. Realists, in the liberal view, are obsessed with treating security as an unobtainable absolute, preparing for the worst, and thus, very often, ensuring that it comes about. Liberals are more inclined to see the security problem as something subordinate to that of self-determination. The concept itself stems from the broader idea of freedom in general and from the potential for individual development in particular. As with security, there are limits to this malleability, a fact accepted by most liberals other than extreme libertarians and existentialists.

The limits to the malleability of self-determination are set by the attributes of identity. If it is said that something has an identity – and for the moment it does not matter whether it is a material object or a human subject – it must mean that it can be recognized for what or who it is across space and time. The only qualification to this statement is that provided by natural processes. Even metal is prone to fatigue and caterpillars change into butterflies. No such luck for human beings, who merely grow old before they die. However, so long as they retain a capacity for even minimal action, their will can be identified as singular. It is this attribute, I suggest, that we normally associate with a capacity for self-determination.

Agency – this capacity for self-willed action – can be exercised in any direction, but its default setting is negative. In other words, what defines a 'free' person is their ability to say no. It is also, one might add, their willingness to suffer the consequences. Slaves are defined by the absence of these qualities. If they rebel because slavery is an unnatural condition and an affront to their human dignity, they will either be killed, forced back into servitude, or become free. Of course a free man, usually a traditional ruler, may be given an offer he cannot easily refuse, or tricked into putting himself under the protection of a stronger power, only to discover that he has surrendered his birthright and, in some cases, consigned his people to extinction. This was more or less what the unholy alliance of American plantation owners, traders, and missionaries did to the Hawaiian monarchy at the end of the nineteenth century. But while possibilities plainly exist, they do not negate the definition of agency as negative freedom. The self may not be given in advance – it may even be imagined or invented – but it is subject nonetheless to a reality test: can it sustain itself, and, if necessary, by resistance?

The dangers inherent in arguing by analogy, that is, in this case, in assuming that collective identities have the same properties as individual identities, are well known. However, how else can we analyse the concept of self-determination, particularly in an age when sovereignty is held to reside with all the people, and not merely with a caste of rulers, whom alone are free? When President de Gaulle signalled his willingness to seek a negotiated end to the Algerian revolt, he spoke of a 'peace of the brave'.[8] Since 1830, Algeria had been defined as part of metropolitan France, but Algerians, de Gaulle conceded, had established their separate identity and their right to independence by being willing to die for it.

Reprise

The ambiguities involved in the relationship between the concepts of security and self-determination should now be reasonably clear. In both cases, there is a wide, but not infinite, discretionary area of interpretation. Its limits reflect the common experience of human beings and the symbiotic relationship of the two concepts, psychologically. This discretionary area reflects the variety of human experience and fuels the contest over how it should be interpreted politically.

With regard to security, an armed attack across the recognized borders of a state is still likely to be interpreted as a threat to human as well as to state security, particularly by those whose homes lie directly in the path of marauding armies, or become targets – intentionally or not – of bombardment from the air. From their perspective, the justifications offered by those who unleash the dogs of war are beside the point. NATO's bombing campaign against Yugoslavia in 1999 was as much an attack on the status quo, and therefore on our common sense understanding of security, as Saddam Hussein's attack on Kuwait in 1990, the genocide unleashed by Hutu extremists against Rwandan Tutsi in 1994, or the US-led coalition's assault on the Iraqi city of Fallujah in December 2004. Unlike Darwin's experience of the Chilean earthquake, these catastrophes were the result of deliberate human action, but their effects are similarly recognizable across time and space – that is, across historical periods and diverse cultures.

This is not so with all security threats. The threat to social stability represented by a rapid rise of unemployment, a shortage of fossil fuels at affordable prices, or the criminalization of society as a result of the burgeoning international drugs trade, is not likely to be perceived as a threat to fundamental security in countries where the majority of the population have little prospect of paid employment or live outside the exchange economy altogether; where they do not possess automobiles and are not dependent on modern technology; or where the opium poppy is the only cash crop that will generate a surplus, and, therefore, even a modest prospect of improving their lot. Only in the industrial West is the concept of social security a public, rather than a purely private, concern (let alone an international concern). Conversely, the destruction of the Amazon rainforest, or the practice of dragnet fishing in the Pacific, is not taken seriously as a security threat in Western countries, even though it threatens indigenous communities in the Amazon basin and the Pacific islands with extinction.

The pattern with regard to self-determination is broadly similar. We are right to be shocked by the fact that the Tasmanians were hunted to extinction in the early nineteenth century, but there is *no* point in claiming for them the right of self-determination. Like many other peoples over the ages, they failed to survive. The odds were too heavily stacked against them and they disappeared as the result of extermination, assimilation, dispersal, or some combination of these and other causes.

Contemporary political consciousness allows us to entertain alternative and less brutal arrangements. Indeed, if, as many now believe, cultural diversity is to be valued for analogous reasons to those advanced in support of bio-diversity, then groups threatened with extinction, either through the destruction of their habitat or by forced assimilation, deserve protection.[9] Environmentalists have joined forces with the representatives of small states and indigenous peoples in an effort to obtain political leverage, or at least to ensure that the voices of the dispossessed are heard. But, whatever *should* be the case, in practice their right to self-determination is conditional rather than absolute. It is dependent on their not threatening the identity and/or physical security of the majority population among whom they live.[10]

Governments seldom have to confront an outright bid for independence from indigenous peoples, whereas they continue to fear that national minorities may seize on any concession as an excuse to destabilize the political order. The reason is that national minorities often look across the border to another state, where their kinsmen or ethnic group are in the majority or control the government. Security and self-determination can be reconciled, but only through arduous negotiation and in a favourable international environment, as in South Tyrol. In many more cases, minority self-determination is viewed by the majority as threatening secession.

The absolute and the relative are thus constantly in tension. The nurturing of an individual's identity to a point where he or she is capable of autonomous action requires protection from danger, particularly during the formative period of infancy. But, because the forging and maintenance of identity requires security, it also necessarily at some point involves constraints on the sovereign will. This in turn opens up the political argument since the trade-off between freedom and safety can be struck at any point along a spectrum. 'Live Free or Die', the New Hampshire license plate logo, summarizes one possible resolution; 'Better Red than Dead', the once popular slogan of the Campaign for Nuclear Disarmament (CND), another and opposite one. The liberal maxim that my (or my country's) freedom, must not harm anyone else's, is a sympathetic attempt to have it both ways. It cannot, however, deal with hard cases.

From individual to collective self-determination: the perils of nationalism

In practice, such cases can only be resolved politically and within a context that shifts the focus from considerations of personal safety and individual autonomy to collective security and national self-determination. Conflict is no doubt inseparable from social life, but in retrospect, its scale and scope seems (paradoxically) to have been more human, or at least more restrained, before the rise of nationalism. When only rulers were free, their ambitions may have been unbridled, but the national security state did not exist. We have paid a high price for the modern insistence on the collective ownership of the state.

Before then, wars were often fought with mercenary armies and affected the lives of the predominantly peasant populations only when their crops were requisitioned or they found themselves having to provide billets for a passing army.[11] Well before full-scale industrialization, let alone the introduction of aerial warfare, Napoleon had initiated the change with the introduction of the *levee en masse*. The nationalist wars of the nineteenth and twentieth centuries increasingly involved the population at large. Democratic government may have introduced a firewall against the bellicosity of earlier warrior societies, but the need for a moral justification for the use of force, and a total one at that, was not unquestionably evidence of progress. As George Kennan once wrote,

> there is nothing in nature more egocentrical as an embattled democracy. It soon becomes the victim of its own war propaganda. It then tends to attach to its own cause an absolute value which distorts its own vision of everything else. Its enemy becomes the embodiment of all evil.[12]

Once – not so long ago – irresolvable conflicts of interest or honour, whether between individuals or states, were settled by combat. Now, judging by the evidence of the Dayton Accords, the only way that such a verdict can be accepted is by diplomatic sleight of hand. The internal and so-to-say lived boundaries of Bosnia were changed by the most time honoured and brutal of methods – Sarajevo and Gorazdne were flattened and Srebrenica, declared a safe haven by the UN, was purged of its Muslim population – but the international personality of Bosnia as the recognized successor state of the Yugoslav federation was preserved. Much the same happened in Kosovo. After NATO's military victory over Milosovic in 1999, the administration of the territory was handed over to the United Nations, but formally it remains part of Yugoslavia, a fact that continues to complicate any final resolution of the territory's status.

Nor is the pattern confined to Europe. India retains the Kashmir Valley by force of arms; the guerrilla conflict between the Tamil Tigers and the Sri Lankan state rumbled on, until an agreement that formally preserved the integrity of the Sri Lankan state while conceding to the Tamils a large measure of internal autonomy, was signed in August 2002 – whether it will hold remains uncertain; north and south Sudan have been at almost continuous loggerheads since independence in 1956; and just as it seemed to be edging towards some kind of resolution at the end of 2004, a ferocious conflict, claimed by many observers to be of genocidal proportions, opened up between the Muslim African and Arab communities in the western province of Darfur.

It would not be difficult to find other examples. Apart from the loss of life, the flood of refugees into neighbouring countries, the internal displacement of huge numbers of people, and the physical destruction of the economic and social fabric of society that has accompanied these conflicts, what is remarkable is how little has changed. Even in those cases where there has been a de facto change of control – in Ngorno Karabach, occupied by Armenian forces, or Abkhazia, wrested from Georgia by its tiny indigenous population – official recognition has been withheld. In the vast majority of cases the political map remains as it was before the outbreak of war. The reason, as we shall see shortly, is that, now that trial by combat is ruled out, international society lacks a recognized way of differentiating between those groups that have a right of self-determination and those that do not.

So why is it so difficult to change the political map, even when to do so might help to resolve an intractable territorial dispute, improve the security of all concerned, and reduce the human suffering that its continuation necessarily entails? Why, further, does it appear to have become more rather than less difficult at a time when the process of globalization has, in many respects, undermined the capacity of governments to deliver the fundamental political, economic, and social goods that provided a major part of the nineteenth century justification of the nation state?

The Japanese Samurai who returned from their European tour determined to transform their ancient society into a modern nation state have no present equivalent. At that time the marriage of territorial statehood with nationalist ideology drove forward the process of economic modernization. It required a territorial base and success was ultimately measured by military victory – in the Japanese case, over the Russians and Chinese.[13] But, these days, ethnic and national conflict is more likely to create an economic wasteland; whereas, in theory, a peaceful resolution, by partition if necessary, could open up the afflicted territory to inward investment and the prospect of economic recovery. But so rational an outcome remains beyond our grasp despite the labours of an army of conflict researchers.

I do not pretend to have a complete answer to these questions, but I contend that part of the explanation is to be found in the view that only nations should have states. Since there is no objective test for deciding under what circumstances a group meets the criteria for nation-hood, this view is widely translated as meaning that only existing states can have nations. The inevitable consequence is that conflicts over self-determination exhibit a tendency to develop pathologically. This potential is present in all versions of nationalism and seems to spring from its propensity to invest territory with symbolic significance to a point where even to contemplate territorial adjustment becomes tantamount to blasphemy. What are the symptoms of this condition? And under what circumstances does it occur?

I shall attempt to explore these questions by contrasting the relationship of territory to statehood before and after the rise of nationalism and national self-determination. Before doing so, though, I should emphasize what I am not arguing. First, I do not claim that nationalism is the root cause of war, either between states or within them. Second, I do not wish to suggest that all nationalism is pathological.

The ultimate causes of war remain beyond the reach of both philosophers and social scientists. Human beings are not the only animal species to prey on each other, but they are, so far as I am aware, the only one which has always organized for war in a systematic and disciplined way and practised intra-species aggression, often in the absence of any self-evident provocation or imperative of natural necessity. The nationalists inherited this disposition from earlier forms of social organization. They then nationalized it in the same way in which they nationalized most other institutions of social life such as education or public health.

The nationalization of security contributed to the sacralization of territory, and hence, under certain circumstances, to a pathological form of nationalism. But the human propensity for war long preceded the rise of nationalism; and although those who advance the democratic peace argument would have it otherwise, we have no reliable evidence that it will not survive. In the meantime, it is hard to improve on Kenneth Waltz's original account, in which he reviewed the debate between those who locate the causes of war in terms of human nature, those who see its origins in the internal structure of state – and thereby claim to have identified an escape – and those who regard it as a consequence of international anarchy, the price that states must pay – and indeed choose to pay – for their independence.[14] It is possible to discover many things about the proximate causes of particular wars, including the part played by nationalist sentiment and ideology since the French Revolution. But, for reasons discussed earlier that relate to the psychological hold on our imaginations of the ideas of danger and freedom, war itself is woven too deeply into the history of humanity to be easily isolated.

Not all nationalism is pathological. At a time when most work on nationalism concentrates on the ethnic origins of nations, it is worth reminding ourselves that it was in the first place a political doctrine of liberation for peoples who shared a common history and culture, but who paid little self-conscious attention to matters of ethnic ancestry. This broadly civic concept was taken over, with varying degrees of success, by anti-colonial nationalists in the revolt against Western imperialism and it survives in most of the Western democracies. However, the idea that constitutional forms of government are somehow uncontaminated seems to me to be based on a fundamental misunderstanding of the modern world.

No form of government, however stable and legitimate, can afford to dispense with the loyalty of its citizens. Moreover, no government that is charged with their welfare can afford to be so cosmopolitan in its outlook and policies, that it can disregard the identity of its national community and pay no attention to those who have and those who do not have a peremptory right to the entitlements of citizenship. Democracies thus rely both on the active patriotism of their citizens and on nationality as a passive classificatory and administrative principle. The current anxiety displayed by most industrial democracies about the threat of illegal immigration may often be neurotic and insensitive. Indeed, in Europe, governments seem to have created a system in which even legitimate asylum seekers have strong incentives to cross borders illegally, so difficult is it to establish their bona fides. But official anxiety is not itself irrational or pathological.

It is sometimes argued that fascism and ultra-nationalism are to be distinguished from the genuine article by their quite different intellectual origins. The attraction of this argument for liberal nationalists is obvious: they can be comfortable with their nationalism. The truth is surely that the intellectual content of nationalist ideas, *qua* ideas, is so feeble that nationalists have always had to contract marriages of convenience with other ideologies in order to translate a popular movement into a political programme. This is because a theory, whose only substantive claim is that every nation should have its own state, not only fails to establish an uncontested definition of the nation; it has nothing to say about how national independence should be achieved or what policies should be pursued once the promised land has been reached. Liberalism and Marxism may not have much to say about identity but they generate social and economic policies that aspiring nationalists find useful. Liberals and Marxists also have intellectual genealogies of their own; indeed, originally they denounced nationalism as a form of irrationalism. But in their pursuit of power, they, like fascists, recognized its emotional power and accommodated it for practical rather than theoretical reasons.

There are states – Liberia under Charles Taylor was one example – where the leadership scarcely bothers to appeal to public opinion (even rhetorically) to justify its hold on power. But wherever such appeals are made, it is the nation that is invoked. Through the films of Sergei Eisenstein, Stalin identified himself with Ivan the Terrible in mobilizing support for the Great Patriotic War; in 1949 Mao Tse Tung announced the success of the Revolution not in the universal language of the Communist Manifesto – 'Workers of the World Unite' but in the language of national regeneration – 'the Chinese people have stood up'. And to this day American servicemen and women cannot be put 'in harm's way' unless Congress has identified a threat to specifically American national interests and, then, only so long as they are under direct US command. This was true even before the events of September 2001 and the invasion of Afghanistan. But with the annunciation of the doctrine of pre-emption as the basis of American foreign policy, and the subsequent attack on Iraq, it has become even more prominent.

Where the great powers lead, the others follow.[15] Rather than trying to distinguish sharply between democratic, communist, fascist, and nationalist regimes, it seems safer – and more accurate – to accept that the nation state, nationalism, and the principle of national self-determination describe the political architecture of the modern world and its social and legal justification. They may not always do so but they do at the present time. We may like or dislike this phenomenon but we cannot sensibly identify it as the disease. This is an important distinction because it means that ethical judgements cannot simply ignore national sentiment.

So much for what I am not arguing: that nationalism is the cause of war and, therefore, of the chronic insecurity in much of the world. Nor is it the root of all evil or a pathological disease, per se, let alone, as Albert Einstein once described it, an infantile disease like measles. If we are to explore some of the reasons – and I confine myself to the international reasons – for the tendency of pathological variants to develop and proliferate, we need to return to the relationship between territory, the state, and the way in which conflicts between states were handled before and after the rise of nationalism.

The pre-history of contemporary international society

The traditional account of the rise of the modern state system locates it at the juncture of two major developments: the break-up of European Christendom and the decline of feudalism in the face of the centralizing state. The wars of religion that accompanied these events and acted as the midwife of our own world not only lasted for thirty years but left a terrible trail of destruction in their wake. The peace the princes made in Westphalia in 1648 sealed a process that had its origins in the Augsburg settlement of 1555, which ended a previous phase of European religious warfare. Indeed, in Adam Watson's words, 'it was in a sense the extension to the whole system of the Augsburg formula.'[16] Like its predecessor, the 1648 treaties were based on the elevation of the principle of sovereignty and its twin entailments. One was non-interference, or in the language of a princely and still religious age: *cuius regio eius religio.* The other entailment was territorial integrity: if sovereigns were to have the right to determine the religious identity within their jurisdiction (subject to tolerating the beliefs of religious minorities to which they had expressly agreed) the boundaries between states had to be clearly marked. A shift had quietly been sanctioned: power over people, still of central importance in a world that was internally organized along hierarchical lines, began to give way externally to power over things, above all to power over territory. The post-Westphalia states system was a real estate system.

At this point in the story we encounter a paradox. The pre-modern period had its own form of pathological excess, but it resulted from a perversion of faith rather than from making a fetish of the land on which the majority of people depended for their livelihood, regardless of who ruled them. 'When we have destroyed the land, then we will make peace.' In his play (*The Camp of Wallenstein*), Schiller, writing at the high point of German romanticism, puts these words into the mouth of Wallenstein, the Swedish General on the Protestant side, who mournfully describes the pathological behaviour to which the religious wars had led. Because the land was a real economic resource – the basis of Ernest Gellner's *Agraria* – self-preservation required that the link between secular administration and spiritual enthusiasm should be broken.[17] Or to put it another way: the princes discovered the importance of loyal subjects and the attraction of national, or at least state-level, administrations and churches. If there had to be enthusiasm it should be attached to the state and not to a theological conception of the good life or humanity at large.

The antidote on which the princes eventually settled, proscription of religious wars between Christian states, was in other respects highly permissive. Saving war had saved civilization.[18] For the first time the acquisition of territory became an end in itself. Political boundaries were redrawn in Europe because of wars fought for reasons of state or to maintain the balance of power. Elsewhere, the European powers began to enclose the rest of the world, a process that often involved them in ferocious competition with one another and acts of great brutality against the local people who got in their way. The forcible removal, and in some cases virtual extermination, of the inhabitants of the Moluccas, when they attempted to frustrate Dutch attempts to wrest the monopoly of the spice trade from the Portuguese, is an all too typical example.[19]

If the non-interference principle nonetheless stabilized the system in Europe, it was no doubt partly because the political order left social relations within the new fortress-like boundaries of the state relatively undisturbed. The mass of the people was not directly involved in politics, even in Northwest Europe where the centralized state had already laid the foundations for its subsequent nationalization. And in most of Southern and Eastern Europe the concept of popular sovereignty lacked any social reality before 1919.[20] The social order in most of the non-European world was even less affected.

It is true that peasant populations, then as now, often lived very insecure lives in the absolute sense of the term described earlier. More than other members of society, they were vulnerable to the ravages of natural disaster, marauding armies, or the extortion of rapacious but usually absentee landowners. Nevertheless, it is not mere nostalgia to suggest that they could also draw succour – and hence emotional security – from traditional folkways and customs that had little to do with church or state. The role of local shrines and saints, and, indeed, of heretical movements that had a tendency to spring up almost as soon as they were suppressed in both Christendom and Islam, is one such example.

The difference between the pre-1914 world and our own is not always, or everywhere, about territory. It is also sometimes about the claims that the state makes on its citizens, even when they do not – and realistically cannot – live the lives of citizens. The recruitment of children to fight in the Iran–Iraq war, or in several contemporary African civil wars, is a case in point. These children are very often abducted from their familiar surroundings and, by all accounts, are so traumatized by the experience of war that it would be folly to suppose that after the war they will easily fold back into the traditional support system of peasant society. In some third world countries – Angola for example – prolonged civil war has arguably so pulverized traditional society that it has created the preconditions for the emergence of a genuine nation, as distinct from an aspiring nationalist movement. It is possible; but in the absence of industrial employment of the kind that mopped up the surplus rural population in nineteenth century Europe, the odds must be on a pathological, rather than a benign, evolution of nationalism.

Nationalist pathology

The fetishism of territory, which lies at the heart of nationalist pathology, stems directly from the elevation of the principle of self-determination to its present position as an allegedly inalienable human right and the only theoretically legitimate basis of statehood. It is true that the phrase 'national self-determination' does not occur in the UN Charter, the Universal Declaration of Human Rights, or in either of its supporting Covenants. The phrase used is 'the right of all peoples to self-determination'. The choice of words seems to have been deliberate, in the hope of avoiding a repetition of the rash of competing national claims that had proved so troublesome after 1919. Presumably the intention was to signal that only populations of existing states – and subsequently of European colonies –

had a right to self-determination. If so, it did not have the desired effect – the definition of a people turned out to be just as contested as that of a nation.

It is irrelevant whether a people or a nation holds the right to self-determination. The theoretical and practical problems to which this elevation of self-determination gives rise are well known, and are the same in both cases. The concept is theoretically incoherent because of the contested nature and boundaries of the nation. Practically, it is impossible to implement because in very few parts of the world does the cultural, let alone the ethnic, map coincide with the political map.

The twin threats of irredentism and secession, to which the nationalization of world politics gave rise, emerged at the end of the nineteenth century. There were early indications of their pathological tendencies, such as the Armenian genocide and the forced population movements between Greece and Turkey. Armenian and Turkish peasants had tolerated one another under Ottoman rule so long as their homeland was not defined in exclusive terms as the sacred patrimony of the Turkish state.

The extent to which the Wilsonian vision of a world made safe for democracy and national self-determination would challenge rather than support the international order also became evident immediately after the First World War. The gruesome consequences of the demands for organic democracy in much of Europe were submerged by the Second World War and the territorial stabilization imposed on Europe by the Cold War division and the reintroduction, in the east, of authoritarian rather than democratic rule. The end of the Cold War put the clock back, revealing that little had been done to resolve the underlying problem in the meantime. Nor is it clear that the US neoconservative project of promoting democracy in the deeply divided sectarian societies of the Middle East will fare much better.

I have already argued that it would be wrong to conclude from these examples that nationalist pathology is confined to Europe. But nor is the current – and increasingly unsuccessful – formula for containing it, primarily a European construct. The withdrawal of European power, first from Latin America in the nineteenth century and then from the rest of the world in two great waves of disengagement after 1919 and 1945, raised the question of who was to succeed to the imperial regimes and within what borders? The first question was answered by equating self-determination with decolonization – the successor regime took over the colonial state. Similarly, they inherited a variety of existing and potential border disputes that had been suppressed, or simply not acknowledged, under imperial rule.

The irredentist wars that followed the withdrawal of Spain and Portugal from South America – most famously the war between Paraguay and the Triple Alliance which killed off a major part of Paraguay's population –

provided a warning of the dreadful consequences of treating territory as a positional good and therefore as non-negotiable. The principle of *uti possidetis juris*, like the European principle of *cuius regio eius religio*, was intended as a practical solution to an otherwise irresolvable ethical problem. Since appealing to the principle of self-determination could not settle the issue of rival territorial claims, what criteria were to be used to decide who had title? The answer was that in the absence of a negotiated boundary adjustment, successor states would accept the borders that they had inherited at independence.

The principle was revived after 1960 when African successor states, whose leaders had often previously called for the redrawing of African boundaries in line with African social and cultural realities, became fearful of opening a Pandora's Box of ethnic claims and counter-claims. The principle did not originally enjoy the same status in post-colonial Asia, where several coercive consolidations occurred in the immediate aftermath of decolonization, and in the case of Indonesia's annexation of East Timor, as late as 1974.[21] However, this annexation was increasingly viewed as an aberration, and in 1999 the conventional interpretation of self-determination as decolonization was used to justify the territory's claim to independence and to distinguish it from separatist demands elsewhere in the Indonesian archipelago. *Uti possidetis* was also imported into the former Soviet Union and Eastern Europe where it was used to transform the internal administrative boundaries of the Soviet Union and the former Yugoslav Federation into internationally recognized borders.

Secession seldom solves the human problem to which it is addressed, namely the need to buttress the identity and enhance the security of a breakaway population. The reason is that it creates disenfranchised minority groups trapped within the new states. To that extent, the application of *uti possidetis* is a useful exercise in damage limitation. But it is a less effective therapy for nationalist rivalry than the non-interference principle was in the case of religious warfare. A post-Cold War legal study of *uti possidetis juris* concluded, somewhat optimistically, that the principle need not trump self-determination because the circumstances that had made it good law in the colonial context no longer apply. The author admitted that in General Assembly Resolution 1541 the Assembly conceded that 'the self government inherent in decolonization need not result only in independence, but that this decision would rest with the colonial peoples alone'.[22]

This line of thought echoed ideas that were raised in 1945 during debates on the framing of the UN Charter and the establishment of the Trusteeship Council.[23] Proponents of imperial trusteeship suggested that the right to self-determination could be respected by drawing dependent peoples into an association with the metropolitan power. The British flirtation with the idea of an imperial federation and citizenship did not last long; what did persist, though, was the idea that Dominion status within the Commonwealth created a relationship closer than that which normally exists between two sovereign states. In contrast, the French clung to the concept of a Franco-African partnership until 1960, when the former colonies – with the sole exception of Guinea – that had voted in 1958 to accept the idea, abandoned it in favour of full membership of the United Nations.

Steven Ratner is no doubt right to argue that 'decolonization did not have to entail adoption of *uti possidetis*' but, strictly speaking, he is wrong to maintain that it was adopted 'because it kept decolonization – a development regarded almost universally as imperative – orderly'.[24] It was not revived by the colonial powers but by successor African governments, although it certainly appealed to state authorities everywhere as a principle of order. It is also true that sometimes there are possibilities for satisfying demands for self-determination – and hence strengthening security – without creating a new independent state. Referenda were used successfully, although not without offering future hostages to fortune, in settling the national identity of the divided Trust territories of Cameroon and Togo at the time of independence from Britain and France. South Tyrol, as we have already seen, is a more recent example. Such cases, however, are more like exceptions that prove the rule that under conditions of democratic government, there is nothing so difficult to change as an international border.[25]

Moreover, what is to happen when such rational solutions are not accepted because a previously internal border that was regarded as tolerable within the framework of a federation is not accepted as legitimate within the context of its dissolution and independent statehood? Or when those who win control of a successor state seek to replace the indirect rule of the former imperial power by forced assimilation and/or centralized nation building? These symptoms presage a slide towards pathological nationalism. When they are present, the flip side of the *uti possidetis* doctrine becomes apparent. Good fences no longer make for good neighbours. Rather the doctrine ceases to operate as an incentive to rational problem solving, and serves instead to legitimize savagery and the militarization of society to a point where the cure is often worse than the disease.

It was unfortunate that the model that was inherited at independence was that of the national security state. In the majority of cases, particularly in Africa, there was no external threat. This inheritance paved the way for the widespread military hijacking of the state apparatus, which was regarded by the new politico-military class as an exploitable resource for their own enrichment. In many countries, the government itself was the major source of insecurity. Nor is it clear that the return to civilian, and ostensibly democratic, rule in many countries during the 1990s has done much to improve either the self-determination or security of the mass of the population.

Uti possidetis is less effective as a therapy than the earlier principle for three main reasons. The first is that popular passions are more likely to be involved. This may be, as in the Serbian attachment to Kosovo, because a territory, or even an entire landscape, is imbued with symbolic significance within a particular nationalist mythology. Alternatively, it may be that changes in the regional and wider international climate provide an opportunity for a majority community to overturn the traditional dominance of a minority, as with the Kosovo Albanians or the Rwandan Hutu. Where political life is organized along lines of communal or sectarian confrontation, the absence of local or international provision for territorial adjustment can lead society to implode. The case of Somalia, where the state disintegrated, once the safety valve of irredentism in the Ogaden was closed in 1978, provides a dramatic illustration of this possibility.

The second reason why the *uti possidetis* principle may backfire is simply that there is no appeal beyond it. Admittedly, it was the central aim of the Westphalian system to remove such an appeal in interstate relations. But in the period between 1648 and the French Revolution, the fact that territory could change hands, without having a cathartic effect on the lives of ordinary people, allowed the system to operate more or less as intended. Once politics were nationalized, military defeat in contested territory such as Alsace-Lorraine began to be followed by mass population transfers. The twentieth century attempts to outlaw war as an instrument of foreign policy amounted to a recognition that in a world of popular sovereignties, territory could no longer be treated as so much real estate, to be traded on the battlefield, brought under new ownership by inclusion in the dowry of royal brides, or literally bought and sold as in the cases of the Louisiana and Oregon purchases and Alaska.

The final unfortunate side effect of the doctrine is that it raises the symbolic value of holding territory at a time when changes in the nature of the world economy are undermining both its economic value and the ability of many governments to resolve internal political problems by economic means. Many of the Mercantilist moorings of the international economy have been sheered with the result that it can no longer be accurately described as primarily a set of interstate relationships and transactions. In these circumstances, states at the losing end of the globalization process also lose much of their *raison d'être*. In many cases ethnic or other groups that seize valuable assets – the diamond mines and logging operations in Sierra Leone for example – are able to operate internationally without the state.[26] When this happens, the central government has little other than its juridical sovereignty to cling to. International recognition still provides access to the institutional order – above all to the international financial institutions – capturing and holding the centre is still a major prize, but, the economic welfare of the population at large can be ignored since it seldom generates much revenue for the political class, and there are therefore few local pressures to seek a political rather than a military solution. For evidence of the legitimacy crisis that has been pro-voked by nationalist pathology one need only turn to United Nations High Commissioner for Refugees (UNHCR) statistics, which draw atten-tion to the plight of 19.8 million people, including twelve million refugees and over five million internally displaced persons.

It is beyond the scope of this chapter to offer a solution. Woodrow Wilson made a parallel diagnosis and proposed a solution in his original draft of the League Covenant. His draft of Article X provided for a peri-odic review of international borders and the creation of a mechanism for bringing about peaceful adjustment. It failed to convince even the Amer-ican delegation to the Versailles Conference and was quickly abandoned. In his *Agenda for Peace*, published by the United Nations in 1992, Boutros Boutros-Ghali argued that the way forward was to redefine national self-determination as the right of democratic participation within existing frontiers, combined with respect for human rights and particularly minor-ity rights.[27] This prescription would no doubt do much to immunize soci-eties against the disease, but except in the minds of the more enthusiastic American neo-conservatives, it remains unclear how it is to be delivered.

Final reflections

What conclusions can be drawn from these reflections on the dilemmas of security in an age of national self-determination? Two are perhaps worth a final comment. The first is to reiterate a point that was hinted at in the first section, namely that while the debate between liberals and realists, about the relationship of the two concepts and its political impact, is about real issues, above all where to strike the balance between prudence and trust, it is not a first order argument. Nor is it one that can be won definitively, one way or the other. Liberals and realists share many of the assumptions about the nature of the social and political world. They also face the same need for protection and harbour the same psychological and material ambition for autonomy. Indeed, the argument between Hobbes and Kant is not merely academic; acknowledged or not, it goes on all the time within the heads of most thinking people.

The dilemmas that are rooted in our psychological make-up are, it seems to me, just that. They are not going to be resolved by a session on a cosmopolitan psychiatrist's couch. In the end, they will continue to call for judgement, based on experience, our capacity for empathy with other human beings, and close attention to the social and political context in which they arise. The subjectivism implied by this conclusion will not satisfy either proactive international lawyers, or the swelling ranks of inter-national moral philosophers. But the onus of proof is on them to show that a better alternative is available.

The second conclusion is that we need to have respect for the argu-ment that holds that international society is evolving away from the pluralist law of coexistence, under which the state can sit as judge and jury in its own case. Throughout the twentieth century there has been a series of crab-like advances towards a more solidarist conception, under which governments – and their leaders – can be held to account. The establishment of the International Criminal Court (ICC) is just the latest manifestation of this evolution. From this point of view it could even be argued that the revival and modification of the principle of *uti possidetis* after the Cold War, to which I referred earlier, is an anachronism. *Uti possidetis* was a device of the traditional society of states, which valued international order over internal peace and civility. These days, however, its invocation invariably seems to provoke internal chaos and violence on a scale which undermines international order. A solidarist might plausibly argue that the principle will have to be abandoned in favour of some new system of international accountability.

Perhaps, although it remains impossible to say what this principle might be or how it would operate. We would be wise, therefore, to retain a measure of cautious scepticism in relation to these claims. This is particularly so with regard to the version of the argument that holds that democracy and universal human rights can be understood – and promoted – without close attention to the culture and values of particular peoples. The negotiation of the ICC was undoubtedly a major achievement, but we need to recall that the governments of the United States, Russia, China, India, and virtually all the Middle Eastern and Asian states have so far rejected it.

There is an abstract sense in which it is probably true that most people would, given the chance, opt for an open and democratic political system, always providing that it was not perceived as a serious threat to their physical security and welfare. Intuitively, democracy seems to be the system that most closely combines the delegation of responsibility for the protection of the community, under civilian control, with the empowerment of its members. But this does not mean that this desirable system will always be available. There seems little to be gained by pretending that it is.

Notes

1 Mill (1991), Chapter 16.
2 Alcock (1994), pp. 46–55.
3 This idea is present in most of Nehru's writings, but is developed at length in the book he wrote while in prison in 1944 (Nehru 1946).
4 The 'line of control' (LOC) is the ceasefire line agreed at the end of the first Indo-Pakistani War in 1947–48. It created a de facto partition of the state along the LOC, which has been monitored by a UN observer force ever since. There is a vast literature on the Kashmir dispute. For a balanced overview, albeit from an Indian perspective, see Raza (1996).
5 Ledda (1975). The film, with the same title, was made by the Taviani brothers.
6 Some of the dilemmas of such interventions are examined in the chapters by A. Roberts (pp. 158–87) and W. Bain (pp. 188–205).

7 Quoted in Moorehead (1971), p. 169.
8 'The majority of insurgents have fought courageously. Let there be a peace of the brave and I am sure the hatred will die away.' The occasion of this remark was the first press conference given by de Gaulle on 28 October 1958, after he has assumed power with the support of the military, who believed, wrongly, that he was determined to keep Algeria French. For text see *Keesings Contemporary Archives,* 28 November–5 December 1959, col. 17129.
9 See J. Jackson Preece's contribution to this volume (Chapter 8) on the value of cultural diversity and its relation to security.
10 The campaign to secure the rights of indigenous peoples, as opposed to similar campaigns to secure rights for national minorities, may have received a more sympathetic hearing at the international level because they are not viewed as a major security threat. See Lyons and Mayall (2003).
11 Contrast with K. J. Holsti's portrait of some kinds of contemporary war (Chapter 3).
12 Kennan (1961), p. 5.
13 See Nish (2000), pp. 82–90. C. Nolan notes that these same victories signalled Japan's entry into the club of great powers, see (p. 73).
14 Waltz (1959).
15 See C. Nolan's contribution to this volume (Chapter 5).
16 Watson (1992), p. 184. Chapters 16 and 17 contain an excellent and succinct account of the emergence of the modern European states system.
17 See Gellner (1988), pp. 11–23, and (1997), pp. 15–24.
18 Three hundred years later Raymond Aron made much the same point about the nuclear stand-off in his numerous writings on international relations in the nuclear age. Had the Cold War turned hot, nuclear war would have destroyed both sides and everything they stood for. As it was, approximate rules of engagement emerged out of a series of superpower confrontations starting with the Berlin crises and culminating in the Cuban missile crisis of October 1962. Although they could not go to war themselves, through proxy wars, covert activity, propaganda etc., they continued to confront one another until the mid-1990s. See Aron (1958), and (1966).
19 For a vivid account of this episode, see Milton (1999).
20 See Gellner (1994), Chapters 15–17 on 'The Time-Zones of Europe', pp. 113–28.
21 See Mayall (2000), pp. 187–96.
22 Ratner (1996), p. 610. For a more orthodox legal defence of the principle as a support of international order, see Shaw (1996), pp. 75–154.
23 See Bain (2003), pp. 121–36.
24 Ratner (1996), p. 610.
25 I have discussed this issue in detail in *Nationalism and International Society* (Mayall 1990), Chapters 3–4.
26 Such activities are also closely related to the changing nature of contemporary war, at least in some parts of the world. See Holsti's contribution (Chapter 3).
27 Roberts and Kingsbury (1993), pp. 468–98.

7   Globalization and security

Much ado about nothing?

Cornelia Navari

Globalization has challenged traditional concepts of security more radically than perhaps any other single contemporary development. Its exponents argue that it has made the traditional paradigm of borders and state interests no longer an appropriate way of thinking about security. The new threats are 'social threats', not military threats; they are environmental threats, threats to rights, and threats to 'food security'. Moreover, the targets are not states, but persons. The new security paradigm evaluates threats in terms of their effects on people, not on their consequences for states. Indeed, the new literature on globalization and security scarcely discusses interstate conflict.[1] It has also challenged security studies. Security specialists are advised to leave behind force configurations and capabilities and to focus instead on social developments with adverse outcomes, and the ways in which they might be circumvented. They are advised to join hands with 'new institutionalists' to explore institutional developments that might ameliorate such threats. They should be looking at new compliance mechanisms and at transnational actors in the belief that they contribute to the social and political environment within which the new threats arise.

But the new paradigm challenges more than method; it also embeds a far-reaching *ontological* claim. It claims that the borders of political community have shifted. According to the globalization literature, we are all in the same boat now – we live in a borderless world. In other words, we are enmeshed in what David Held has called 'communities of common fate' and we have to learn to become cosmopolitan citizens.[2] Threats are indivisible as between one people and another so that it is no longer relevant to speak of 'them and us'. Security is indivisible; it is something enjoyed in 'common'.

But in spite of the apparent consensus, globalization theory is a slippery animal. It has different disciplinary roots and contains, in some cases, opposed postulates. It also confuses causal theories with discursive theories. Not all of those in the globalization business are concerned to identify actual processes and not all globalization theory is intended as empirical theory. Some is intended as *critical theory*, which, to utilize a useful distinction made by Martin Hollis and Steve Smith, is concerned with 'understanding' rather than 'explanation'.[3] This approach to security sees 'security effects' as belonging to a rhetorical mode that is intended to secure a political programme. The rhetoric is intended to change our minds, not to identify a currently existing state of affairs.

The two concepts are often confused, since the discourse of globalization frequently has recourse to a kind of loose 'causal' language to elucidate the implications of globalization. But they are separable, and capable of being distinguished, certainly with regard to security. Still, there is no doubt that security as traditionally conceived is being degraded as a value in globalization discourse. The discourse demands that we rethink security: towards human security, human welfare, and common security. However, with regard to its causes, it is not clear that anything very remarkable is occurring with regard to security, or if it is, that it has much to do with globalization.

Globalization as causes and effects

Much globalization theory is the product of traditional social science. In this sort of theory, some things are causing other things to happen. We may call this 'causal theory' since it is concerned, variously, with causes and outcomes. (Some in this orientation argue from outcomes to causes; others argue from causes to outcomes. In either case, these are social scientists seeking to *explain something*.) But there are also different understandings of globalization as a process, with different implications for its supposed security effects.

Disputed causes in globalization processes

As causality, globalization may be understood in terms of the question: what is it that is impinging on what? As soon as we pose this question, it should become apparent that there is no single subject that constitutes globalization. Globalization theorists point to different trends, propose different outcomes, and imply or posit different causal motivators. In terms of time span alone, some date globalization from as early as AD 500, while others see it as a much more recent vintage. Simplifying a complex picture, we may note three broad periodicities, which are associated with different subjects, and these, in turn, with different disciplinary perspectives.

The main disputants are sociologists, political economists, and institutional economists. The sociological approach casts globalization in terms of large trends that may have begun as early as the onset of modernity. They focus on *deep changes in society*. This approach should be distinguished from middle-range theories where globalization is identified with a particular *cycle in the productive process*, such as 'post-Fordism' (or alternatively, a truly integrated world financial system). This domain tends to be occupied by political economists who are looking at the development of modern capitalism, usually within the last half century. Finally, there are short-range theories that see it in terms of more recent, and in some cases, very recent *policy choices*, such as the Uruguay Round. These theorists are typically institutional economists who are concerned with the contemporary organization of the world economy and the development of new rules of economic transaction.

The long-range sociological view generally bundles together long-term social trends, primarily the expansion of communication, the rationalization of government, and the internationalization of production and consumption. Together, these produce a distinctive, and new, social form described as 'the globalized society', which is characterized by more internationalized forms of governance, various forms of interdependence and intense transnational pluralism. In this theory, which is identified as the mainstream in Water's key text for Routledge, the transnational (or global) society is the proper unit of analysis.[4]

Globalization as a long-term trend is difficult to distinguish from *modernization*; indeed, some regard globalization as simply a contemporary expression of modernization: for many of the trends identified by the sociological globalists are the same trends long identified in the modernization literature, and some of the posited outcomes are similar as well. Relating the two has become a subject of some contention. There is Anthony Giddens' robust defence of globalization as modernity, which portrays globalization as simply the latest stage of modernization, and the signifier that makes more precise the outcomes of modernization processes.[5] Others, however, distinguish the orientation of 'traditional' modernization theory from its new form as represented in globalization theory, for example, Ulrich Beck's reference to globalization as the 'second' modernization.[6] However, for Giddens, this 'new theory' simply tracks modernization processes as they have manifested themselves further down the historical timeline.

The medium-range, more economistic, theories concentrate on the mode of production rather than on broad social trends. This is, moreover, a particular mode of industrial production with clear generative properties. It may be 'post-Fordism' that is driving government policies; it may be the increasing internationalization of capital; or it may be the specific form of modern production, such as technology-dependent industrial processes. Political economists tend to be agnostic on whether the development in question was immanent in industrialization from its earliest days. More frequently, it is simply the way things have turned out. But in any event, the economic form has consequences.

Susan Strange, whose *Retreat of the State* advances a popular middle-range theory, derives the phenomena associated with globalization (retreat of the state, new patterns of violence, etc.) from what she calls the 'new' internationalization of production. By this she means not a division of labour among different plants in different parts of the globe, nor the multinational company; rather, its central feature is the *transnational company* – the company that looks to a world market as its normal market, wherever it is located.[7] She means that, now, producers take for granted an international (or more accurately global) market for their goods. (She has no views on whether this development is a necessary aspect of capitalism.)

In the short-range view, globalization is simply the system of international settlements that replaced Bretton Woods. It is post-Uruguay; it is 'dirty floats' creating a vast international currency market; and it is the World Trade Organization. In this variant, it is also, possibly, hyperliberalism such as that developed and encouraged by successive American administrations. In any event, it is more of a policy than an underlying social or productive trend.[8]

Within each of these approaches, the significant variable and, accordingly, the explanatory referent, differs. We may note among the long-range sociological theorists the quarrel between Giddens, and Held and McGrew.[9] Each sources globalization in long social trends, but Giddens puts the emphasis on communication systems while Held and McGrew prefer other long-term changes. (These different foci affect both the time span and dynamic of the process. The development of *global* communications is relatively recent, and Giddens would see further development of global communications as the central dynamic in the process.) Within the middle-range economistic theories there is the difference between changing industrial *organization*, as proposed by Robert Cox,[10] and changing industrial *reach* (and sometimes changing technology), as favoured by Susan Strange. Among the short-range theories, some associate the new policy orientation with the creation of the Eurodollar market, and accordingly with the role of state mandarins in the growth of a global financial market. Others, however, emphasize the Uruguay Round and the emergence of a new universal trading system.[11]

As for explanatory strategies, again we see different modes. Giddens is a full-blown causal theorist who sees the relevant processes being moved along by specific changes which 'cause' other changes. Others, such as Susan Strange, stress *intentions* rather than causes. Strange sees globalization as being driven by the decisions of specified actors at specified moments, generally for rationally understood reasons. Finally, there is Held and McGrew's functional approach, perhaps the most common approach, which presents institutions and modes of thought as simply adapting to long-range social changes without a clear specification of either agents or determinants. In the functional type of theory, there are neither agents nor causes; the configuration just moves along, via processes of adaptation.

Globalization and its security effects

If we turn from disputatious causes to undoubted consequences, it should be noted that none of the major globalization theorists are primarily concerned with security. Giddens barely discusses it, while Held and McGrew merely infer some possible security effects from the social changes they discuss. Susan Strange's remarks on security are contained in a single article. The security implications have been drawn by international relations theorists, inferring from the broader social changes proposed mainly by the sociological globalists.

Ignoring for the moment the risks of inferring from inferences, the international relations literature has highlighted three major security effects, with a variety of intra-specific progenitors. First in prevalence, and primarily of material origin, is the increased incidence of ethnic conflict, which, though unsourced, is generally related to the 'local' and uneven effects of global processes. This is primarily a *material effect* since it is rooted in the unevenness of material life chances associated with rapid globalization. Second, there are the 'human security' effects, material as well as perceptual. On the material side, there is environmental security, which is demanded in light of the enhanced risks that come with a new, globalized environment. For example, concerns about 'food security' stem from inadvertent outcomes of modern supply and demand patterns in world agriculture. On the perceptual side, globalization is credited with calling forth a view of security as something more than 'state' security. In a globalized world security means personal security. For example, human security theorists argue that it is individual human beings, rather than states, who should enjoy freedom from fear, hunger, and ill-heath. Finally, there is the 'decline of the state' thesis, which is inferred from the state's loss of regulative capacity in a global market and from the associated idea of 'common security'. The latter is evinced by efforts to address questions of security, not in terms of states and their alliances of convenience, but in international regimes endowed with independent capabilities directed to conflict resolution and institutionalized peacekeeping. Thus, 'common security' is sourced in the state's inability to deal with the new security threats alone.

Quite apart from their inferential nature, there are a variety of problems with these effects, the most important of which is their precarious empirical grounding. In short, it is not clear that some of these effects are actually occurring; and it is not clear that what is occurring has much to do with globalization.

The rise of ethnic conflict?

The increased incidence of ethnic conflict is one of the most frequently cited entailments of globalization and is also the most remarkable for its shaky foundations. Nowhere in the globalization literature is it demonstrated that ethnic conflict is, in fact, on the rise. Ethnic and separatist conflict has been prevalent since serious counting of war began.[12] There is nothing new in this fact. Equally, there is no evidence of an increase during any time period that might be coincident with globalization. There is, for example, no evidence of a 'blip' or intensification associated with any new trend in material production, such as 'post-Fordism'. On the contrary, apart from an immediate blip in the three years after the fall of the Soviet Union, there appears to have been *less* ethnic conflict in recent years.[13]

Of course, there is something new: the recent *distribution* of ethnic conflict.[14] On the one hand, Europe – a relatively war-free zone between 1945 and 1990 – became war-prone after 1990. Also, the new pattern within this previously war-free zone, while capable of being represented as boundary or border or 'political' conflict, seems to have been shaped primarily along ethnic lines. Accordingly, the new European conflicts seem, at a superficial level, to be more 'social' than 'political'. It is the re-emergence of European war, and especially war on separatist or ethnic lines, which has provided globalization theorists with the firmest support for both the 'new social forces' thesis and the 'globalization-produces-disparate-local-effects' postulate.

But if this is a new pattern there is also something about it which is, if not old, certainly familiar. This is the 'end of empire' phenomenon. The occasion of the new ethnic conflict in Europe has been the dissolution of the Soviet Union's formal and informal empire, and exclusively so. Moreover, in terms of its causes, it is not primarily an 'economic' phenomenon (though economic calculation may have played a part in it). Nor is it a 'social' phenomenon, if by that an autonomous social development is implied. On the contrary, it is essentially a 'politicist' phenomenon, in that it developed in the context of different struggles on the part of various social forces and governments within the former Soviet zone to enlarge their scope for political autonomy. For its part, Soviet policy consisted of a series of de facto imperial retreats, until eventually the former zones of Soviet influence, and some regions under direct Soviet governance, gained effective freedom to manage their own affairs. As such, it is scarcely far-fetched to regard the dissolution of the Soviet Union in the light of the dissolution of empire more generally, and accordingly as the latest in a series of imperial dissolutions following in turn the dissolution of the Ottoman, Austrian, British, and French empires.[15] Moreover, each of those earlier retreats was also followed by a period of ethnic conflict, as groups within the former imperial zones fought to establish ascendancy within their respective political spaces. (We may recall North Slavs versus South Slavs, Mau Mau in Kenya, Magyarization in Hungary, the Irgun in Palestine, Muslim expulsions from Greece, etc.)

Accordingly, what we have seen since the end of the Cold War may be nothing more than an entailment of the retreat of empire, and a repetition of the consequences of the Russian, Ottoman, Austrian, and British imperial retreats. Indeed, it is more likely to be a post-imperial phenomenon than a globalization phenomenon, since what is new is being defined primarily by the European (and central European) context. Moreover, as a post-imperial phenomenon, it may be nothing more than the entirely 'modern' outcome of the liberal thesis regarding the self-determination of national groupings.[16]

If the rise of ethnic conflict is a post-imperial, and not a globalization, phenomenon, it still may be affected by something related to globalization. In other words, we might be witnessing *two processes* in which one (globalization) acts as an intervening variable. For example, when the Soviet Union collapsed, it did so in a global environment where the prevailing norm was marketization and the prevailing policy orientation neo-liberal. This norm and the policies associated with it were powerful factors affecting the nature and pace of the Russian decolonization. Among other things, it meant that Russia did not have that wide range of policy choices with which to manage the decolonization process that France and Britain enjoyed in the immediate post-war period. Then, prevailing notions of the planned welfare state afforded space for a wide range of social and economic experiments. For example, France was 'allowed' to construct a monetary zone between it and its former colonies, which would not have been possible in the Russian case, even had it been able to do so.

Another genuinely new factor, analysed most notably by Mary Kaldor, is the modern weapons productive system, identified by her as one of the progenitors of the 'new wars' phenomenon.[17] New wars are wars of irregulars representing different social factions and marked by social disarray and high degrees of interpersonal violence.[18] In 1971, Istvan Kende found that civil wars tended to last longer and become more intense than inter-state wars. But he associated it with the involvement of major power state backers in local wars, which made weapons more easily available to rival factions in 'backward' areas than would otherwise have been the case.[19] It may be that Kaldor is quite right in one respect – that the new deregulated market is now making 'weapons of choice' more easily available, irrespective of state wishes; and that, accordingly, weapons provision (and higher degrees of interpersonal violence) will be more difficult to regulate or contain.

Environmental insecurity?

If 'ethnic conflict' requires more specificity, the apparent trend towards increased environmental insecurity is no less suspect. The general tendency in the globalization literature is to ignore natural disasters, focusing instead on human and institutional failures; that is, where human management systems fail (oil spills, nuclear plant explosions, global warming). But it is not clear whether systemic failure is one failure (the hubris of modern science) or different types of failure (institutional, scientific, political, etc.).

There is also a good deal of confusion as to the origins of such failures. They may be the outcome of an unregulated market; that is, a phenomenon associated with hyper-liberalism (a policy choice). Alternatively, they may be the accumulated effects of industrialization, irrespective of industrial form. Moreover, it is not clear which general paradigm might be most useful in understanding such systemic failures. They might, for example, be more usefully understood in terms of chaos theory (that in increasingly complex systems something is bound to go wrong) and not as a specific feature of some specific institutional/ideological pattern called globalization.

The retreat of the state?

With regard to the inadequacies of the modern state, the causes are less confused but the trend is confusing. On the one hand, there is the 'hollowing out of the state' thesis, according to which traditional state functions are being shifted, or displaced, to either the market or public (and non-governmental) corporations. The decreasing salience of the state is a constant refrain in the globalization literature, and is treated as an inevitable outcome of the specifically political processes associated with globalization (pluralism, the victory of the market etc.). On the other hand, if we regard globalization in terms of 'long' processes, we should rather be surprised at the emergence of hollowing out since, in terms of long trends, the more striking feature would appear to have been the obverse. The prevalent pattern, over the long duration, has been the growth of state competencies and the state's increasing intervention in and regulation of society (as opposed to its rivals – religion, entrenched corporate bodies, and 'tradition'). This long process is reflected in the appearance, variously, of the developmental state, the welfare state, the 'father state', etc.; and within this long process we see, not a steady advance, but rather a flux whereby the state advances and retreats so that at times there is more market and at others times less.

Karl Polanyi, often treated as the forerunner of globalization theory, first theorized the cycle or flux of state growth and retreat in terms of what he called 'the double movement' of modernity.[20] This was an intra-process dialectic related to the contradictory demands of modernity, in which free movement set up disturbing effects and inspired calls for control, while controls had other disruptive effects and inspired calls for more openness. It was a flux between nationalism and internationalism, in which nationalism, by a complex series of factors, 'caused' internationalism, and internationalism, in a likewise manner, caused nationalism. Moreover, there was no inevitable resolution or synthesis. Polanyi concluded that the flux was the prevailing feature of modernity.

Within Susan Strange's middle-range theory (globalization as a feature of modern production) the causes become somewhat more precise. First, she has defined power in terms of effects, not in terms of capabilities. It is not that the state has fewer capabilities today, but that the structures of modern production cause different effects or outcomes, irrespective of state capabilities. These turn, first, on a set of policies, by which Western aid donors ceased making funds available for modernization transformations (this was a policy choice) and, second, on the growth of transnational corporations (TNCs) operating in a different, more globalized production structure. According to Strange, TNCs have moved in to fill the 'gap' left by the state's retreat, often with the willing collusion of the major powers. This has made the decisions of TNCs as to where and how they choose to invest very important for outcomes. They have more 'power' in the sense that whether a country develops or fails to develop is related more to the decisions and investment policies of TNCs than with those of state development agencies or the wishes of major aid donors.

The care that Strange has taken in defining her terms allows her to identify three effects, or causal outcomes, of state retreat and TNC expansion. First, she predicts a growing disparity between major and minor states, the significant variable now being global reach. Second, power has moved sideways, from states to markets, and to the disorganized plethora of market actors, with differential effects, particularly as regards the 'failed state' phenomenon (i.e. fragile states become more fragile). Finally, some power has evaporated, due to the 'marketization' of many social forces. The overall argument rests on an apparently necessary relationship between the retreat of the state and the decline of the rule of law and regulation.

The security implications, defined as violence and risk to life and property, are also well specified. Strange postulates a set of differentials and a set of 'expectations' (which should be more properly understood as hypotheses). The differentials involve a recasting of the zones of peace and zones of war (first identified, in those terms, by Kende). The new zone of peace, as identified by Strange, is signified by an absence of war among those global and regional powers that are increasingly absorbed into market relations. According to Strange, it is less the democratic transition thesis that explains the relative absence of war among liberal states as their being locked into complex market relations and developmental agendas. The other zone is the *zone gris*, or failed state zone where, as a result of civil wars and failed state authority, risks to life and property have substantially risen. Viewed in terms of violence, the significant fact would be not that violence has become more frequent, but that it has been relocated and, in the *zone gris*, has become more difficult to control.

That violence has become more difficult to control one may certainly grant. But whether global marketing is the sufficient or even a necessary factor in explaining it one may doubt. Strange mentions, almost in passing, that the 'grey zones' were created by the end of the Cold War,[21] a phenomenon that no serious theorist has, as yet, related to the inter-nationalization of production. On the contrary, its main explanations appear to be overwhelmingly politicist (and often quite historically contin-gent). In relating the creation of grey zones to the end of the Cold War, one may be forgiven for observing that Strange has inadvertently slipped into the Waltzian mode, where change is related to changing global power distribution and not to any specifics of the productive system. There are, moreover, good reasons for this shift. The more convincing view of the matter, in terms of the retreat of the state, is that this has been a retreat not in the face of market forces, but out of a series of politicist calcula-tions concerning the value of engaging less-than-strategic peripheries. In other words, a free-for-all has been created in areas formerly regulated by bloc interests, with the consequence that market forces may now operate with greater freedom (along with all the other resurgent political forces that have emerged within the new non-regulated zones).

If Strange's drift into the Waltzian mode evinces a certain doubt that the relocation of violence can be explained by market factors alone, her notion that modern forms of capital evade regulation is also contestable. Let us suppose that the trend is correct, but also subject to correction. To give merely one example: during the 1970s it was widely predicted that sovereignty was becoming 'hollow', largely in response to the growth of the multinational corporation. (We should recall that we have been here before.) It should also be recalled that, by the end of the 1970s, the end-of-sovereignty thesis was being revised. (And we should be alert to the fact that state withering has been a constantly failed prediction in the liberal era.) One explanation for the absence of state decline was that the state had learned to deal with the multinational company (the state-learning thesis).[22] Another hypothesis was that marketization itself was subject to economic forces: at the time, Fred Bergson related the 'recovery' of state sovereignty to the increasing scarcity of good sites for overseas operations and hence to the increasing ability of states to set the terms of inward investment.[23] Today, by contrast, one might draw attention to *risk aversion.* In the Asian turmoil, money demonstrated not that it was powerful but that it was scared, and regulation has once again become a mantra. In other words, we should be cautious of the idea that deregulation implies a permanent curtailment of the state's legislative capacity.

The other puzzle in respect of deregulation is the *intentional* aspect of the process. As Strange has observed, one of the notable features of the present deregulation drive is that states (or at least some powerful liberal states) chose it (and, one might add, often in the teeth of 'social' opposi-tion, which fought it every step of the way).[24] Some might regard this as evidence of an alliance between the state and some capitalist 'factions' (although this alliance was not much in evidence in Britain during much of the post-war period). Alternatively, one might regard it in *politicist* terms, as relating to the governing task. It is generally wise when considering state policy to start with the assumption that state policies serve state interests. Accordingly, if the state has been giving up functions, or devolving them to the market and/or non-governmental organizations, it might be that this is good for the state. For example, it may be that the redistributive drudge was running out of resources for redistribution. It may be that the old welfare state, faced with the prospect of increasingly scarce resources, found it better and more resourceful to raise capital for social projects from the market instead of from over-stretched national budgets. One might even postulate that this sort of deregulation has actually increased its autonomy.

The undoubted development effect of the action of TNCs, pointed out by Susan Strange,[25] is a case in point. The fact that more states are developing, and being incorporated into the World Trade Organization (WTO), without the resources of the traditional aid donors, is good news for the Western states, since it produces a positive effect without the use of Western resources. As such, however, the phenomenon has nothing to do with long trends, nor with a particular cycle in the mode of production, but with specific policy choices related to state resources and to political judgements as to how best to provide those resources.

Human security?

One may express a similar scepticism regarding the 'human security' effects of globalization. Human security is not a causal outcome; it is a policy prescription and, in fact, a *discourse* as to how we should conceptualize security. But it has a 'causal' history that is worth recalling. It came to prominence in the real world of policy in the context of the UN Development Programme (UNDP) report of 1994.[26] A complicated story lies behind the production of this report, but not least was the fear among UN development agencies that development was being permanently sidelined. This arose not only from the demands of hyper-liberalism but from the relative indifference of the United States to the development agenda following the end of the Cold War. 'Human security' was intended to reinvigorate the development agenda by presenting development as a security issue.

This report has been given much play in the globalization and security literature (where it frequently evidences globalization processes). It has also had a concrete effect on some government policy. Both Norway and Canada have reoriented important aspects of their security policies in terms of a 'human security agenda'. But in terms of reorienting 'global governance' more widely, as was clearly intended by the UNDP report, the effects have been very limited – not least because the United States has continued to view security in more traditional terms.[27]

More recently, the mantra has been revived, albeit in a new form and in new contexts. Now it is appearing in the human rights context, where 'human security' has come to signify civilian immunity in the ferocious civil rebellions that have characterized the post-Cold War era. But in this form, it has nothing to do with any widened agenda of security; it means nothing more than civilian or non-combatant immunity. Moreover, it appears to have been taken up, as it seems to have been, because it allows some states to take civilian immunity seriously without at the same time committing them to a widened human rights agenda. It is a way of talking about non-combatant immunity without talking about rights.

If we are really looking for the undoubted security effects of globalization, where they are most clearly registering is in enhanced concerns for state coercive capacity in a global technology market. Here, the concern is with the civilianization of military equipment, through computerization and other multiple use technologies, in the context of the deregulation of the weapons market. (There is also, significantly, the packing up of the Coordinating Committee on Multilateral Export Controls (COCOM), or the 'restricted technology' list, which controlled the export of technologies during the Cold War.) The new threat lies in the widespread civilian usage of what are at the same time also military technologies and their diffusion to a global market. Both present states with the possibility that, for example, the communication systems necessary to advanced warfare may be increasingly vulnerable to disruption by any teenage hacker. But here, it is state capacity, and capacity to fight war, which is guiding the concern – a very traditionally conceived concept of security.

Common security?

Along with human security, there has emerged the idea of 'common security'. But common security is quite a different case. As opposed to 'human security', the idea of 'common security' has a long and important history. Moreover, its re-emergence in the present climate might indeed signal that something very significant, and genuinely new, has occurred. But it might not have very much to do with globalization.

In its historical aspect, common security is part of the family of concepts known as 'collective security', which came to the fore at the beginning of the twentieth century. Originally, collective security implied a legalized security system, where an international 'crime', for example aggression, would be met with a swift and obligatory collective response. However, with the development of the bloc system following the Second World War, the term underwent a significant shift. It became associated with the idea of opposed alliances and forces-in-being. In other words, it became associated with the idea of a balance of power between opposed coalitions of states, not with legal redress. Viewed historically, the idea of 'common security' represents not a new development, but a return to older ideas, which would seem to have become possible following the collapse of the antagonistic blocs. But what is new, and quite remarkably so, is that there was no specific enemy when the term emerged. At the end of the Cold War, when the idea of common security re-emerged, there was no immediate source of endangerment to which the idea of common security might plausibly refer.

To clarify this important point, we should recall that in the immediate post-First World War period, when the idea of collective security first gained widespread currency, concern for resurgent German power was much in evidence, despite Germany's defeat. There was also the rise of Bolshevism in Russia. There was much to fear, particularly on the part of what was then a still relatively small number of liberal states. Today, liberalism has achieved a hegemonic position and there are no 'enemy' states threatening the countries of Europe, where the idea of 'common security' seems to have the most resonance. Accordingly, its re-emergence might signal that something very important has occurred. It might mean that security has come to be considered a form of 'common good'; that is, a good that cannot be secured by one state alone, in any environment. As such, it would be a genuinely historic development, and sourcing it would be one of the most important tasks for scholars of international relations.

But if we treat 'common security' as part of the family of collective security concepts, we have an explanatory field bounded by 1917–19 at one extreme and by contemporary conditions at the other. It was during and following the First World War that the call for collective security became prevalent, and it was the League of Nations that first attempted (unsuccessfully, in the event) to construct a collective security system.[28] In explaining it, therefore, we must look to conditions that span the twentieth century.

In terms of a twentieth century field, there are three main contenders. One is the rise of German power and the creation of superpoweredness; that is, a power which might overwhelm all other powers or coalitions of powers. The second is the *rise of the liberal powers*, and the specific foreign policy choices of liberal states. The third possible explanator concerns the consequences of industrialization as it has affected war, and the 'impossibility of fighting modern wars' thesis, which has been a recurring theme of strategic writing during the twentieth century. The impossibility of fighting a 'rational' war has been a major refrain in twentieth century strategic discourse; it has been so since even before the invention of the nuclear bomb, and the main concern in twentieth century strategic writing has been to 'save' war and tame it to rational purposes.

For our present purposes, it does not matter where we put the emphasis. The point is that all of these potential candidates point away from either long trends or short-term policy calculations. They also point us away from those mid-range economic changes associated with globalization (post-Fordism etc.). In terms of 'deep' forces, the closest economic referent would be what Norman Angell (one of the first theorists of the need for common security) called 'economic civilisation'. By this, however, he meant something much closer to interdependence, and the interpenetration of national economies, not the transnational developments that are usually associated with the globalized economy.[29]

The idea of a common security (that is, permanent security arrangements among states even in the absence of an immediate threat) has become at least thinkable in the contemporary era; it is notable, however, that it also has a specific geographical focus. Those who are voicing the most interest in common security, and who are most concerned to avoid autonomous national defences, are the states of Europe. This points to an explanator related to the particular demands of the European political space.

In short, while many things have happened with regard to security in the last decade and other things within the last century, which are significant in their own right, there is little reason to assign them to globalization. On the contrary, there is every reason to suppose that the reputed security effects are rather the outcomes of other causes, or processes. A short list would include the end of the Cold War, the ascendancy of the liberal state, hyper-liberalism as it has affected the arms trade, and the desire (and pressure) for greater autonomy among the European states.

Discourses of globalization

This body of theorizing is concerned less with causes than with how those processes are to be understood in the sense of their broader implications for social and political organization. Here we are looking less at causes than at outcomes: the downstream effects as opposed to the upstream progenitors.

According to Hay and Marsh, globalization is not a process at all but a discourse; it is, moreover, an historically located discourse, associated primarily with the attack on the welfare state.[30] The new discourse of globalization, they argue, has nothing to do with large-scale social changes, much less with intermediate changes in the mode of production. It has arisen, in Britain at least, in response to the needs of political legitimation following the Thatcher era.[31] Here, globalization is presented in terms of a specifically political device related to the construction of 'new' Labour. It is intended to conceal 'new' Labour's neo-liberalism by presenting its, essentially neo-liberal, policies as a response to apparently ineluctable global forces. It is a sign that 'new' Labour has itself fallen to the ideological hegemony of Thatcherism.

Hay and Marsh represent most accurately the post-Marxist approach, with its inherent scepticism concerning prevalent discourses. What they imply is that globalization is in fact a form of political ideology and, by extension, that what is being produced via globalization discourse is a form of false consciousness.

As a discourse related to a 'structure', discourse theorists are pressed to identify the relevant political/social form that is generating the discourse. But any number of other potential social developments might also be producing the new discourse.

The origins of the idea that globalization is a form of discourse lie with Hirst and Thompson's very influential *Globalization in Question*.[32] Hirst called it a myth, and, specifically, a 'necessary' myth that rose out of events much larger than Britain's particular political transition. It had to do with perceptions, and fears, of an ungovernable world economy. Those fears, in turn, derived from a set of historical conjunctures – events that are not necessarily, but only contingently, related – such as the collapse of the Bretton Woods arrangement, the internationalization of financial markets, and the shift from standardized mass production to more flexible production methods. There are some 'deep forces' here, but others are merely 'happenings'. What matters are the ideational features of globalization discourse as they relate to fears of ungovernability. Thus, according to Hirst, the notion of an ungovernable world economy is a response to the collapse of expectations 'schooled by Keynesianism and sobered by the failure of monetarism to provide an alternative route'. It is a 'myth suitable for a world without illusions'.[33]

But this anxiety is also indicative of a form of false consciousness in that many of the changes claimed by the employers of this discourse are overstated. The purpose of Hirst's work is to set the record straight, essentially by disentangling the conjunctures. Indeed, attacking the 'inevitability thesis' is a common move among those who see globalization in terms of political ideology. So if it can be demonstrated that there is nothing inevitable in many globalization 'predictions', they can be shown up as forms of either ideology or moral panic, and falsified, allowing either the welfare state, or in Hirst's case, the liberal rational project, to proceed.

Hirst's main opponents are Held and McGrew, and the argument they advance in *Global Transformations*.[34] Held and McGrew do not argue that globalization is not a discourse. They accept that there is a widespread language out there; they also accept that they are engaging in a form of social theorizing which requires 'understanding' as well as explaining. What they contest is the extent to which Hirst ignores the real effects of the specific spatial transformations, the 'particular spatial attributes',[35] being created. Thus, they also raise a question of considerable interest: why is the discourse of globalization so widespread but for these wide-ranging social changes?[36]

But Held and McGrew also ignore some other 'large' social developments to which the globalization debate might be related. For example, the globalization debate grew in the context of the 'victory of capitalism', and within a prevailing triumphalist discourse which posited 'the end of history'.[37] Liberal triumphalism following the end of the Cold War presented 'marketization' as 'development', and 'economy' (or 'civil society') as 'peace'. Accordingly, it threatened (and in many cases actualized) the marginalization of a whole range of hitherto dominant projects, including not only social democracy, Marxism, and the welfare state enterprise, but also, in international theory, the neo-realist revival, with its reinvigorated focus on power distributions. The defeat of socialism left many social theories beached, while the triumph of 'economism' and 'societization' in their neo-liberal forms left many politicists out in the cold. What options are available to the marginalized? One option is to reinterpret the old enterprise within a new frame, a move that social theorists refer to as 'reframing'.

The idea of social framing developed within that branch of social theory concerned with the rise and fall of social movements, where it is used to explain the re-emergence of apparently defeated or outflanked social movements in new forms and with new alliances.[38] Reframing involves not so much the articulation of new ideas. Rather the new frame allows for the restatement of old ideas in new contexts, as well as the building of new alliances around areas of common ground or common concern.[39] It allows for communication and advocacy coalitions among social movements that find themselves in positions of shared opposition (albeit on different grounds). In other words, old theories, or 'social discourses', may regain saliency and place within wider more general frames that re-legitimate their aims in changing social climates. These new frames then act as bridges, reconnecting the old enterprise to the new mainstream.

Viewed in this light, globalization may be a framing device, related neither to the present realization of long social trends, nor to the specific endangerment of the welfare state, but to the hegemony of neo-liberalism and its discourse of triumphal liberalism. Thus, it may serve as a bridge that connects those threatened with marginalization by linking them with the new mainstream, which invests in defeated projects a renewed saliency.

If we consider globalization discourse in terms of an ideological bridge, allowing for the re-entry of marginalized political movements into the mainstream of political debate, we may also comprehend Held and McGrew's 'large numbers'. First, it is a very broad bridge, allowing many potential claimants to climb on board. There is room for postmodernists, post-Marxists, constructivists, supporters of traditional development agendas, and radical political economists. In its aspect as a communication enabler, it also joins that erstwhile radical fringe with a 'more legitimate' critical element – in the case of globalization it joins 'eco-freaks' with sceptical neoclassical economists and even traditional realists who have long been suspicious of 'globaloney' discourse. Finally, it sets up a dialogue between the critics, on the one hand, and the 'establishment' supporters, on the other; that is, between the sceptics of and the enthusiasts for globalization.

There are reasons besides saving professional reputation for taking the framing thesis seriously, especially those deriving from Karl Mannheim's theory of ideology.[40] Mannheim theorized ideology in terms of power and its alternatives. In his construction ideology and utopia were functional correlates. Ideology was the social discourse of the party in power; it was part of the control mechanisms of power. In contrast, utopia was the social discourse of the party out of power and it was used to critique both the prevailing ideology and its institutionalized expression. In the light of Mannheim's distinctions, we may observe that a good deal of globalization literature, while scarcely utopian, is something just as good in a climate of triumphal liberalism. Much of it is dystopic – it is a literature of endangerment. But it is dystopic with a difference: much of it issues a call to change.

To get at this aspect of globalization theory, we might recall that treating discourse as either false consciousness or political justification is not the only route to understanding discourse. Discourse also refers to a specific literary form and to the internal structures of that form. Here, we are not concerned with the 'hidden' motives of the players, nor with the broader structures to which the discourse may be related, at least not in the first instance. Discourse-as-literature considers discourse primarily in its own terms, as a form of text, and it asks what the text is doing. Applying this approach to the body of theorizing known as globalization is revealing, and not only in the light of Mannheim's distinctions.

As text, as in so many other respects, globalization discourse comes in different forms. Along the bridge there are different modes of expression. Near the right is the liberal–rational mode, characteristic of the liberal globalists, such as, for example, Robert Keohane or Stephen Krasner.[38] Here the text inscribes a cautious acceptance of change that might require institutional adaptation and the tone is that of a balance among alternatives. Just beyond them is the scientist methodological tone of the neoclassical economists. Here the form is the sceptical interrogative: it asks what has changed. But they are in the minority; they are clustered at merely one point on the bridge. What is occupying most of the bridge is a prophetic literature, a literature that tells us we are going somewhere.

As prophecy, globalization discourse points in two radically different and opposed directions. At one end of the bridge is a 'road to salvation' literature, which heralds a more prosperous global future where inequalities of wealth and life chances can be managed through a form of international 'new dealism'. Notable in this tendency would be Kenichi Ohmae's *Borderless World*.[42] At the other end, and occupying a good deal of its length, is the 'road to damnation' literature. Here, the destination brings no good news. Our present course is leading to oppression, to social division, to increasing disparities of rich and poor, and to new and disturbingly unfamiliar forms of identity. We are not going to a utopia but to a dystopia.

A prevalent feature of these dystopias is the play of retribution. There is much allusion to past warnings that have gone unheeded; there are a lot of chickens coming home to roost. Capitalist chickens prevail, perhaps. We are alerted to the many warnings we have already received of the inherent divisiveness of capitalism, that it created social divisions and sharpened the difference between rich and poor. Now, it seems, we are creating a 'new poor' and along new fractures: there is a new impoverished periphery appearing in the global economy as more advantageously sited third world states enter the semi-periphery. Moreover, the new poor are also in our very midst. While old capitalism exported its divisions, 'turbo-capitalism' reproduces them at home.[43] There are also the unheeded warnings concerning the limitations, and dangers, of the rationalist, utilitarian mode of calculating social risk, implicated in environmental disasters, among other things.

But the 'road to damnation' literature differs in significant respects from the pure form of dystopic literature. The latter reveals the future in the present and is essentially backward-looking. It tells us that the utopia is irretrievably lost. The 'road to damnation' literature is, paradoxically, forward-looking. It is an integral part of 'road to damnation' literature that it is not intended to leave us on the road, much less to get us to the destination. This particular literary form outlines how we might avoid the inevitable. There are forks in the road; there are still choices to be made; and, indeed, there are cues as to how to regain our footing on the road to salvation. Between the two literatures there is a stark contrast. In the 'good news' literature, we can do no better than to go on as we are now. In the 'bad news' literature, salvation is possible; there are alternative routes, but only through a change in our attitudes as well as in our institutions. This call to change rhetoric is not exactly euphoric. The tone is slightly doom-filled. It is not clear that if we do change, the actual Promised Land will be before us (not least because the seriousness of our present condition might be called into question were salvation too easily achieved). The scales are precariously balanced: in some variants the best we can hope for is moderated perdition.

Held and McGrew's contribution to what is considered by some the definitive work on globalization is a fairly standard exemplar of the mode.[44] The Valhalla is the republican notion of civil society. Its enemies, taken at random and in no particular order, are the growing intensity of the arms trade; the ever-present possibility of reversals in democratization processes; and, within the liberal democracies, non-democratic coalitions of governments, corporate interests, and technical specialists which dominate political–industrial policy making. There is also an environmental catastrophe in the making, a residual nationalism impeding both cosmopolitanism and multiculturalism, and deterritorialization and reterritorialization (instability in borders and ambiguity with regard to the political spaces of effective decision making). Moreover, there is no evidence of the generalizable effects of wealth creation (on the contrary, wealth is being concentrated), and there is the indeterminate loss of state power (or inadequate internationalized power) to control such effects.

It is, however, possible to 'civilize and democratize globalization'. The routes (again in no particular order) include the development of an international human rights regime; increasing inter-consciousness among communities of common fate; growing interrelations among separate political orders which may link communities of common fate; and new differentiated levels of political decision making responsive to common fate communities. However, to realize these potentialities, we must get rid of those insider/outsider distinctions, which are the legacy of the nation-state mentality. Here, we have the real devil in the globalization story. It is not so much the processes of globalization that are the problem, but a *mental structure* that is impeding our way of understanding and dealing with the present conjunctures. One of the reasons we have difficulty dealing with the challenges of globalization is that we are still locked within a nation-state discourse and with nation-state conceptions of political structures and social identities. If this changes, there is hope.

The balance of probabilities appears in the last lines of the work. On the one hand, there are 'plenty of reasons for pessimism' but, on the other hand, we may also detect the faint outlines of a barely perceptible new world order, evident in the new voices of an emerging transnational global society. There are possibilities evident in past redemptions and past restructurings of nation-state identities, notably in the establishment of the European Union following the Second World War.

Ankie Hoogvelt also cultivates the theme of dystopia: the road to damnation is 'imploding capitalism'. Far from a generalized process of globalization, he detects an intensification of trade and capital linkages within the core of the capitalist system and a withdrawal of such linkages from the periphery.[45] This produces extreme marginalization in the largest portions of the globe, and the growth of poverty, exclusion, and anarchy, with spill-back effects into the core. These effects include the growth of anti-development in primarily Muslim areas, without, however, much hope of constructive rebellion 'from below'; similarly, they are implicated in highly politicized processes of impoverishment in Latin America along with the loss of state capacity to deal with either. So far as East Asia is concerned, the struggle to achieve economic maturity will be constantly threatened by the differential wage levels between it and the rest of the core. These differentials create tensions in the core as workers fight against the loss of work and industrial relocation. Thus, salvation in Hoogvelt's story is found in regionalization, which acts as a barrier to marginalization within a global economy.

Rooted in this prophetic literature is a call to arms; it is dystopia with change integrated into it. It is a utopian literature into which a theory of social change and a political theory of the good society are enmeshed, which aims to gain force from a predictive element rooted in a set of causal inferences. In this context, it uses the sure and certain evidence of damnation to tell us that salvation is also at hand. The problem is that the evidence for damnation is not so certain. Susan Strange insists that globalization has delivered both more development and more widespread development, compared to the record of the 'trade-and-aid' policies that characterized the 'pre-global' economy. Others insist than negative effects of globalization are merely transitional phenomena that lay the foundations for future correctors. Thus, Ohmae argues that the emerging 'competition state' will deliver greater global wealth overall, and that the African 'basket cases' will eventually be accommodated by varieties of international welfarism.

Prophecies and causes

Viewing the range of globalization theory, what can we say it contributes to an understanding of security in the post-Cold War era? Before we answer, 'not much', we might pause to consider some of the ways in which social knowledge advances. For example, it might provide a new and valuable research agenda without committing us to any clear answers yet. It might even be poor social science but worthwhile as *normative inquiry*. And it might call our attention to worrying trends which, while causally uncertain, still require normative reorientation.

On the social science side, one approach that might help clarify its scientific status is the Popperian approach, according to which globalization theory would be included as a part of a genuine scientific endeavour, albeit one with rather weak scientific credentials.[46] For Popper, the scientific process consists of two stages, a conjectural stage, which lays down a range of hypotheses, and a refutation stage, which subjects them to scrutiny. Viewed in this light, globalization theory belongs to a clearly identifiable stage in the research process in so far as it establishes conjectures that are to be refuted.

But there are problems in this Popperian reconciliation. One of Popper's main concerns was to establish the criteria for taking conjectures seriously, the most important of which is 'testability'. Popper observed that some theories were so indeterminate in the specification of their terms that they were non-testable, and, hence, non-refutable. Here, we may find grounds for unease in at least some of this literature. Many globalization claims resist testability; others are so large that they must be first reduced in scale, and then translated into hypothetical postulates, in order to be rendered refutable. Of course, this can be done, and the result, as I hope this chapter has demonstrated, may not be uninteresting.

More problematic, though, is the non-repeatability of globalization processes. Testing requires repetition and comparability among like processes; in other words, it requires more than a single instance of the phenomenon in question. But many globalization claims involve one historically specific transformation only: the move from Thatcher to 'new' Labour, from 'tradition' to 'modernity', or from one type of productive mode to another. Unique historical events require, not the devices of Popperian positivism, but historical imagination, historical comparability, and a commitment to plausibility among contending explanations. Thus, it is not surprising that one of the effects of globalization discourse has been the recovery of the historicist mode in which events are judged in comparison with the past.

If we turn to the discourse side, our dilemma is somewhat more complex. Some globalization theory is not intended as social science at all; it is intended as critique of the present organization of international society, its growing inequalities, and its relentless emphasis on state interests and national identities. In respect of security, it raises many normative issues, even metaphysical issues. What is security? How is human security to be conceptualized? What values should security policies secure? It demands new structures that entrench democratic values and it demands a new security architecture that is somehow 'more equal'. In these domains, empirical accuracy is not the test of good theory: the test of a good normative theory is in the moral choice it specifies. Good normative theory should explicate moral dilemmas, propose agents of change, and specify alternative institutional arrangements.

Here, the problem is that, while the discourses of globalization are quite good at raising normative issues, they are not very good at presenting convincing accounts of either moral agency or moral choice. Too much of globalization theory as discourse mixes metaphysical questions, such as 'what is security?', with theoretical postulates which, in effect, answer the question. It tells us that security is (common, human, etc.) in statements that are supported by a mass of empirical data. But answering such questions in empirical terms actually stops normative inquiry. For example, globalization discourse endorses a new normative orientation, away from nationally oriented or state-centred defence, to human defence in a global community. Value pluralism is rejected in the process, albeit not as the result of a moral choice. On the contrary, the demise of value pluralism is presented as an ineluctable outcome of globalization's generative processes. In philosophy, this is called the 'naturalistic fallacy', which repositions the normative debate by locating it at the empirical level of what is or what is not happening.

Quite apart from whether this sort of move can be deemed to constitute moral inquiry at all, there are consequences that are worthy of notice. Since what is or what is not happening is at the centre of globalization theory, the moral force of the discourse becomes lost in a maze of (inconclusive) empirical data. Globalization theory is also far too 'agency-free' at the explanatory level, while placing unrealistic demands on human agency as a means of correction. At the explanatory level globalization theory presents many of its processes as the result of ineluctable social and economic forces; and it does so to demonstrate the analytical soundness of insights gleaned from these processes. However, human agency suddenly reappears at the corrective level in order to respond to the demand that we change our ways of doing things. How human agency, something which is absent throughout the generation of globalization processes, can halt or reverse the baleful consequences is seldom addressed.

It is evident that globalization theory cannot for long carry such burdens. The globalization bridge is already being abandoned by political economists who are tired of being associated with the explanation of everything, when their aim is to postulate the plausible effects of changing industrial modes of production for a range of (limited) state, and inter-state, practices. It will have to be abandoned if security theory is to address the normative issues involved in contemporary security practices, or guide us to the requisites of a new, possibly more desirable, set of security structures.

Notes

1 The paradigmatic account is Scholte (1993a), especially Chapters 6 and 9. Other, systematic, accounts are notably scarce. See Scholte (1993b); Dewitt *et al.* (1993); Shaw (1997), pp. 253–69; Clark (1999); and Strange (1996). Among the sceptics, note Freedman (1998).

2 Held (1995).

3 See Hollis and Smith (1990).

4 Waters (1995).

5 Giddens argues that 'modernity is inherently globalizing'. See Giddens (1990), p. 63.

6 Beck (1999).

7 Strange (1996), pp. 46–54.

8 Among an enormous literature, Wachtel (1986); Helleiner (1994); Lipsey (1996); Eichengreen (1994); and Jackson (1998), 157–88. On globalization as hyper-liberalism (and policy), Krasner (1985); and Hirst (1997), pp. 409–25.

9 Held and McGrew (1999).

10 Cox (1987).

11 Among the former, Porter (1993); and Kapstein (1994); among the latter, Martin and Winters (1996). Illustrating both, Michie and Grieve Smith (1995).

12 See, for example, Wright (1965). Civil wars were not included in the first attempts to count wars. However, Istvan Kende was the first to conduct an empirical study that included civil wars in a general count; of 120 since 1945, he identified ninety-six as ethnic or separatist. See Kende (1982).

13 This finding is reported in Gurr (2000); see also Booth (1998), pp. 29–55.

14 See Holsti's contribution to this volume for an extended discussion of changing patterns of contemporary war.

15 C. Nolan also sees the break-up of the Soviet Union in the context of the dissolution of empire, see (p. 84).

16 See J. Mayall's chapter for an exposition of the liberal theory of self-determination (pp. 94–7).

17 Kaldor (1999).

18 See Holsti (pp. 41–4).

19 See Kende (1971), pp. 5–22.
20 Polanyi (1944).
21 Strange (1996), p. 189.
22 Moran (1978), pp. 79–100; and Sunkel (1978), pp. 517–31.
23 Bergson (1975), p. 38 where he announced that 'sovereignty is no longer at bay'.
24 Strange (1996), pp. 54–7.
25 Strange (1996), p. 58.
26 The UNDP report defined the 'new security' as 'safety from chronic threats such as hunger, disease, and repression, and protection from sudden disruptions in the pattern of daily life': United Nations Development Programme (1994), p. 3.
27 See Campbell (1992), p. 7.
28 C. Nolan argues that the failure of the League of Nations is attributable to the defection of certain great powers, most significantly, the United States, see (p. 81).
29 See Angell (1911), pp. 152–4.
30 Hay and Marsh (2000).
31 Hay (1998); and Hay and Marsh (1999).
32 Hirst and Thompson (1999).
33 Hirst and Thompson (1999), p. 6.
34 Held and McGrew (1999); and Held and McGrew (2000), pp. 1–50.
35 Held and McGrew (2000), p. 6.
36 Held and McGrew (2000), p. 5.
37 Fukuyama (1992).
38 I am grateful to Antje Wiener's 'Constructivism and the Social in Political Science' (2001), drawing on Snow and Benford (1992), pp. 133–55, for alerting me to the concept of social framing.
39 Wiener, quoting Snow and Benford, notes: 'what gives a collective action frame its novelty is not so much its innovative ideational elements as the manner in which activists articulate or tie them together'. See Wiener (2001), p. 6.
40 Mannheim (1936).
41 See Keohane (2000), pp. 108–34.
42 Ohmae (1992).
43 The term is Edward Luttwak's, but the thesis is not patented. See Luttwak (1999).
44 Held and McGrew (1999).
45 Hoogvelt (1997).
46 Popper (1963).

8   Cultural diversity and security after 9/11

Jennifer Jackson Preece

For many political commentators the Al-Qaeda attacks on New York and Washington provided confirmation that we had entered a new era of global civilizational war in which cultural differences between peoples threatened chaos and disorder on an hitherto unprecedented scale.[1] As the *Washington Post* noted in December 2001, 'For Huntington, a clash of civilizations was a worst-case scenario. For bin Laden it was a game plan.'[2] Statements like these tend to exaggerate what remains a highly controversial argument about the limitations of international and especially inter-civilizational understanding. Nevertheless, Huntington's characterization of politics as being as much about culture and identity as power politics remains important and timely:

> In the post-Cold War world, the most important distinctions amongst peoples are not ideological, political or economic. They are cultural. . . . People define themselves in terms of ancestry, religion, language, history, values, customs and institutions. They identify with cultural groups: tribes, ethnic groups, religious communities, nations and, at the broadest level, civilizations. People use politics not just to advance their interests but also to define their identity. We know who we are only when we know who we are not and often only when we know whom we are against.

Not surprisingly, questions of identity and culture have featured prominently in debates about security that followed on from the events of 11 September in the United States and, indeed, elsewhere.

Accordingly, this seems an opportune moment to consider how the leading security paradigms – national security, international security, and human security[3] – respond to questions of cultural diversity within states. Why is cultural diversity so often regarded as a threat to security? Does security really require cultural homogeneity? Or can it be maintained in the presence of diverse cultural groups? Huntington himself has suggested that the 'clash of civilizations' might be avoided or at least ameliorated by 'renounc[ing] universalism, accept[ing] diversity, and seek[ing] commonalities. . . . The security of the world requires acceptance of global multiculturality.'[4] By way of conclusion, I will offer some reflections on what a multicultural paradigm of security might look like:[5] How would it differ from existing security paradigms? What sort of policies would it entail? And, finally, is there any evidence to suggest that a multicultural paradigm of security is gaining adherents in the wake of September 11?

Identity, culture, and security

Questions of identity and culture are among the most contested issues in political life because they speak to an inherent tension in human affairs between competing desires for freedom and belonging. Human beings do not exist as atomistic individuals abstracted from society, but rather as socialized individuals embedded within a well-defined social and political order. For this reason, most contemporary political theorists, following John Rawls, assume that people are born into and lead a complete life within the same society and culture, such that this context delineates the scope within which people must be free and equal.[6] Thus, the desire for social belonging is an essential human characteristic and a prerequisite for that condition of peace and stability that is necessary for human flourishing.

There is of course a fundamental paradox implicit within this characterization of the human condition. Freedom and belonging may be equally important for human flourishing, but they nevertheless remain mutually incommensurate and potentially competing values. Freedom requires autonomy of action; belonging requires coordination and, in some situations, subordination of autonomous action to preserve the social relationship on which it is based. Freedom necessitates and perpetuates a diversity of choices and so promotes a variety of values, beliefs, and identities; belonging necessitates and perpetuates social cohesion and so constrains choices to preserve a common identity and its concomitant values and beliefs. Freedom encourages innovation; belonging encourages orthodoxy. Freedom creates diversity; belonging creates uniformity. At some point, these values will collide and that collision is likely to foster uncertainty, suspicion, fear, and even conflict. It is precisely this collision of values that makes the existence of diversity within humankind, especially the religious, racial, linguistic, and cultural diversity which has long been a hallmark of distinct human communities, a potential source of insecurity and conflict.

This potential for conflict arises because of the intrinsic incommensurability of belonging manifested as community, and freedom manifested as diversity. This explains both the tendency towards suspicion and fear of those who are different and why such fears are often politically manipulated within highly developed political communities like states, wherein social complexity is assumed to require a correspondingly increased degree of conformity. Hannah Arendt explains this tendency in her study of the origins of totalitarianism:

> Our political life rests on the assumption that we can produce equality through organization, because man can act in and change and build a common world, together with his equals and only his equals. The dark background of mere givenness, the background formed by our unchangeable and unique nature breaks into the political scene as the alien which in its all too obvious difference reminds us of the limitations of human equality. The reason why highly developed political communities, such as the ancient city-states or the modern nation-states, so often insist on ethnic homogeneity is that they hope to eliminate as far as possible those natural and always present differences and differentiations ... because they indicate all too clearly those spheres where men cannot act and change at will, i.e., the limitations of the human [political] artifice. The 'alien' is a frightening symbol of the fact of difference as such, of individuality as such, and indicates those realms in which man cannot change and cannot act and in which, therefore, he has a distinct tendency to destroy.[7]

Political order is precisely as Arendt describes it: it is a human artifice that is a consequence of human conduct rather than a part of the natural, physical world around us. Political discourse and action is fundamentally moral discourse: it deliberately constrains freedom defined as the ability to do exactly as one pleases with reference only to one's own esoteric and idiosyncratic needs, desires, ambitions, and so forth, by establishing a common ethical standard. Such normative constraints on individual behaviour are the foundation of an ordered and, therefore, secure collective existence. As Thomas Hobbes reminds us, without this human artifice, which he terms 'Leviathan', there is 'no place for industry ... no arts, no letters, no society; and which is worst of all, continual fear and danger of violent death; and the life of man, solitary, poor, nasty, brutish and short'.[8] It is the abiding fear of a return to the natural (non-social) order (what Hobbes describes as a 'war of all against all') that makes the existence of diversity, especially that diversity which challenges the normative basis of the prevailing political community, so controversial.

Where diversity is understood to contradict, weaken, or destroy collective belonging and social consensus, it becomes a subject of policies designed to ameliorate these socially and politically destructive effects. In other words, this perspective views culture in zero-sum terms such that cultural coexistence and toleration is not an option. Such circumstances resemble the classical Hobbesian paradigm: international relations is defined as a war of each culture against all others in a struggle for territory, people, and resources – what Huntington so evocatively terms a 'clash of civilizations'.[9] Avoiding such a scenario would therefore seem to require rethinking the relationship between diversity and security in the manner suggested by Huntington when he urges the rejection of 'universalism'.

Cultural diversity and state or national security

The idea of state and later national security has its origins in the sixteenth and seventeenth century fragmentation of the universalist social order of Catholic Christendom and the emergence of sovereign, territorial states in Western Europe. Since this time, the dominant security paradigm has viewed the state as the fundamental source of social belonging and, by extension, personal well-being. From this perspective, the state is the provider of peace, order, and – by implication – good governance. Thus, personal security becomes dependent upon and even analogous to state security; and insecurity is understood as an external threat located outside the state–citizen relationship. Therefore, in theory, if not in fact, the state cannot pose a threat to its own citizens whose personal interests are synonymous with state interests. Crucially, though, the state may legitimately discriminate against, oppress, or even attack non-members who threaten its political stability, territorial integrity, or political interest.

The emphasis on social conformity as a matter of state security is apparent even in the early history of the state. In an attempt to control the destabilizing effects of the Protestant Reformation, the Peace of Augsburg (1555) territorialized religious affiliations as the purview of each individual sovereign. This practice was later confirmed and consolidated in the Peace of Westphalia in 1648. According to the principle of *cujus regio ejus religio* (like sovereign, like religion), princes determined the religious practices within their territories. Subjects either complied with the established religion of the sovereign or migrated to another jurisdiction where their religious beliefs prevailed. An extensive transfer of populations within Germany followed.[10] These migrations of religious dissenters reinforced both the doctrine of *cujus regio ejus religio* and the prevailing assumption that religious homogeneity within the state ought properly to be maintained in the interests of peace and stability.

Contemporary usage refers not simply to state or sovereign security but rather to *national* security – a shift that reveals more than mere semantics, for it draws our attention to the principle of self-determination which, in turn, explains why cultural diversity is particularly problematic within contemporary politics.[11] The current preoccupation with cultural diversity is a consequence of the revolutionary change in political thinking that took place in Europe from the late eighteenth century to the mid-nineteenth century, which, by 1945, had become the basis of a global international order. It is only at this point (i.e. from the late eighteenth century) in the history of political ideas that the concept of the 'nation' achieves political salience. Who are the people in whom sovereignty and, indeed, liberty, ultimately resides? The people are the nation and the state exists as an expression of the national will, which, in Article 3 of the 'Declaration of the Rights of Man and of Citizen' was expressed as '[t]he principle of all sovereignty rests essentially in the nation. No body and no individual may exercise authority which does not emanate from the nation expressly.'[12] The national state places a premium on homogeneity with respect to those characteristics which define its distinct national identity and thus support its claim to popular sovereignty. The precise nature and extant of these characteristics will vary enormously from case to case as will their location in either the social or the non-social sphere.

In the classic liberal account the state is created through the mutual consent of free and equal individuals. This way of thinking corresponds with – indeed emerges out of – the civic national tradition. Here, the nation is predominantly viewed as a corollary of democracy and citizenship rather than ethnicity and culture. This understanding was inherited from an earlier period of state building in which England and France had been created, over centuries, by the territorial consolidation and increasingly effective administration of the great medieval monarchies. In this earlier period, jurisdiction had determined and defined the people and not the other way round.

National identity in the civic tradition is thus primarily defined through a shared political experience and common constitutional guarantees. Accordingly, linguistic or cultural programmes – which nevertheless have featured prominently in the political programmes of many civic nationalists – are generally understood in terms of civic virtues and not the defence of ethnic purity per se. This position is best summarized by John Stuart Mill, who famously argued that,

> Free institutions are next to impossible in a country made up of different nationalities. Among a people without fellow-feeling, especially if they read and speak different languages, the united public opinion, necessary to the working of representative government, cannot exist.[13]

The civic nation state tends to relegate ethnicity, like religion, to the private sphere. Minority ethnic and cultural identities may be tolerated within the home where distinct languages, traditions, myths, and memories may be preserved, provided they do not conflict with, nor in any way undermine, the prevailing civic culture. Obviously, such private identities do not receive public recognition from the civic nation state. Instead, public institutions actively support the civic national culture and language within public life to the exclusion of all others. And assimilationist or paternal policies may be directed towards nonconformist ethnic groups, where necessary, in order to defend this civic culture.

Nevertheless, within civic nation states security policy per se is less likely to be a reflection of ethnic or cultural attachments. Such a state may go to war in defence of national territory, institutions, or liberty, but it is less likely to do so in the quest for 'lost' ethnic homelands. In extreme circumstances (war or threat of war) it may both restrict the civil liberties of resident aliens and even its own national citizens, as well as use armed force to put down popular resistance in the interest of national security. We see evidence of such policies in the American response to the threat of international terrorism after 9/11. A report by the Washington-based Lawyers Committee for Human Rights, published in 2003, documents post-9/11 restrictions in several key policy areas, including government openness, personal privacy, immigration, and security-related detention.[14] Most notorious of these restrictions are perhaps the set of extra-legal institutions established by executive order to bypass the federal judiciary in cases relating to the 'war on terror'. In such circumstances, the civic nation state may single out individuals belonging to ethnic or racial minorities for security-related reasons. For example, the American Civil Liberties Union claims that security screening of immigrants and refugees since 9/11 has disproportionately targeted males who fit a specific 'racial or ethnic profile' (i.e. of Arab origin).[15]

Once the ethnic bond is accepted as the *raison d'être* of the state, cultural diversity is a fundamental threat. Thus, although the freedom of minorities to express and develop their distinct ethnic and cultural identities may be limited in either civic or ethnic nation states, the latter are arguably far more hostile towards ethnic minorities and thus potentially more destructive, not only of ethnic minority identities but, in extreme circumstances, their physical survival as well. In order to preserve its territorial integrity and domestic stability, the ethnic nation state tends to act as if it is a homogenous ethnic community. If (as is often the case) such a state is not in fact ethnically homogeneous, than it must 'endeavor to make the facts correspond to the ideal', regardless of the rights and liberties of those among its citizens who do not belong to the majority ethnic group.[16] Consequently, where the ethnic community predominates, those cultural groups that do not share its ascriptive characteristics cannot belong and, therefore, must be eliminated.

This process of elimination can take different forms, including separation ('ghettoization'), expulsion, or extermination. Separation or 'ghettoization' is a practice that predates both self-determination and popular sovereignty – the origin of 'ghettoization' goes back to the medieval practice of confining Jews within particular quarters of otherwise Christian cities. It was notoriously revived by the Nazi regime as an element of their Final Solution against European Jewry. More recently, it has been suggested that the Israeli 'security fence' is an instance of 'ghettoization' aimed at separating Israeli Jews from the Palestinian population. In July 2004, the International Court of Justice ruled that the construction of this fence is contrary to international law.[17] Expulsion featured prominently in Hitler's policy of *Lebensraum* and was also used by Stalin, both in the Soviet

Union itself and Soviet occupied Europe. Since the end of the Cold War the practice has been most closely associated with events in former Yugoslavia, from which the term 'ethnic cleansing' originates. The Jewish Holocaust remains the most widely known example of genocide, but there are both earlier (e.g. the Turkish genocide against the Armenians during the First World War) and later (e.g. the Hutu genocide against the Tutsis in Rwanda in 1994) episodes.

The assumption underlying all of these responses is that political stability cannot tolerate cultural pluralism, as such divisions will undermine the integrity of the overarching political order by calling into question the ethnic and cultural characteristics on which it rests. This perspective, as previously indicated, views culture and ethnicity in zero-sum terms so that coexistence between ethnic and cultural groups within the same jurisdiction is not an option.

Cultural diversity and international security

The international security paradigm aspires towards a general condition of peace, order, and lawfulness within the society of states.[18] States which form an international society agree to conduct their sovereign affairs in accordance with specified normative standards; these include, for example, non-intervention, *pacta sunt servanta*, the procedures of international law, the customs and conventions of war, and the practice of diplomacy. The common objective of these various rules is the preservation of international order defined as the continued existence of international society as a whole – although not necessarily the independence of particular states.[19]

Significantly, international society has struggled with the problem of diversity from its very inception – indeed, international society itself is largely a response to the emergence of diversity within early modern Europe. It originates in the

> disintegration of a single community [the *imperium* of Pope and Emperor], the waning on the one hand of central authorities, and on the other hand of local authorities, within Western Christendom, and the exclusion of both from particular territories by the princely power.[20]

Although the Reformation shattered the religious unity of Medieval Christendom, the old principle of divine right to rule was not lost. Instead, it was translated into a desire for religious affinity and even conformity between sovereign and subjects. Hence, the status of religious minorities – Catholics in the territories of Protestant princes, and Protestants in the territories of Catholic princes – became a source of international concern and even conflict. For this reason, the Peace of

Westphalia – which restored order to Europe after the Thirty Years War, and in so doing gave final form to the European states system that had been slowly developing over the previous century – confirmed the *grundnorm* of non-intervention so as to prevent religious diversity being used as a pretext for war.

Cujus regio ejus religio (like sovereign, like religion) – and its later incarnation *cujus regio ejus natio* (like sovereign, like nation) – became the organizing principle within and between states. From this time onwards, international society has assumed a contradictory stance towards cultural diversity depending upon the level – state or sub-state – at which it exists. On the one hand, international society seeks to preserve that cultural diversity reflected in its plural state membership. On the other hand, there is a tendency to control or suppress cultural diversity within states that threatens to disrupt or destabilize order between states.

This dualistic response to cultural diversity is apparent in the international history of self-determination. The idea of self-determination as applied in international society may be traced back to Woodrow Wilson's vision of a post-First World War peace. The creation of nation states in the territories of the defeated and discredited Hapsburg and Ottoman Empires was a major component of his plan: accordingly, a dozen new or enlarged states in Central and Eastern Europe were admitted to international society during the interwar period. However, a fundamental weakness in Wilson's ideas for restructuring international society was his failure to realize how indeterminate a criterion nationality was and what little assistance it could actually give in delineating frontiers.[21]

The methods used to define nation states in 1919 were contradictory. Plebiscites evocative of the civic tradition were employed while at the same time ethnographic and linguistic evidence suggestive of the ethnic tradition were also taken into account. On certain occasions decisions were made on the basis of *realpolitik* and even punitive justice – as, for example, in the incorporation of majority ethnic German Sudetenland within Czechoslovakia (despite Sudeten German requests for assignment to Austria) and the gift of majority ethnic Hungarian Transylvania to Romania. Once it became clear that not all claims to self-determination could or would be recognized in the 1919 territorial settlement, the potential for ethnic dissatisfaction with the territorial status quo to escalate into domestic and even international violence was obvious.

During the interwar period there were two distinct, albeit related, international security responses to this dilemma: population transfer agreements and international minority rights guarantees. Both of these ideas reflect the then widespread assumption that, wherever possible, ethnic homogeneity within states was to be preferred to diversity in the interests of international peace and stability. Similarly, where homogeneity was not immediately obtainable, it was thought that international supervision and collective security measures could be used to encourage group coexistence and thus prevent ethnic conflicts from destabilizing that territorial status quo on which the new international system was based.

Population transfer (the movement, sometimes forcible, of minorities between states) was viewed as a legitimate means of improving the fit between national boundaries and the ethnic composition of the population within them.[22] National minorities that remained outside the boundaries of their ethnic group's nation state could simply be relocated. It was hoped this would ease tensions both within and between states by reducing the incidence of disruptive minority claims for self-determination. At the same time, the transfer of minorities to their ethnic group's nation state was considered the fulfilment of that minority's right to self-determination – once moved, they would become a part of that body politic which reflected their particular ethnicity.

In circumstances where population transfers either could not be used, or were considered to be undesirable, provisions were made for internationally supervised minority guarantees. The interwar minority rights system was based upon a series of treaties which linked the recognition of new or enlarged states in Central and Eastern Europe, the Baltics and, exceptionally, also Iraq, with undertakings to protect ethnic minorities. Such treaties were then placed under the guarantee of the League of Nations. In theory, this legalistic procedure was designed to ensure compliance through a combination of collective decision making and the moral approbation of international public opinion. In practice, though, this consensual conflict resolution formula broke down because the international goodwill it relied upon was not forthcoming. As a result, minority questions degenerated into a political struggle between, on the one hand, minorities and kin-states with revisionist aims towards the international boundaries set by the treaties of 1919 and, on the other hand, those treaty bound states that wished to preserve the territorial status quo where it was to their advantage. Consequently, and ironically, the League of Nations System of Minority Guarantees – with few exceptions – satisfied neither the minorities they were intended to protect nor the states on which they were imposed.

After 1945, the United Nations was reluctant to adopt the interwar rhetoric of national self-determination and its concomitant language of minority rights. Inis Claude contends that the 1945 Charter of the United Nations was formulated 'without consideration of the questions of principle' which arise from the existence of national minorities in a 'world dominated by the concept of the national State as the . . . unit of political organization'.[23] More than this, however, there was at San Francisco a deliberate move to discredit the idea of self-determination as it had been understood in ethnic terms. This was in large measure a reaction against the failure of the League experiment and indeed the 1919 system of nation states and national self-determination that underscored it. Understandably, in the aftermath of the Second World War, national self-determination – and the secession and irredentism it could provoke – were viewed as serious would-be threats to international security. Such fears were only heightened by the prospect of widespread decolonization and the creation of new, and potentially weak, states in Asia and Africa.

As a result, the UN Charter incorporates the vague phrase 'self-determination of peoples', as distinct from the more familiar and discredited 'national self-determination', in the hope of avoiding that sort of minority controversy that had plagued the League of Nations system. Articles 73 and 76 further define such 'peoples' in terms of the pre-existing colonial territory and not according to ethnicity. The use of civic criteria for assessing claims to self-determination was clearly motivated by a desire to preserve the colonial territorial status quo and in so doing international peace and stability. This position was specifically expressed and affirmed in United Nations General Assembly resolution 1514 (1960), the Declaration on the Granting of Independence to Colonial Countries and Peoples, which clearly states that 'any attempt aimed at the partial or total disruption of the national unity or territorial integrity of a country is incompatible with the purposes and principles of the United Nations Charter'.[24]

The international legitimization of pre-existing territorial units remains a fundamental practice of international society. Thus, while Czechoslovakia, Yugoslavia, and the Soviet Union were replaced by successor states in the 1990s, the new boundaries follow those of the defunct domestic political structures.[25] Just as with decolonization in Latin America, Asia, and Africa, internal boundaries were inherited without regard to ethno-national demographics. Consequently, regions that were not highest-level constituent units of the old polities – e.g. Kosovo within Yugoslavia, or Chechnya within the Soviet Union – were not entitled to sovereign statehood, despite their distinct ethnic populations, and remain as ethnic minority enclaves in the successor states of Serbia-Montenegro and Russia respectively. Similarly, the territorial integrity of post-war Iraq has been affirmed by both the American and British occupying powers and the United Nations, with the clear implication that any Kurdish demands for secession will not be recognized. Such an interpretation is directly aimed at preventing further fragmentation and the additional political instability that might unleash. Territorial integrity determines which claims to independence will take priority, and so order continues to trump self-determination except where the states involved so agree (as in the Czechoslovak 'velvet divorce').

In sum, to the extent that international society maintains a global states system, it facilitates the political expression of a diverse range of ethnic and cultural identities. However, it is much less able to accommodate that cultural diversity which remains at the sub-state level because such measures might threaten the territorial integrity and political stability of existing states – and by extension international order itself, which is based on territories, not peoples. In those circumstances where a hard choice between competing norms of self-determination for sub-state groups and the sovereignty and territorial integrity of existing states is required, those who espouse an international security paradigm will usually choose the latter. The only exception to this rule applies to those circumstances where the sacrifice of one state is considered necessary to preserve stability within the society of states as arguably happened when the breakaway Yugoslav republics were recognized as independent states, and again when the Dayton Agreement (1995) created that strange entity known as the Serpska Republik within the territory of Bosnia-Herzegovina.

Cultural diversity and human security

Both the national security and international security paradigms reflect the classic liberal assumption that the state, properly understood, is protector rather than oppressor of its own citizens (although, as previously indicated, the same reasoning does not necessarily apply to non-members including those on the territory of the state who should otherwise be eligible for the rights and protection of citizens). For example, once the Hobbesian *Leviathan* is co-opted by particular, private interests – as in civil war – the social order can no longer be said to exist. In such circumstances, the individual is, once again, in the state of nature, subject only to the laws of nature. Thus, what today is termed a failed state (e.g. Sudan, Somalia, Sierra Leone) is – in Hobbes' rendering of things – no state at all; it is a reversion to the profoundly insecure state of nature. The insecurity of those individuals who find themselves in such places is simply the natural circumstances of humankind without the social artifice. Their plight may be worthy of sympathy from those more fortunately placed within a social order, but it does not present any serious moral challenge to the idea of Leviathan (or the state) as such. Nor does it pose any immediate dilemmas for those who espouse a national or international security perspective unless it threatens the political order existing elsewhere.

It has been recently suggested that the human security paradigm offers a better way of conceptualizing the problems that arise in circumstances like those noted above than the more traditional approaches of national and international security. From this perspective,

> security extends beyond the protection of borders, ruling elites, and exclusive state interests to include the protection of people. . . . To confine the concept of security exclusively to the protection of states is to ignore the interests of people who form the citizens of a state and in whose name sovereignty is exercised. It can produce situations in which those in power feel they have the unfettered freedom to abuse the right to security of their people. . . . All people, no less than states, have a right to a secure existence, and all states have an obligation to protect those rights.[26]

The search for a global human community, which transcends international frontiers and 'trumps' the rights and interests of particular (national or other) communities, has a noble pedigree in the historic search for an alternative to international anarchy. Suggestions of this kind, which one can trace back to Kant, accept the description of international society while insisting that such circumstances can, and should, be overcome. They are usually constructed either in terms of the memory of Roman or Western Christian unity (as in the 'new Mediaevalism') or in the language of progress, whether moral or material (as in the 'new interventionism').[27] The aim of this discussion will be to interrogate whether such a human security paradigm can be usefully applied to those conflicts that have their origins in ethnic or cultural differences.

This human security paradigm is not intended to promote the security of ethnic or cultural communities as communities (whether these are states or sub-state groups) but instead the security of individuals as human beings. Human security recognizes and advocates the rights of those individuals who have been victimized (oppressed, tortured, expelled, or worse) because they do not belong to the ruling or dominant community. Neither the national nor the international security discourses are able to address these circumstances in as powerful a normative language precisely because they are first and foremost predicated upon and, indeed, directed at, either states or citizens.

The great achievement of the human security paradigm – as embodied since 1945 in humanitarian law, crimes against humanity, and human rights – is that it has created a normative discourse in which those who abuse their power, regardless of who or where they are, may be condemned. The rapidly expanding body of international norms that reflect this human security perspective is certainly dramatic, and perhaps even revolutionary. Take, for example, the various provisions outlining the rights of combatants that can be found in the Geneva Convention III Relative to the Treatment of Prisoners of War (1949), the Geneva Protocol I Relating to the Victims of International Armed Conflicts (1979), the Convention Against Torture (1984), and the UN Resolution on the Body of Principles for the Protection of all Persons under any form of Imprisonment or Detention (1988).[28] The widespread international condemnation of American practices towards detainees held at Camp X-Ray in Guantanamo Bay and at Abu Ghraib in Iraq underscores the normative authority of these provisions even if the fact of abuse itself points to the ongoing problem of enforcement.

Yet despite its many laudable achievements in championing the rights of oppressed individuals, wherever they might be, the human rights perspective may be less well suited to dealing with problems of ethnic or indeed other forms of diversity.

> The problem with the concept of human rights is not that it gives the wrong answer to such questions. It is, rather, that it often gives no

answer at all. The right to freedom of speech, for example, does not tell us what language policy a society ought to have. The principles of human rights leave such matters to majoritarian decision-making, and this may result in minorities being vulnerable to injustice at the hands of minorities. Human rights may even make injustice [directed at minorities] worse.[29]

For this reason, there is a tendency for the proponents of human security to promote equality rather than freedom (which would of course perpetuate and even promote diversity) when these two values conflict. This tendency can be seen in the failure, until very recently, to include measures aimed at the preservation of minority languages, cultures, identities, and ways of life alongside equality and anti-discrimination guarantees within international human rights texts. Until 1992, there was no human rights instrument devoted exclusively to minority concerns. The only specific mention of minority rights to identity and culture, as distinct from equality provisions, prior to this time was in Article 27 of the 1966 International Covenant on Civil and Political Rights. However, this formulation has been criticized as a minimal guarantee, not least because it gives state signatories the freedom to determine whether or not ethnic groups in their jurisdictions constitute minorities. This contrasts with the generous provision for equality guarantees at the United Nations and within many regional organizations, including the Council of Europe, the OSCE, the Association of Commonwealth States, the Organization of American States, the Organization of African Unity, and its successor organization, the African Union.

It is also evident in the recent criticism of human rights by representatives of non-Western states and cultures who have alleged that these provisions disproportionately reflect a Western, Judeo-Christian morality. According to this perspective, to impose on non-Western societies norms taken from the Universal Declaration of Human Rights involves 'moral chauvinism and ethnocentric bias'.[30] Often, such criticisms are made by non-Western states in the deliberate attempt to deflect criticism away from domestic human rights violations and can therefore be dismissed as rhetorical political posturing. However, those cases where the controversy involves practices that are internally defensible within the cultural system, but unacceptable by external standards, ought properly to be taken seriously as hard choices between competing values.[31] For example, the legal requirement within many Islamic countries for women to wear the veil in public as stipulated in the *shari'a* may be in that context a legitimate restriction of the universal right to gender equality guaranteed in the Universal Declaration of Human Rights.[32]

> What is clear is that values can clash – that is why civilizations are incompatible. They can be incompatible between cultures, or groups,

or between you and me.... We can discuss each other's point of view,
we can try to reach common ground, but in the end what you pursue
may not be reconcilable with the ends to which I find that I have
dedicated my life. Values may easily clash within the breast of a single
individual; and it does not follow that, if they do so, some must be
true and others false.[33]

In sum, the potential for controversy regarding cultural diversity
remains within the context of the human security paradigm. Indeed, to
the extent that human security is inherently solidarist, while the existence
of cultural diversity is an undeniable reminder that the human condition
is, in this respect at least, fundamentally pluralist, the two are logically at
odds.

Cultural diversity and multicultural security

None of the three security paradigms discussed thus far – national security, international security, or human security – is able to fully accommodate the distinct requirements of cultural minorities per se because each
privileges a social relationship which, in varying degrees, is inimical to the
existence of diversity. Both the civic state and international society tend to
subsume culture and ethnicity within the private sphere; consequently,
they are often ill-disposed towards the public recognition of diversity
except where this is absolutely necessary to preserve social cohesion. The
ethnic state incorporates ethnic and cultural characteristics into the very
foundation of its social existence; consequently, it publicly recognizes one
ethnic identity while deliberately excluding (often forcibly) any others
that might exist within its jurisdiction. And while the idea of a universal
humanity confers equal dignity on all individuals, in so doing it tends to
downplay, and in some instances, ignores ethnic and cultural distinctions
regardless of whether or not these are valued.

The predicament of ethnic and cultural minorities in circumstances
where diversity is considered undesirable implies much more than the loss
of universal human rights: it involves the loss of specific rights; the loss of
a cherished ethnic, linguistic, or cultural identity; the loss of membership
in a particular community in which that identity is recognized and
affirmed; the loss of a place in which they can feel fully and completely 'at
home'; and the loss of meaningful belonging. It in this context that
Arendt writes:

> Something much more fundamental than freedom and justice ... is at
> stake when belonging to the community into which one is born is no
> longer a matter of course and not belonging no longer a matter of
> choice.... Not the loss of specific rights, then, but the loss of a
> community willing and able to guarantee any rights whatsoever, has

been the calamity which has befallen ever-increasing numbers of people. Man, it turns out, can lose all so-called Rights of Man without losing his essential quality as man, his human dignity, only the loss of a ... [community] expels him from humanity.[34]

In other words, we are never more vulnerable than when we are deprived of our distinct identities and communal relationships.

The proponents of minority rights (as distinct from those of states, citizens, or human beings) advocate what might be viewed as a fourth paradigm of security that aims to protect and promote the identity and culture of ethnic communities within states, while also protecting the freedom of their individual members. We might appropriately call this approach multicultural security since it is broadly comparable to the multiculturalism espoused by liberal theorists such as Isaiah Berlin, Will Kymlicka, Joseph Raz, and Judith Shklar. The multicultural security paradigm regards cultural diversity within states as the consequence of a political desire for territorial inviolability in the context of a normal human propensity for belonging that makes sociological pluralism in ethnic and cultural terms a usual and indeed normatively desirable state of affairs. The guiding principle of this way of thinking about cultural diversity, to echo liberal theorist Judith Shklar, is that 'social diversity is something that any liberal should rejoice in and seek to promote, because it is in diversity alone that freedom can be realized'.[35] From the multicultural perspective, ethnic and cultural minorities are not considered to be prima facie threats to the prevailing social order at either the domestic or international level. Instead, the main premise of multiculturalism is that minorities who are recognized and supported by the state, and by extension international society, are far less likely to challenge existing modes of authority. The multicultural paradigm recognizes the importance of the ethnicity and culture, while at the same time striving to ensure that the public space remains characterized by a discourse of freedom predicated on mutual respect, and which does not degenerate into tyranny on the part of either majorities or minorities.

Although of relatively recent origin, the multicultural approach to problems of ethnic and cultural conflict is becoming increasingly apparent in international relations. The hitherto dominant response to cultural diversity within states (territorial inviolability coupled with individual equality guarantees) has come under growing criticism, not least owing to the increasing incidence of ethnic and cultural conflict around the globe. Ironically, that tendency may have strengthened the multicultural position; in this changed world order, the old fear that recognizing cultural diversity might precipitate inter-communal violence has now become a moot point. Consequently, a growing list of minority rights including *inter alia* provisions for identity, culture, language, participation, and a limited degree of autonomy, have now been recognized within international standard setting documents. Examples of such provisions may be found in the UN Declaration on the Rights of Persons Belonging to National or Ethnic, Religious and Linguistic Minorities (1992), the European Charter for Regional or Minority Languages (1992), and the Framework Convention for the Protection of National Minorities (1995).

At the same time, whereas previously democratic assumptions tended to discredit minority claims for special rights in addition to those of equal citizenship, the idea of democracy has itself been re-evaluated, and indeed redefined, in light of the growing recognition that a social consensus must be determined by more than a majority decision if it is to be stable and long lasting. This outlook is apparent in many of the recent agreements intended to create stability and good governance in plural societies following the cessation of ethnic conflict. Since 1990, there have been a number of cases where international mediation has sought to resolve self-determination disputes through power-sharing agreements, such as the Dayton Agreement (1995); the Northern Ireland Peace Agreement (1998); The Constitutional Framework for Provisional Self-government in Kosovo (2001); and the Bougainville Peace Agreement (2001).[36] It appears that Kurdish leaders in post-war Iraq are hoping to secure a similar arrangement under any future Iraqi constitution. Their key political demand is to maintain the high levels of autonomy enjoyed during the 1990s and to formalize this status within a federal Iraqi state, with the contested city of Kirkuk as the capital of the proposed Kurdistan region.[37]

Agreements like these recognize those normative entitlements that are considered fundamental for the well-being of the various individuals and communities who have been involved in or affected by ethnic and cultural conflict. Accordingly, they identify a variety of right holders – humans, citizens, members of ethnic and cultural communities, the state, and the various ethnic and cultural communities that fall within its jurisdiction – and provide each of them with substantive guarantees that address their particular circumstances. While distinct, these categories are also overlapping and so create a web of rights and obligations that cut across civic and ethnic divisions. Such provisions aim to establish a lasting series of rules and relationships in which competing normative claims may be articulated and resolved, thereby promoting both social cohesion and cultural diversity. In this way, cultural diversity is understood to support rather than subvert security.

Conclusion

Problems related to cultural diversity within states may have received renewed interest in the aftermath of 9/11, but such issues have been the subject of public policy for a much longer period of time. Once popular identity becomes the locus of political authority, then those cultural identifications at odds with the public persona of the state tend to be viewed as a potential threat. Accordingly, the belief that cultural diversity is inimical to peace and stability has been pervasive for several centuries.

The multicultural security paradigm offers a potential way out of this problematique by rethinking the relationship between diversity and stability. From this perspective, ethnic and cultural minorities who are recognized and respected by the state – and thus become integrated (but not assimilated) within it – are considered less likely to challenge existing political arrangements. So instead of viewing cultural diversity as a threat that must be contained or, if possible, eliminated, the multicultural approach sees diversity as a value that should be affirmed and protected.

Admittedly, this scenario may not be what Huntington had in mind when he advocated 'global multiculturality'. A curious feature of the 'clash of civilizations' argument is its affirmation of cultural homogeneity within states, even while it affirms respect for diversity between states. Huntington is highly critical of domestic policies designed to perpetuate ethnic and cultural diversity for the very reasons usually associated with the national and international security paradigms – fear of instability resulting from the erosion of shared values. For this reason, he recommends the assimilation of immigrants and other minorities into the dominant (majority) culture. However, history demonstrates that such attempts to enforce conformity are at best temporary and incomplete due to the recalcitrant nature of individual and collective identities and the constant movement of peoples within and indeed across political frontiers. Ultimately, cultural diversity is remarkably resilient; and, consequently, assimilationist policies often exacerbate the very conflicts they hoped to avoid. For this reason, 'renounc[ing] universalism, accept[ing] diversity, and seek[ing] commonalities' may be a more effective way of managing value clashes within states as well as between states.

Notes

1 Huntington (1997).
2 'The Clash', *Washington Post*, 16 December 2001, http://www.washingtonpost.com/.
3 The concepts of national security and international security have a long history within international theory and practice where they represent the dominant security paradigms. Both terms are commonly used in the media and in public policy documents as well as in academic analysis. Human security is a more recent paradigm that deliberately seeks to challenge the state-centred perspective of national and international security with a view to promoting the universal human rights of individuals. In 1991, for example, an independent Commission on Human Security was established with the initiative of the Government of Japan; its final report entitled *Human Security Now: Protecting and Empowering People* was presented to UN Secretary-General Kofi Annan in May 2003.
4 Huntington (1997), p. 318.
5 The idea of multicultural security as presented here is extrapolated from the growing literature on multiculturalism and minority rights as well as recent

international policy documents concerning self-determination and minorities. See among others: Council of Europe, *Charter for Regional or Minority Languages* (1992); Council of Europe, *Framework Convention for the Protection of National Minorities* (1995); Council of Europe, *Parliamentary Assembly Report 7228 on the Protection of the Rights of National Minorities* (1995), all of which are available at http://www.coe.int/DefaultEN.asp; Gutman (1992); Jackson Preece (2005); Kymlicka (1995); Musgrave (1997); Organization for Security and Cooperation in Europe, *Copenhagen Document* (1990) and Organization for Security and Cooperation in Europe, *Geneva Report on National Minorities* (1991), both of which are available at http://www.osce.org/; Raz (1986); Thornberry (1991); United Nations, *Declaration on the Rights of Persons Belonging to National or Ethnic, Religious or Linguistic Minorities* (1992); United Nations, *Study of the Rights of Persons Belonging to National or Ethnic, Religious or Linguistic Minorities* (1989); Young (1990). The multicultural paradigm aims to promote the interests of cultural communities and their members, including those of sub-state groups.

6 Rawls (1999), p. 277.
7 Arendt (1972), p. 301.
8 Hobbes (1988), p. 66.
9 Huntington (1996).
10 Watson (1992), p. 173.
11 For an in-depth discussion of the dilemmas posted by national self-determination, see J. Mayall's contribution to this volume, Chapter 6.
12 LeFebvre (1988), p. 221.
13 Mill (1999), p. 392.
14 *Assessing the New Normal: Liberty and Security for the Post-September 11 United States* (Washington: Lawyers Committee for Human Rights, 2003), http://www.humanrightsfirst.org, date accessed: 11 September 2005.
15 *Sanctioned Bias: Racial Profiling Since 9/11,* (New York: American Civil Liberties Union, 2004), http://www.aclu.org/, date accessed: 19 September 2005.
16 Cobban (1970), p. 109.
17 International Court of Justice, 'Legal Consequences of the Construction of a Wall In the Occupied Palestinian Territory', 9 July 2004, http://www.icj-cij.org, date accessed: 19 September 2005.
18 R. Jackson addresses this idea at length (pp. 24–8). See also Jackson (2000), p. 199.
19 Bull (1977), pp. 16–17.
20 Bull (1968), p. 37.
21 See J. Mayall's chapter, (p. 109).
22 This perspective is discussed at length in Newman (1943); and Schechtman (1946).
23 Claude (1955), p. 113.
24 See Brownlie (1992), pp. 28–30.
25 This principle, *uti possidetis juris,* is discussed by J. Mayall (pp. 110–14).
26 *Our Global Neighbourhood: The Report of the Commission on Global Governance,* (Oxford: Oxford University Press, 1995), p. 84.
27 Bull (1966), p. 38.
28 K. J. Holsti discusses the development of these norms in the context of changing moral sensibilities about the place of war in international society. See Chapter 3.
29 Freeman (2002), p. 117.
30 Pollis and Schwab (1979), p. 14.
31 Donnelly (1989), p. 114.
32 Mayer (1995), pp. 98–100.
33 Berlin (1990), p. 12.

34 Arendt (1972), pp. 296–7.
35 Shklar (1964), p. 5.
36 See the Carnegie Council Funded Project on Complex Power Sharing in Post-Conflict Divided Societies: http://www.ecmi.de/cps, date accessed: 11 September 2005.
37 'Kurdish Aims for a Post-Election Iraq', *Oxford Analytica*, 10 February 2005, http://www.forbes.com/, date accessed: 11 September 2005.

9 Intervention

Beyond 'dictatorial interference'[1]

Sir Adam Roberts

Military intervention, one of the enduring institutions of international relations, has a notable capacity to mutate. Indeed, the very meaning of the term has changed over a relatively short period of time. In 1984 Hedley Bull opened the introduction to his edited book on intervention with a definition of its subject matter as 'dictatorial or coercive interference, by an outside party or parties, in the sphere of jurisdiction of a sovereign state'.[2] The word 'dictatorial' did not imply that the intervening state was a dictatorship: it was to be taken as referring simply to the fact that the intervening state or states forcibly imposed their policies and personnel on the target state. At the time the definition was relatively uncontroversial. Today, however, the word 'dictatorial' seldom appears in definitions of intervention. It is hardly the appropriate adjective to describe some of the interventions since 1990, the purposes of which have included: assisting delivery of humanitarian aid, preventing ethnic cleansing and genocide, and introducing democratic changes. 'Dictatorial' also seems especially inappropriate given that interventions today are often defended by their protagonists as implementing the principles of the international community as a whole, and as helping to liberate the inhabitants of the territory concerned from dictatorial government. Something fundamental has happened which powerfully affects thinking about the law and ethics of intervention. The decline of the epithet 'dictatorial' is emblematic of wider changes in the nature of intervention that are explored in this chapter.

The changes in the terms of debate about intervention are not confined to 'humanitarian intervention'. They also relate to other actual or proposed types of intervention addressing different (if sometimes overlapping) problems: for example, intervention in states where there has been a military *coup d'état*, in failed states, in states undergoing civil war, in states harbouring terrorist movements, or in states deemed to have violated disarmament terms. In these cases, too, the word 'dictatorial' is not always the most appropriate term to define interventions.

When such changes of practice occur, there is often a tendency to take them as proof that the very nature of international relations has been transformed, and to adjust the language of international political discourse accordingly. Since the end of the Cold War there has been no shortage of terms, often connected with the idea and practice of intervention, which suggest such a fundamental transformation. For example, there has been unprecedented emphasis on the concept of 'international community' and its values; 'human security' is presented as having supplanted, or at least significantly supplemented, state security; the 'responsibility to protect' is widely discussed, even if its application in any particular case remains hugely problematic; and, especially in the United States, there has been a revival of the idea of intervention to assist democratic transformation. Yet alongside this language of a new era, old realities have endured: military interventions remain problematic and controversial. The changed facts and language of a new era show no signs of completely supplanting familiar and enduring difficulties surrounding the subject of military intervention.

The changes in the practice of intervention, and in its characterization, raise tough questions about the adequacy or otherwise of contemporary international ethical and legal norms regarding the use of force. Such norms, especially as they bear on the question of intervention, are sometimes seen as having evolved significantly. Ethics may have moved faster than law, whose movements are by nature slow and cumbersome, and which in its written form is sometimes seen as out of date. If intervention has changed significantly, is it realistic to suppose that it is still governed by a body of written international law based on the six-decades-old United Nations (UN) Charter that has been widely seen as hostile to interventionism? Could it be that today the principal intervener and the world's most powerful state, the United States, is in some undefined yet all too observable way above the existing body of international law? Or, alternatively, is there still some wisdom in the existing provisions of international law?

Despite the sense that the post-Cold War era is characterized by some genuinely new practices and norms, there is remarkably little formal consensus on what these actually are. There have been no formal modifications of the existing written law. Because of the difficulties of securing any agreed legal doctrine of intervention, it is tempting to say that if there is a case for intervention today on humanitarian or other grounds, it is more in the realm of ethics than in that of law. Yet the problem is not just one of ethics versus law: it is also a problem within international law itself.

The *jus ad bellum*, which can be seen as encompassing both law and ethics, has a centuries-long and distinguished record of providing one basis for making and judging decisions for or against the use of force. The experience of certain interventions in the 1990s, with their emphasis on certain core principles and values of the international community, has confirmed certain inadequacies within this body of thought. This chapter offers an exploration of those inadequacies as they relate to intervention, what they tell us about the role of norms in the contemporary international order, and what might be done in respect of them.

The central questions addressed here are simple. Is this really a revolutionary era so far as the practice of intervention is concerned? Is a 'solidarist' conception of international society emerging, whether regionally or globally, that could justify intervention to enforce the norms and values of that society? Or do contemporary practices, despite their trappings of multilateralism and of progressive purposes, in fact reflect thoroughly 'realist' considerations of state interest and pursuit of power politics? Is the body of international law addressing the question of intervention still relevant in the new circumstances of the post-Cold War world? Can the law evolve to overcome any limitations? Or, if the law cannot be changed, can some conception of ethics provide a useful guide to states in addressing questions about the justifiability of military interventions? The exploration of these questions is covered in eight sections:

1   Military intervention: an old problem with new dimensions
2   Restrictions on intervention in international law
3   The UN Security Council as an intervener
4   Humanitarian intervention: not a 'right'
5   Ethics and law apparently out of step
6   Problems beyond humanitarian intervention
7   Criteria for intervention
8   General issues and conclusions.

Military intervention: an old problem with new dimensions

Military interventions have always posed problems for the branches of international law and ethics that set out basic rules about the use of force. There never was a 'golden age', in which the principles governing intervention were completely clear, or in which principle and practice operated in perfect conjunction. There has long been tension between the norm of non-intervention and the recognition that states do occasionally, and sometimes for good reason, resort to intervention.

The term 'intervention' defies neat definition. It can encompass military action in a country with the consent of the government. It can also encompass certain non-military types of action directed against the government of a country, for example, economic sanctions and support to opposition movements. The main, but not exclusive, emphasis here is on one particular type of international intervention, namely military action within the territory of a state without the approval of the government of that state. This type of intervention has assumed many different forms in the years since 1990. The military action may be by the armed forces of one or more countries, and it may or may not have authorization from a regional international organization or from the UN Security Council. It may include the incursion of armed forces into the territory of a state, or the use of external military pressure, for example, in the form of bombing. It can have many different types of purpose.

Over the centuries, interventions have taken place for a wide range of purposes, many of which have been seen as constituting possible legal justifications. The range of purposes has traditionally included:

1 assistance to an incumbent government (e.g. in a civil war);
2 counter-intervention (i.e. intervention to reverse the effects of an earlier intervention by a third state);
3 protection of threatened nationals of the intervening state;
4 self-defence of the intervening state (e.g. following attacks on it from the territory subject to intervention);
5 support for the self-determination of the inhabitants of a colony, province or region (e.g. in cases where they wish to establish their own state);
6 ending situations of lawlessness, especially ones that pose a threat to other states and their nationals (e.g. if a territory was a haven for terrorists or pirates), and;
7 prevention or cessation of gross human rights violations.

The idea that the last two categories are wholly new, and evidence of the superiority of our own times, is much too simple. That intervention for human protection purposes is hardly new can be illustrated by three nineteenth-century cases: (1) in Sierra Leone, from the late eighteenth century onwards, an important purpose of the British presence was to provide a haven for freed slaves;[3] (2) in Greece, the Franco-British-Russian military involvement in 1827, culminating in the Battle of Navarino and the liberation of the Greeks from Ottoman rule, reflected humanitarian concerns based on outrage at Turkish and Egyptian atrocities in Greece and widespread sympathy with the Greek national cause – the growth of Hellenophile societies in many European states contributing to popular support for military action;[4] and (3) in 1853 Russia claimed a general protectorate over the Christians in the Ottoman Empire – a claim which was rightly viewed by others as evidence of Russian designs on Turkey, and which contributed to the outbreak of the Crimean War.[5]

Traditional as they may be, all seven types of purpose indicated above have been cited in connection with interventions in the post-Cold War period. However, as compared with earlier periods, the last two of these seven purposes (ending situations of lawlessness and prevention of human rights violations) have been particularly emphasized. Here lies a strange and disturbing paradox: these two purposes of intervention, both so prominent since the early 1990s, have been in tension with each other, and especially so since 2001.

On the one hand, in the post-Cold War period the category of 'prevention of human rights violations' has been enlarged and enriched by the addition of some new purposes, closely related to it: the protection of victims of armed conflict, especially civilians; the prevention or punishment of violations of the laws of war (international humanitarian law); assisting the delivery of humanitarian assistance; and the creation of conditions enabling refugees to return home. In addition, restoration of a democratic political system, and assisting in democratic electoral processes, have been important considerations in several interventions since the Cold War, including in Haiti in 1994, Afghanistan in 2001, and Iraq in 2003. Even if these factors do not prove that intervention in the post-Cold War period is qualitatively new, and even if the fear that intervention might assume a dictatorial character has not disappeared, these cases do confirm that intervention can no longer be defined as necessarily being 'dictatorial interference'.

On the other hand – and here lies the paradox – the interventions that come into the category of 'ending situations of lawlessness' were conducted in such a manner as to lead to criticisms that human rights considerations were being violated. In the US-led 'war on terror' there were numerous such accusations, both generally and in relation to the interventions in Afghanistan and Iraq. The maltreatment of prisoners by the US and its allies was among the most negative consequences of these wars. It is true that these wars also had human rights purposes, and also had some undoubtedly beneficial outcomes – including the return of 1.8 million refugees to Afghanistan in 2002. Overall, though, the 'war on terror' and its associated interventions have cast a shadow over the statements of legal and humanitarian principle that were made in connection with interventions in the decade before 11 September 2001.

Intervention is thus still a divisive issue in international relations in the twenty-first century. Today, as in other eras, international debates on the matter are intense and acrimonious. Many states and individuals are suspicious of the motives of states intervening, and are also sceptical about the results. States doing the intervening are conscious of the criticisms to which their actions lead, the costs they incur, and the overstretch that their armed forces experience. As reactions to the US-led intervention in Iraq in March 2003 confirm, foreign military occupation remains a highly contentious issue.

For many countries the new pattern of international interventionism presents special and difficult problems. Some states with a history of intervening abroad have learned much from their own imperial history about the short duration, limited achievements, and high costs of engaging in interventions. France, Germany, Japan, and the United Kingdom have had such sobering experiences, but have drawn very different conclusions from them. Other states, including China, have learned from their history to be suspicious of interventions against them by foreign armed forces.

Even the United States – the most interventionist state of the post-Cold War period – still has living memories of its disastrous involvement in Vietnam, and even now it may once again be learning, in Iraq, the dreadful costs of running an unpopular empire. Most other states, having emerged in the past sixty years from one or another kind of colonial domination, are sceptical about any pattern, or doctrine, of interventionism.

However, a simple rejection of all forms of intervention is simply not a convincing policy for governments to pursue. Faced with major crises, they have to make policy choices involving life-or-death decisions. In particular, since 1990 many representatives of countries elected to non-permanent membership of the UN Security Council have found decisions regarding intervention to be among the most difficult that they have had to address. Although most states now recognize the changed character of intervention, they remain understandably suspicious of it, and continue to look to law as a means of restricting and limiting a potentially destabilizing phenomenon.

Restrictions on intervention in international law

Legal prohibitions on forcible military intervention in the territory of sovereign states have a long history, and are one of the key foundations of the system of sovereign states. The undoubted fact that their effect was limited does not negate their fundamental importance. They helped to establish the principle that non-intervention was the norm; and when interventions did occur, those responsible generally felt it necessary to produce detailed justifications based on the special and pressing circumstances of the case at hand.

The UN Charter reinforced existing legal prohibitions on intervention, and is still seen, sixty years after its adoption, as the key encapsulation of international law on the subject. It is fundamentally non-interventionist in its approach. Taken as a whole, the Charter essentially limits the right of states to use force internationally to cases of, first, individual or collective self-defence and, second, participation in UN-authorized or controlled military operations. Nowhere does the Charter address directly the question of intervention for humanitarian or other purposes, whether under UN auspices or by states acting independently. However, the Charter does set forth a number of purposes and rules, which could point to the legitimacy of certain types of intervention.

The strongest and most frequently cited prohibitions on intervention are those in Article 2 of the Charter. These provisions create a strong presumption against forcible military interventions by member states. Article 2(4) states: 'All Members shall refrain in their international relations from the threat or use of force against the territorial integrity or political independence of any state, or in any other manner inconsistent with the Purposes of the United Nations.' Article 2(7) states:

> Nothing contained in the present Charter shall authorize the United Nations to intervene in matters which are essentially within the domestic jurisdiction of any state or shall require the Members to submit such matters to settlement under the present Charter; but this principle shall not prejudice the application of enforcement measures under Chapter VII.

Notwithstanding the strong presumption against the use of force against a state, these Charter provisions leave some scope for intervention in two main ways.

The first concerns the phrase in Article 2(4), 'or in any other manner inconsistent with the Purposes of the United Nations'. What then happens if an intervention is presented as having as a primary goal the implementation of the UN's purposes? These purposes, as outlined in the Preamble and in Article 1, are broad to the point of being all-encompassing. The UN includes in its purposes, in Article 1(2): 'To develop friendly relations among nations based on respect for the principle of equal rights and self-determination of peoples, and to take other appropriate measures to strengthen universal peace'; and in Article 2(3): 'To achieve international co-operation in solving international problems of an economic, social, cultural or humanitarian character, and in promoting and encouraging respect for human rights and for fundamental freedoms for all without distinction as to race, sex, language or religion.' These provisions inevitably raise the question, not addressed directly in the Charter, of what should be done if these fundamental purposes are openly flouted within a state.

The second way in which the Charter may leave scope for intervention concerns the possibility of such intervention under UN Security Council auspices. The final phrase in Article 2(7), 'this principle shall not prejudice the application of enforcement measures under Chapter VII', leaves at least some scope for the Security Council to take action within states. Chapter VII itself is much less restrictive than had been the equivalent provisions of the Covenant of the League of Nations (1919) about the circumstances in which international military action could be authorized.[6] In particular, Article 39 empowers the Security Council to take action in cases deemed to constitute a 'threat to the peace, breach of the peace, or act of aggression'. In practice, a wide range of crises within states can encompass or coincide with any or all of these threats. Articles 42 and 51 leave the Security Council a wide range of discretion as regards the types of military action that it can take.

The actual practice of states during the UN era, including in the Cold War years, does not suggest that there was a complete, universally accepted, and effective prohibition on intervention. The phenomenon of intervention, deeply engrained in the international system and capable of endless mutations, was not about to disappear completely.

Many interventions occurred, most of which were condemned at the UN. Due to the existence of the veto, agreement on such condemnations could only rarely be obtained in the Security Council – at least as long as the Cold War lasted. It was therefore the General Assembly that issued most of the condemnations. Military interventions that were condemned by the General Assembly included: the Anglo-French invasion of Suez (1956); the Soviet invasion of Hungary (1956); the Indonesian invasion of East Timor (1975); the Moroccan invasion of Western Sahara (1975); the Vietnamese invasion of Cambodia (1978); the Soviet intervention in Afghanistan (1979); and the US-led interventions in Grenada (1983) and Panama (1989). However, not all interventions were condemned by the General Assembly. For example, it failed to criticize the Indian invasion of Goa (1962), partly because of sympathy with the principle of retrocession of colonial enclaves; and it did not condemn the Soviet-led occupation of Czechoslovakia (1968), because the Czechoslovak government, acting under duress, asked that the matter not be discussed.

In many cases, although UN bodies condemned interventions, or demanded a ceasefire and withdrawal of forces, their members tacitly accepted the results of intervention. This was the understandable if unheroic response at the UN to the Indian intervention in East Pakistan that began on 3 December 1971. India justified its actions in terms that, apart from encompassing an element of self-defence, referred repeatedly to the urgency of responding to a situation that had resulted in ten million refugees fleeing from East Pakistan to India. After the Security Council decided on 6 December to refer the matter to the General Assembly under the 'Uniting for Peace' procedure, the General Assembly passed a resolution calling for a ceasefire and withdrawal of armed forces to their own side of the India–Pakistan border.[7] This appeal was unsuccessful. New Delhi continued its military operations in East Pakistan, and the war ended only on 16 December with the surrender of Pakistani forces there. In the ensuing months and years UN members accepted the outcome and indeed admitted the resulting new state, Bangladesh, to UN membership. Here was a case in which the UN's members, having expressed doubts and anxieties about a military intervention, were prepared to tolerate its results.

The war over Kosovo in 1999 reignited concern about the apparent disjunction between the actual practice of states and a legal system that largely prohibits intervention by states. The disjunction was especially stark because, given the circumstances of the Kosovo crisis, it would not have been convincing for NATO members to claim that they were acting in self-defence. Many observers, including those who opposed it and those who favoured it, saw the decision to use force over Kosovo in breach of the non-intervention rule as an epoch-making event. Professor Michael Glennon of Tufts University wrote that,

Kosovo represented as momentous an event for the legal order as the fall of the Soviet Union did for the geopolitical order.... The received rules of international law neither describe accurately what nations do, nor predict reliably what they will do, nor prescribe intelligently what they should do when considering intervention.[8]

This view is interesting but exaggerated. The Kosovo war did not prove that the non-intervention norm was dead, but rather confirmed what was already evident from other cases, namely that occasionally, in extreme circumstances, it might have to be overridden by other considerations, which themselves included concern for international legal norms.

Professor Michael Reisman, an exponent of the so-called 'New Haven School' of international law, took a different approach to the question of the lawfulness of the 1999 war over Kosovo. He argued that acceptance of human rights law by the international community creates a conflict of legal obligations whenever extreme repression within a state leads to calls for external intervention.[9] On this point he is right. He is also right in his belief that lawyers need to understand the nature of governmental decision-making processes, and the difficulties of the dilemmas faced. However, the approach of the 'New Haven School' is vulnerable to certain criticisms. This school represents an intellectual tradition of interpreting international law in a way which is not merely contextual but also highly subjective – and frequently favourable to particular US military interventions. Some work within that School has had such a lofty view that it has risked losing sight of such mundane things as treaties, and of the continued significance of the non-intervention norm.[10]

The strength of the non-intervention norm throughout the UN era has not depended on its perfect implementation, but rather on the fact that it has been, and remains, a closer approximation to the facts of interstate relations than any other actual or proposed norm. As John Vincent put it in the concluding paragraph of his study of non-intervention, written a quarter of a century before Kosovo, 'the doctrine of nonintervention bears a closer relation to reality than the progressive doctrines predicated on the disappearance of the state, its civilization by law, or the establishment of a super-authority over it'.[11] On that admittedly modest basis, the non-intervention rule is likely to outlive those of its critics who have pronounced it dead and ready for burial.

The UN Security Council as an intervener

Although the UN Charter is widely viewed as a non-interventionist document, it contains a set of purposes, a structure, and set of procedures that have proved compatible with a pattern of intervention. Even during the Cold War the Security Council agreed on sanctions (though not military intervention) against Rhodesia and South Africa over what was an essentially internal issue: racial domination and discrimination within these states. Since the end of the Cold War the UN Security Council has authorized interventions of many types – both by forces under the control of the UN and by states or coalitions of states.

One innovation has been the setting up of certain peacekeeping operations in such a manner that the host state cannot terminate them by withdrawing consent to their presence. The first such case was the UN Iraq–Kuwait Observation Mission (UNIKOM), established in the wake of the 1991 Gulf War. The authorizing Security Council resolution stated that UNIKOM could be terminated only if there was a Security Council vote to that effect. Marrack Goulding, UN Under-Secretary-General in charge of peacekeeping, has written:

> This was a historic departure from (some would say 'betrayal of') the principle of consent so laboriously established by Hammarskjöld with Nasser when the first UN Emergency Force in Sinai was set up in 1956. But it was justified by the fact that UNIKOM was the first peacekeeping operation to be deployed in the aftermath of UN-authorized enforcement action.[12]

The Security Council established some subsequent peacekeeping operations in such a manner as to imply that they were not completely dependent on the continued consent of the belligerents. This approach was necessary in certain complex civil wars in which it was unrealistic to make the continuation of a major UN operation dependent on the will, or whim, of any of the numerous parties to the conflict. The UN Protection Force (UNPROFOR) in the former Yugoslavia was a case in point. The original Security Council resolution of February 1992 authorizing the establishment of UNPROFOR, while containing evidence of elements of consent, also specified that the Council was acting under its responsibility 'for the maintenance of international peace and security' – a coded reference to Chapter VII of the Charter; and, by referring to Article 25 of the Charter, the resolution reminded states of their formal obligation to accept and carry out the decisions of the Security Council. Further, this resolution set UNPROFOR up for 'an initial period of 12 months unless the Council subsequently decides otherwise', thus indicating that renewal was a matter for decision by the Security Council. All of this implied, at the very least, that although the operation began with a degree of consent of the parties, it might continue even without that consent.[13] Subsequent resolutions continued along similar lines.

In a number of cases where there has been an oppressive or chaotic situation within a supposedly sovereign state, the Security Council has authorized intervention on largely humanitarian grounds. Sometimes it has done so without the consent of the host state: the authorizations of US-led coalitions to intervene in Somalia in 1992 and Haiti in 1994 are the clearest examples. In the case of Haiti, the explicit purpose of military action was to change the government of the target state.[14]

Regarding Iraq from 1991 onwards, the Security Council was thoroughly interventionist in its imposition of disarmament terms. Resolutions required Iraq to comply with provisions on nuclear, chemical, and biological weapons. The precise nature of the pressures and threats against Iraq to secure compliance with these requirements was and remains the subject of dispute: certainly they involved more than the economic sanctions that were imposed on Iraq from 1990 to 2003. Some, mainly in the US and UK governments, claimed that perceived Iraqi violations entitled the US and allies to view the 1991 ceasefire between them and Iraq as no longer in force, while others – with the support, it appears, of many states on the Security Council – argued that any resumption of major hostilities against Iraq, especially in the form of a full-scale invasion and occupation, would require firmer evidence of violations, and a new decision of the Security Council.

It is striking that in all these and many other cases, the right of the Security Council to either initiate military interventions, or to authorize interventions by states, has not been seriously contested. Nor has there been much questioning of the right of the Security Council and its members to apply pressure to states to accept a UN-authorized presence – as was done with Indonesia over East Timor in September 1999. This does not mean that the Security Council is viewed uncritically. There is concern about the wisdom of many Security Council decisions, about the procedures by which they are reached, and about the notable selectivity of the Security Council's actions, but for the most part this concern does not extend to challenging the Council's right in international law to intervene, or authorize intervention, in a wide range of situations.

However, the involvement of the Security Council in matters relating to intervention can lead to major problems. Some of the most serious problems relate to those cases in which the Security Council wills the end but does not will the means. In the humanitarian field, northern Iraq in 1991 and Kosovo in 1999 are clear examples. The Security Council, concerned about grave situations producing huge numbers of refugees, proclaimed explicitly that the target states had to change their policies, but was not able to agree on military intervention. The Security Council thus contributed to pressures for intervention, but the subsequent military action lacked its formal approval. It is not surprising that the question of the lawfulness or otherwise of humanitarian intervention when not backed by a Security Council resolution became the main focus of debate about intervention. Similarly, but in much more fraught circumstances, in the case of Iraq in 2003 the Security Council could not agree on the means to be used, even though there had been substantive agreement on its aims in respect of Iraq. Again, the lawfulness of the action was subject to intense debate.

Humanitarian intervention: not a 'right'

While many possible grounds for justifying interventions have long been recognized to exist, it is humanitarian grounds that have attracted most attention from writers. Traditionally, humanitarian intervention has been discussed in terms of whether states have a 'right' to engage in such action. Hugo Grotius helped to frame the debate in this way when, almost four centuries ago, he wrote in *De Jure Belli ac Pacis*:

> The fact must also be recognized that kings, and those who possess rights equal to those kings, have the right of demanding punishments not only on account of injuries committed against themselves or their subjects, but also on account of injuries which do not directly affect them but excessively violate the law of nature or of nations in regard to any persons whatsoever.[15]

Ever since Grotius' time, humanitarian intervention has been discussed in terms of 'right'. Although his great work is widely seen as pre-eminently a legal text, it is hard to determine whether the 'right' that he is advancing, based as it is on a 'fact', is presented as part of international law, natural law, or ethics. These three categories overlapped in his writings, as indeed they did more generally in his time, and as they still do in many areas of life. They also continue to overlap in discussions of intervention. Through the intervening centuries international law has developed a separate identity, with its own texts and methodologies. In the course of its development, and especially in the twentieth century, restrictions were placed on the use of force that left little scope for any purported right of humanitarian intervention. What Grotius asserted as a 'right', and as a 'fact' that 'must be recognized', has become a debatable and possibly distorted interpretation of law.

It is time to abandon, or at least modify, this particular part of the Grotian inheritance. It has never been, and is not now, fruitful to try to argue in terms of a general legal 'right' of humanitarian intervention.[16] This is first and foremost because there is no chance of reaching agreement among states about such a right. The history of debate on these matters at the UN amply confirms this much. In the General Assembly, as its debate in late 1999 showed, the concept is viewed with extreme suspicion. As for the Security Council, when it has explicitly authorized particular interventions within states (e.g. Somalia, Haiti), it has included in its resolutions wording to the effect that the case concerned is exceptional and does not constitute a precedent. Even in negotiations on humanitarian issues states have continued to guard their sovereignty jealously: a number of provisions in international humanitarian law treaties, and in UN General Assembly resolutions on humanitarian assistance, strongly reaffirm the sovereignty of states. Moreover, there has never been any serious sign that the major potential intervener in the contemporary world, namely the United States, has any interest in the emergence of a doctrine based on a general legal right of humanitarian intervention: probably this is because any such doctrine might oblige it to act even in certain situations in which it did not wish to get involved.

Thus, while the legitimacy or otherwise of humanitarian intervention has been a central issue in international political and legal discourse since the early 1990s, discussing it in terms of a 'right' seems to lead to an impasse.[17] Writings and debates on this topic convey more than a hint of an irresistible force (the emphasis on universal norms) running into an immovable object (state sovereignty). In an extraordinary paradox, the result of a vast amount of legal development in the post-1945 period is an irreconcilable clash of two impressive bodies of international law. On the one hand, there is a body of law restricting the right of states to use force and, on the other hand, a body of human rights and humanitarian law. Following the development of these bodies of law, it is inherently no less difficult than in earlier times to resolve the clash which occasionally arises between the principles of non-intervention and humanitarian inter-vention. Several investigations have confirmed how difficult it is to arrive at a clear answer to the general question of the legality of interventions on humanitarian grounds not based on UN Security Council authorization.[18] Because this is so, there is reason to doubt the common assumption that any view of the legality of a particular intervention, such as that in respect of Kosovo in March–June 1999, depends on an answer to this general question rather than on the unique set of issues raised by the particular situation. The justification for a particular military action, if it is deemed to stand or fall by reference to the question of whether there is a general legal right of intervention, is likely to be in even more difficult than it would be if legal considerations were balanced in a more *ad hoc* manner.

There being no prospect of securing agreement on a general right of states to intervene in other states on humanitarian grounds, there is a natural tendency to seek authority for intervention within some concep-tion of ethics rather than law. This appears to have been part of the think-ing behind the conclusions of the December 2001 report of the International Commission on Intervention and State Sovereignty (ICISS), whose establishment had been announced by the Canadian government at the UN General Assembly one year earlier. The ICISS suggested that there was a need to shift the terms of the debate about 'humanitarian intervention'. It decided not to use that term, preferring instead 'to refer either to "intervention", or as appropriate "military intervention", for human protection purposes'. It suggested this course partly because of 'the very strong opposition expressed by humanitarian agencies towards any militarization of the word "humanitarian"'.[19] Most importantly, it sought to focus the debate about intervention for humanitarian protec-tion purposes not on 'the right to intervene' but on 'the responsibility to protect'. This was seen above all as a 'responsibility to react' in some manner, not necessarily by intervention.[20] The responsibility to protect (which has become known colloquially as 'R2P') is first and foremost that of the incumbent government, and only when it has failed to exercise it should others even contemplate intervention. Even then, it is suggested, an intervention is unlikely to be seen as unambiguously within the framework of international law, but may rather have the character of a legally doubtful pursuit of a serious ethical principle. In short, this proposed shift in the terms of the debate implies a shift towards recognizing the weight of the ethical principle of 'responsibility to protect'. This has been widely recognized as a commendable suggestion for reframing a difficult debate. However, there has so far been no definite outcome of the various attempts since 2001 to secure formal recognition of this concept by the UN General Assembly.

Ethics and law apparently out of step

On intervention, as on other subjects, it might appear reasonable to expect law and ethics to march in step. International law is more definite than ethics in the sense that, for the most part, it is written down in the form of treaties and other authoritative texts that are accepted by states, and is a basis for the work of a number of international decision-making bodies and tribunals. However, in other respects, the similarities and interconnections between law and ethics are striking. Both are properly viewed, not as high-minded external impositions on the international system, but rather as outgrowths of it. Both reflect practical needs, not least reducing the hazards of inherently dangerous situations. Both seek to balance long-term against short-term interests, and the general against the individual good. Both are based on recognition of the necessity of predictability and restraint in the conduct of international relations. Both encompass underlying principles of conduct. Both can be viewed as a form of institutional memory, distilling from violent historical events some basic rules of the road to reduce the risks, or costs, of future conflicts. Much international law, especially in matters relating to human rights and humanitarian norms, is actually similar to systems of ethics and morality, both in the language in which it is expressed and in the subtle nature (or possible non-existence) of mechanisms of enforcement. Returning the compliment, much ethical discussion of international relations shows at least a nodding acquaintance with international law.

Yet on the subject of intervention, the relation between law and ethics has become peculiar. Many writers on international law have brought in ethics to justify something that they find hard to defend on the grounds of black-letter international law alone, namely a right of intervention. It is as if, stuck in a legal bind, they need an ethical fillip to help them reach a clear conclusion. For example, Fernando Tesón, in his advocacy of humanitarian intervention, explicitly relies on 'an ethical theory of international law' to interpret the UN Charter.[21] It may be doubted whether UN member states, most of which put a more orthodox legal spin on the Charter's provisions, are likely to accept an ethical theory the effect of which would be to weaken the prohibitions on intervention.

In summoning up ethics to bolster an argument for intervention, Tesón is by no means alone among international lawyers. Frits Kalshoven, in an authoritative exposition of common Article 1 of the four 1949 Geneva Conventions, argues that there may be a moral if not legal right of intervention. After presenting conclusive evidence that the negotiators at Geneva in 1949, in drawing up Article 1, did not have in mind anything approaching a legal right of states parties to take action regarding violations in conflicts in which they were not involved, he suggests that a moral right of intervention for such purposes has slowly emerged.[22]

Answers given at the time to the question regarding intervention raised by the 1999 Kosovo war – whether there is a right to intervene in a humanitarian crisis in the absence of a Security Council authorization – indicated that there seemed to be a remarkable disjunction between law and ethics. Three respected specialists on international law suggested that the NATO action was contrary to the UN Charter, and was thus extremely doubtful in legal terms, but may have been morally necessary. Bruno Simma, a leading German international lawyer, wrote:

> 'humanitarian interventions' involving the threat or use of armed force and undertaken without the mandate or the authorization of the Security Council will, as a matter of principle, remain in breach of international law. But such a general statement cannot be the last word. Rather, in any instance of humanitarian intervention a careful assessment will have to be made of how heavily such illegality weighs against all the circumstances of a particular concrete case, and the efforts, if any, undertaken by the parties to get 'as close to the law' as possible. Such analyses must influence not only the moral but also the legal judgment in such cases.[23]

Simma added that 'only a thin red line separates NATO's action on Kosovo from international legality'.[24] He went on to cast doubt on the value of trying to change the law on the basis of the hard case of Kosovo in order to bring the law into line with morality.

Antonio Cassese, who had been the first President of the International Criminal Tribunal for the Former Yugoslavia, agreed with much of Simma's analysis, but criticised him for opposing any attempt to turn an exception into a general policy. He put the problem starkly: 'from an *ethical* viewpoint resort to armed force was justified. Nevertheless, as a legal scholar I cannot avoid observing in the same breath that this moral action is *contrary to current international law*' (emphasis in original).[25] He then went on to suggest that 'this particular instance of breach of international law may gradually lead to the crystallization of a general rule of international law authorizing armed countermeasures for the exclusive purpose of putting an end to large-scale atrocities'.[26] He indicated certain conditions that might have to be satisfied for intervention to be permissible, but he said little about the process by which the proposed general rule of international law might in fact crystallize.

In similar spirit, the Austrian specialist in international law, Hanspeter Neuhold, concluded that NATO's operations over Kosovo in March–June 1999 were 'contrary to international law as it stands today'. He went on to say:

> NATO's air raids against the FRY were morally acceptable and politically necessary. This view is easier to live with if one does not consider compliance with the law – not only international law for that matter – as the supreme value. Law and justice do not always coincide. If they conflict with each other it may be wiser to call illegal behaviour a breach of the law instead of opening the Pandora's box of trying to somehow squeeze the violation into *lex lata*.[27]

It is not always clear exactly what ethical system or norms were being advanced as a makeweight for the perceived weaknesses of international law. Indeed, one might even suspect that in the minds of these lawyers it was actually certain legal norms (especially in the human rights field) that had informed their views of morality. Yet it is interesting, and worrying, that such respected specialists took the view that law and morality were out of step on a matter of great public importance. The episode seems to illustrate a remarkable contrast between ethics and law – a contrast that relates to their basic form as well as particular message on the subject of intervention.

On the one hand, ethical considerations float more or less freely, are not precisely defined as a single agreed set of rules, and are able to adapt to new circumstances. This flexibility, while it has obvious merits, also has defects. Since ethical ideas vary greatly, have no single indisputable written source, and lack a recognized procedure whereby they are identified, they are hardly a secure set of guidelines for international action. Although in the past ethical ideas have often been seen as essentially a restraint on the application of force, they can also assist in its justification, especially when the target state is deemed to have violated fundamental norms. It is striking how in the post-Cold War era, when Western states have ceased to fear a superpower adversary, the idea that certain forcible interventions may be desirable and ethically justifiable has gained ground. On the other hand, contemporary treaty-based international law relating to the use of force has the character of an ocean-going liner: the product of vast labour, and of painful multilateral negotiations involving large numbers of countries over decades, the vessel has huge momentum and cannot change course quickly. The non-interventionist thrust of this body of law remains.

One possible response to the apparent disjunction between law and ethics as they apply to intervention would be that indicated by Professor Neuhold: to let law and ethics carry on their own sweet ways, and live with the disjunction as an uncomfortable fact of life. A second response would be to try to reform or reinterpret public international law, perhaps in the manner indicated by Cassese, so that a legal right of intervention in certain tightly defined circumstances might come to be explicitly accepted.

There is a third possible response, which is based on questioning the whole premise that what is at issue is a simple disjunction between law and ethics. What is also involved is a disjunction between different branches of international law. Given the simultaneous existence of law prohibiting the use of force, and law recognizing a wide range of constraints on the actions of governments even within their own territories, it is obvious that in particular crises legal considerations may point against, and also in favour of, intervention. This means that law may not always provide the basis for a one-word answer on the legitimacy of a particular intervention; or, to put it another way, that it may not prohibit interventions quite so absolutely as Simma and colleagues imply. Even the UN Charter, mainly through its statement of Purposes and Principles, may leave some scope for some interventions by states. There is little chance that this ambiguity within international law can be resolved. The prospect of reaching formal international agreement on a right of intervention, whether humanitarian or otherwise, and on the circumstances in which it could be permissible, is close to zero. What law will continue to offer is countervailing principles that will have to be interpreted in each case. In other words, by a paradox resulting from its own development, international law has become, so far as intervention is concerned, less precise and absolute in its prohibition than it once appeared to be.-In this respect, law may have some of the flexibility that is sometimes seen as an attribute of ethics.

Problems beyond humanitarian intervention

The preoccupation with the issue of humanitarian intervention may distract attention from other forms and purposes of intervention. There are two types of reason why humanitarian intervention should not be seen as a separate and distinct category. The first is that some interventions, not originally justified in humanitarian terms, may have significant humanitarian consequences – a possible example being the US-led intervention in Afghanistan from October 2001 onwards, which created conditions in which 1.8 million refugees returned to Afghanistan in 2002. The second reason is that in many cases that were justified using the language of humanitarian intervention, those intervening may be motivated by other considerations (which might be perfectly respectable) besides those of a strictly humanitarian character. Neither the UN Security Council, nor states acting independently, have ever cited humanitarian considerations alone as a basis for intervention: they have always, and justifiably, referred to other considerations as well. These have included considerations of international peace and security. This is not only for the obvious procedural reason that reference to 'international peace and security' is a *sine qua non* for any action by the Security Council, but also because many different issues do overlap in practice. In the case of Kosovo in 1999, factors impelling NATO states to take military action included not only humanitarian concerns, and considerations of peace and security, but also anxieties about the sheer difficulty for many states of coping with so many refugees, and about their own loss of military credibility if Milošević continued to ignore their diplomatic demands.

In many cases, humanitarian considerations are intermingled with support for a political goal of self-determination, or autonomy, for a particular part of the population of the target state. The debate about humanitarian intervention cannot for ever be separated from the debate, which reached its height in the 1970s, regarding intervention in support of self-determination struggles.[28] If an intervention is in support of one particular part of the population of the target country, inhabiting a particular region within it, the effect (intentional or otherwise) is likely to be a strengthening of demands for the independence of that region. In 1971, India was open about supporting secession in what is now Bangladesh. In the 1990s, Western powers formally declared themselves against secession by northern Iraq and Kosovo, yet their actions then and subsequently have contributed to demands for independence in the territories concerned.

Pressures for intervention can of course arise from a wide variety of considerations that are different from, or even unrelated to, those normally covered by the term 'humanitarian'. Sometimes such considerations are of a legal character. The expanding scope of the subject matter of international legal agreements, and the growing emphasis on implementation mechanisms, point clearly in this direction. For example, a wide range of international agreements in fields as various as the environment and international criminal law impose requirements on what should be done by governments within their own states; violation of such provisions may, in exceptional cases, come to be seen as one possible ground for intervention. Some agreements contain provisions that could be interpreted as providing a possible basis for future interventions to enforce implementation. Thus the 1994 Convention on the Safety of UN Personnel contains this stipulation: 'States Parties shall cooperate with the United Nations and other States Parties, as appropriate, in the implementation of this Convention, particularly in any case where the host State is unable itself to take the required measures.'[29]

A further issue giving rise to pressures for intervention is terrorism. International concern over terrorism is not a new development. The First World War began after the assassination of Archduke Ferdinand in Sarajevo, after which Austria-Hungary was determined to stamp out what it perceived as the 'hornet's nest' of terrorists in Serbia. Israel's intervention in Lebanon in 1982 was defended almost entirely in anti-terrorist terms, as was the US raid on Tripoli in 1986, which followed Libya's involvement in an attack on US servicemen in a discothèque in Berlin. Today, the global range of terrorist actions means that the pressures may not only be for intervention in neighbouring territories, but also in distant lands.

The United Nations was one focus of a debate about whether intervention is justified as a response to certain acts of terrorism. Traditionally, the UN General Assembly has been hostile to military attacks on countries presumed to have been involved in terrorism, but in the wake of 11 September 2001 there were signs of a change of attitude. In a resolution and statement approved the day after the destruction of the World Trade Center, the General Assembly condemned the attacks unequivocally.[30] There was no move in the General Assembly to oppose the US-led action in Afghanistan that started in October 2001, and very little rhetorical opposition by states. As for the Security Council, one day after 9/11 it too passed a resolution – in this case not merely condemning the bombing, but actually (by referring to the right of self-defence) giving a green light to military intervention.[31] The requirements of international collaboration against terrorism led also to the further UN Security resolution of 28 September 2001 that made unprecedentedly detailed and intrusive demands on states for cooperation and assistance.[32] However, there was no formal agreement on the general issue of a possible right to intervene against states harbouring major terrorist movements. The prospects for such agreement were to be diminished by many aspects of the US-led 'war on terror', including the invasion and occupation of Iraq from 2003 onwards. All US attempts to justify this action on the grounds of alleged Iraqi involvement in major international terrorist activities were found unconvincing by the majority of states. Thus, if there was in 2001–02 the beginning of an international consensus on how to deal with terrorism, by the end of 2003, due to international disagreement over intervention, it was under threat.

The 2003 invasion of Iraq was at the heart of another key issue bearing on the legitimacy of military intervention: the debate about preventive war and the imposition of disarmament terms. The question of whether it is legitimate to intervene against countries on account of their development or deployment of weapons systems is the subject of hot debate. Preventive attacks on states, before they have actually used the weapons concerned for attacks on others, is difficult to square with the international legal justification of self-defence. This has always been a difficult area of law and policy. For example, in the 1962 Cuban Missile Crisis the US was determined to stop the massive transfer of nuclear weapons and delivery systems to Cuba, but the precise international legal basis for US action against Cuba was a matter of some complexity. In a number of episodes since the end of the Cold War, there has been discussion of possible interventions against North Korea, Iraq, and, most recently, Iran, on account of their development of weapons of mass destruction, with much emphasis being placed on these states' violations of arms control arrangements. A key practical difficulty with plans for intervention to impose disarmament arrangements is that in many cases the state against which an intervention might be directed is itself well armed and determined: that is, after all, precisely why that state is a cause of international concern. Intervention to impose disarmament, unlike some other forms of intervention against relatively weak states, carries a serious risk of major international war.

Criteria for intervention

Many attempts to enunciate criteria for intervention have been rooted in that well-known and dangerously prevalent form of internationalism, according to which the world would be a better place if everyone else thought as we do and was preoccupied with the same problems as we are. There was more than a hint of this in an essay in *The Economist* at the beginning of 2001. Its central argument is summarized in the following quotations:

> If wars of intervention are to be a serious part of tomorrow's agenda, they will have to be based on a simple, straightforward and more or less universally accepted set of rules.

> The first ground for intervention is when a clearly definable people in a clearly definable geographical area is being violently denied the right to govern itself by another, stronger lot who say that the smaller group is part of their own 'sovereign' territory.

> The second fairly solid argument for intervention, also illustrated by recent events in the Balkans, reaches even deeper into the supposed sanctuary of the sovereign state. Here the target is not the authoritarian ruler's control over a subject territory attached to his homeland, but his control over the homeland itself. If it becomes reasonably obvious that a government has decided to hold on to power against the wishes of most of the people it governs, and is not going to change its mind, it should not think that its denial of the democratic principle will be allowed to go unchallenged.[33]

There are three main problems with this approach: (1) while the article does in passing indicate some awareness that there are other possible

grounds for intervention, it does not do justice to their range and importance; (2) the two grounds it seeks to advance would offer no comfort to a
persecuted minority that is not neatly arranged in a 'definable geographical
area' or to the inhabitants of occupied territories; and (3) the assertion that
the two grounds could be 'universally accepted' is stunningly naive.

Most attempts to develop criteria for justifiable intervention have dealt
exclusively with humanitarian intervention. Extensive agreement on criteria would be evidence of an emerging doctrine, might make the idea of
humanitarian intervention more acceptable to critics, and could also be a
safeguard against abuse. In the period 1999–2001 when Kosovo and East
Timor were, very properly, major preoccupations, there were numerous
attempts to agree a general doctrine of, and criteria for, humanitarian
intervention – including many contributions from writers and research
institutes. Significant official and semi-official expositions of criteria for
humanitarian intervention included those advanced by UK Prime Minister
Tony Blair in his speech in Chicago on 22 April 1999; UN Secretary-
General Kofi Annan in his report of 8 September 1999; Canadian Foreign
Minister Lloyd Axworthy in his Hauser Lecture at New York University
School of Law on 10 February 2000; UK Foreign Secretary Robin Cook in
a speech in London on 19 July 2000; and the December 2001 report of
the ICISS. Since then the subject has ceased to be at the top of the international agenda but it has by no means disappeared.

Even if there is doubt about the possibility of obtaining general agreement on a right of humanitarian intervention, it is useful to consider criteria for intervention. Given that such interventions may occasionally
happen, and are likely to involve a conflict with the law restricting the
resort to force, it is especially important to clarify the legal and moral basis
of such intervention. By contrast, in some cases criteria may usefully
provide a basis for deciding against rather than for intervention.

The idea of general criteria by which to evaluate decisions on the use of
force has a long history, including in the 'just war' tradition. It is certainly
useful to bear such criteria in mind and adapt them to the question of
humanitarian intervention. Most attempts to develop criteria for humanitarian intervention address the following issues:

1   scope of atrocities;
2   responsibility for atrocities;
3   exhaustion of peaceful and consent-based remedies;
4   authorization and legitimation of intervention;
5   the interests and concerns of intervening powers;
6   purposes and results of intervention; and
7   observance of humanitarian norms by intervening forces.

When examined closely against the background of actual cases of intervention, these seven issues constitute critical factors, all of which have to

be considered in any decision to use force for humanitarian purposes. However, they are no more than criteria for consideration. They do not constitute a simple checklist which, if it were to accumulate enough ticks, would be seen as legitimizing intervention. At best they suggest some necessary but not sufficient conditions for deciding on intervention. Each issue involves problems and is likely to be perceived differently in different states. Such criteria are inherently difficult to develop, and can at best only be a set of rough guidelines.

If criteria are hard to crystallize for the relatively well-defined category of humanitarian intervention, they are even more problematic as regards intervention and the use of force more generally. In December 2004, the report of the UN Secretary-General's High-level Panel on Threats, Challenges and Change contained, among a wealth of proposals, a thoughtful updating of criteria for the use of military force.[34] One of the merits of its list of five criteria is the emphasis on the underestimated virtue of prudence, which is particularly clear in the fifth point. However, the Panel's criteria are not free of problems: for example, there is obvious tension between the first criterion (seriousness of threat), and the third (force as a last resort). If terrorist attacks are actually being launched from a territory, or a government is killing people in its own territory, waiting until every non-military option has been explored may not be realistic. A further weakness of the five criteria is that they are put forward as being for use by the UN Security Council, not by states more generally. This is a reflection of the optimistic assumption permeating the report, in which the UN can be at the centre of a system of collective security – an assumption that places too high a burden of expectation on the UN.

In sum, the dilemmas faced by states in considering questions of intervention are so difficult, and the circumstances of interventions vary so hugely, that any statement of criteria for intervention could at best be a small part of the process of decision making. The very difficulty of the twin exercises of drawing up criteria and then applying them in a crisis points to a conclusion: rather than develop a doctrine of justified intervention, it makes sense to continue with the non-intervention rule as the template. This requires a tacit understanding that if and when states do decide to intervene, they need to produce extremely convincing reasons for their actions.

General issues and conclusions

Is this really a revolutionary era so far as the practice of intervention is concerned?

Since the end of the Cold War some forms of intervention have increased – especially intervention that is either authorized by the UN Security Council, or is carried out by a coalition claiming to pursue goals consistent with those proclaimed by the Security Council. It is doubtful whether other forms of intervention, such as unilateral action by states in pursuit of their interests, have increased in the same period.

Although there has been some increase, the interventionism seen since 1990 is not wholly new in either form or justification. Many recent acts of intervention have been defended rhetorically in terms similar to those used in past eras; and if the UN framework for some of today's interventionism is new, it has no shortage of precursors in the use made of regional organizations and, in the nineteenth century, the Concert of Europe. Moreover, the suspicion endures that, even when interventions are justified in terms of high international principle, they reflect the interests of particular states. The US-led intervention in Iraq since March 2003 has been widely denounced in such terms.

Nor is modern interventionism new in the reactions that it evokes. Even in a case in which an intervention has explicit authorization from international bodies, and impeccable humanitarian objectives, it is likely to arouse resistance both in the country concerned and internationally. Somalia in 1992–94 and Iraq since 2003 are the clearest examples of interveners facing, and even provoking, violent opposition within the territory concerned. Such opposition is not surprising. A foreign military presence always involves the wielding of power by outsiders with a limited understanding of a society, and it is naturally perceived as a threat not only by indigenous would-be wielders of power, but also by the population more generally.

The reasons for the growth of interventionism in the past sixty years, and especially since the end of the Cold War, are extraordinarily diverse, relating as they do to the interests of particular states in particular crises, to the principles and treaties that states have adopted, and to the structure of the international system. Four are singled out here: (1) the growth of global media has made it more difficult than before for governments to ignore distant crises; (2) international terrorism – often emanating from weak or failed states, but also from some dictatorial ones – has contributed to a number of decisions to intervene; (3) in many cases since about 1970, one fundamental reason has been the concern of virtually all states to tackle the causes of massive refugee flows at source; and (4) the development of an international legal order in the UN era – governing such matters as arms control, democratic governance, self-determination, human rights, and humanitarian conduct in war – raises the question of how states are supposed to act when this body of international norms is persistently violated in a state.

If the period since 1990 is a revolutionary era as regards intervention, it is not because there is arguably more intervention than before, but rather because it has been so closely associated with international norms and organizations. It has also assumed some special forms which, while not entirely new, have been emblematic of contemporary interventionism: multinational military and peacekeeping operations; close association with regional international organizations as well as the UN; assistance in the management and verification of elections; and provision of administrative services, even transitional administration.

Is a 'solidarist' conception of international society emerging, whether regionally or globally, that could justify intervention to enforce the norms and values of that society? Or do contemporary practices, despite their trappings of multilateralism and of progressive purposes, in fact reflect thoroughly 'realist' considerations of state interest and pursuit of power politics?

The pattern of intervention since 1990 is sometimes presented as evidence of the emergence of a new solidarist conception of international society, characterized by shared values, common participation in international organizations, and a growing density of international contacts at all levels. In this vision, intervention is seen as progressively overcoming the worst defects of a system of untrammelled state sovereignty. This enticing vision, although it does capture certain aspects of contemporary reality, is deeply misleading. Intervention on the one hand, and sovereignty on the other, should not be presented as opposites, between which a decision has to be taken. On the contrary, it has often been considerations of national power and interest that have led to decisions to intervene. For example, in 1991, Turkey's refusal to accept a large influx of Kurdish refugees from Iraq was a key factor in precipitating the US-led intervention into northern Iraq.

This is not to say that the motives and purposes of those intervening correspond to what so-called 'realist' theory might suggest. NATO did not get into war over Kosovo in 1999 because of the ruthless pursuit of interest, the need to expand eastwards, or the inevitability of confrontation between major powers. It was not geopolitics that triggered this war, but rather guilt that Europe and the US had done so pathetically little in over seven years of wars in the former Yugoslavia. This was reinforced by legitimate concern that a large new influx of refugees could destabilize neighbouring states, especially Macedonia. All these considerations, however, exist within a realist carapace: intervention is only likely to be contemplated at all when it is by the powerful against the relatively weak. One consequence of the interventionism since 1990 could be to impress on relatively weak states the importance of developing their national military power.

Indeed, the realist perspective still has considerable relevance in explaining the reactions of certain third parties to acts of intervention. In this respect the case of Kosovo is typical. The NATO powers may have been convinced that they acted from the highest of motives, and without any intention of expanding their power or threatening any other states. That was not how their action was viewed in Belgrade, Moscow, Beijing, New Delhi, Baghdad, or Tehran. NATO was widely seen as hypocritically and selectively using its armed force to serve its own interests, to weaken

Yugoslavia, and to undermine Russia's position in the Balkans. The bombing of the Chinese Embassy in Belgrade added insult to injury. Many in the Islamic world – notwithstanding the fact that the US was once again acting in support of a beleaguered Muslim population – viewed the US military operations as just one more proof of US dominance.

Whether or not such criticisms illuminate the motives of the NATO member states, it is hard to deny that an important consequence of the Kosovo war was an expansion of NATO involvement in the Balkans – especially in Kosovo itself, and in Albania and Macedonia. True, some of that involvement took a cooperative and non-exclusive form, with Russian and many other forces operating side by side with those from NATO states in the NATO-led Kosovo Force (KFOR). However, the ghosts of power politics, with all the jealousies and rivalries of earlier eras, still haunt the Balkan region.

Similarly, the US-led intervention in Afghanistan in 2001–02 may have had an impeccable justification in terms of self-defence, but it involved the establishment of US military bases in Afghanistan and neighbouring countries, including Kyrgyzstan, Pakistan, and Uzbekistan – which naturally caused a totally reasonable and impeccably realist concern in Russia and China. On 5 July 2005, the Shanghai Cooperation Organization (SCO), a regional security body whose members include China, Russia, Kazakhstan, Kyrgyzstan, Tajikistan, and Uzbekistan, issued a declaration calling for the United States to set a timeline for its withdrawal of military forces from Central Asia – i.e. from Kyrgyzstan and Uzbekistan. Power politics have not been eclipsed by new elements in contemporary wars and justifications of wars.

There was one other familiar realist feature in the international landscape after the Cold War: the tendency for the management and use of force to remain under the control of states rather than the UN. Whenever force had to be used on a large scale and against significant opposition, the UN did not wield that force itself but instead authorized individual powers or regional alliances, generally leading coalitions. This was true of the US role in Kuwait, Somalia, and Haiti; the French role in Rwanda; the NATO role in Bosnia and later in Kosovo; the Australian role in East Timor; and the British role in Sierra Leone. This realist triumph reached a curious high point in the wake of the 1999 Kosovo war, which left many in the US subscribing to the belief that it alone understands how to wage war, and that it cannot wholly trust or rely upon its allies. The US appears to have found the process of waging coalition war against Yugoslavia through NATO's decision-making processes cumbersome and frustrating, especially as the other NATO states had very little air strike capability to offer. Thus a multinational humanitarian operation, supposedly enshrining new norms in international relations, had the unanticipated effect of heightening US appreciation of the unilateral application of power – as the largely unilateral US conduct of the war in Afghanistan in 2001–02 was to confirm.

Indeed, the pattern of interventions since 1990 can be interpreted as reflecting a steady decline of solidarism. The terrifying fact is that each of the four major US-led military coalitions of the period contained a smaller number of serious participants than the previous one. There was a process of continuous decline from the 1991 Gulf War coalition, the 1999 Kosovo war, the 2001–02 Afghan war, and the 2003 Iraq war.

Yet another realist sting in the tail of the international interventionism of the post-Cold War years has been the persistence of patterns of violent and fractured politics in many of the territories in which intervention has taken place. While some interventions, as in Kosovo and East Timor, have undoubtedly secured the removal of external forces responsible for much violence, and have built up at least the foundations of democratic systems, other interventions have had much more ambiguous results. For example, in northern Iraq, Somalia, and Haiti, deeply-ingrained habits of political violence show little sign of disappearing. One of the curiosities of the realist tradition of thought about international relations is that it has had little to say about the practice of violence within states. Thus, if the interventionism since 1990 is at best a limited and ambiguous demonstration of the idea that there are universal norms and values, it also throws down a challenge to realists to get to grips with the phenomenon of power politics within as well as between states.

Is the body of international law addressing the question of intervention still relevant in the new circumstances of the post-Cold War world?

There is a tendency to view international law as uniformly non-interventionist. This is too simple. Existing law is consistent with authorizations of intervention by the UN Security Council, and these can assume a wide variety of forms. In addition, international law encompasses a wide range of provisions which, if seriously violated by a recalcitrant state, inevitably provide a legal argument for at least considering intervention. Moreover, the fact that states have had varied – and in respect of some actions not at all unfavourable – responses to certain military interventions not approved by the Security Council comes close to an acceptance in customary law that some such interventions may be justified while others certainly are not.

The increase in interventionism, including in cases not authorized by the Security Council, does not make the non-intervention rule redundant. Indeed, it may add point and urgency to the rule as a brake on any tendency for interventionism to get out of hand. An occasional practice and justification of intervention should not necessarily be seen as a threat to the whole principle of non-intervention. It can be seen as a means of saving the non-intervention rule from being discredited, as could happen if it were observed rigidly irrespective of circumstances. The rule remains at the heart of contemporary *jus ad bellum*, and indeed at the heart of the system of sovereign states. It is what makes the world go round. The society of states appears to strongly prefer the situation in which there is a valid but occasionally violated norm to the situation of trying to replace this old norm with something new and more complicated.

Ideas about the place of intervention in the contemporary world might be intellectually better grounded, and accepted by more states, if they were set more explicitly against the background of the still valid norm of non-intervention. For the way in which humanitarian intervention is frequently presented as an alternative to non-intervention, and as taking the world beyond existing conceptions of sovereignty, naturally arouses antagonism. There is a case for reaffirming strongly the principle of non-intervention, and recognizing that any forceful intervention on humanitarian or other grounds is a very occasional exception to that principle.

Can the law evolve to overcome any limitations? Or, if the law cannot be changed, can some conception of ethics provide a useful guide to states in addressing questions about the justifiability of military interventions?

Many writers, politicians, and lawyers would naturally like to tidy up a chaotic situation by developing new norms, but they have no convincing vision of what the new norms would be or how agreement on them might be secured. Consideration of whether there is a 'right' of intervention in certain defined circumstances is not merely doomed to failure, but is the wrong way to think about the problem anyway. Intervention may best be considered a very occasional necessity that involves a balancing of different and even contradictory international legal considerations, not as a 'right' of states or even of the UN Security Council. A 'common law' approach, based on degrees of assent to a slowly emerging and occasional practice of intervention, is a more promising means of trying to build elements of international consensus regarding intervention.

The debate about criteria for intervention remains important. If there were no conception of criteria at all, an emerging practice of intervention would be deprived of any element of intellectual and moral consistency. Yet the unavoidable limits of the search for criteria must be recognized. Quite apart from the improbability of securing international agreement on them, general criteria are likely to be of limited relevance to the numerous crises in which very different types of intervention are contemplated for a bewildering variety of reasons. Indeed, the search for criteria, like the search for a 'right' of intervention, may represent an understandable but probably hopeless pursuit of a greater degree of legal tidiness than can be found in this world.

Ethical ideas – especially the principled rejection of dictatorship, mass slaughter, and ethnic cleansing – have had an important impact on the international politics of the post-Cold War world. If international law is found wanting in the light of such ethical approaches, it may need to be modified: indeed, it may already be in process of modification. However, the non-intervention rule itself has a very strong ethical basis, as a means of avoiding war, restraining dangerous crusading instincts, and accommodating the fact that we live in a world with different cultures and political systems.[35] Any modification of the non-intervention rule is not likely to take the form of a triumph of ethics over law, but rather a recognition that law itself is subtly evolving, and has long incorporated key ethical principles, especially in the human rights field.

The conclusions to which this discussion inescapably points is that in matters relating to the justification for military intervention, important legal principles frequently clash with each other; that, as a result, the simple classification of particular cases of resort to force as either legal or illegal can in certain instances be of limited value; that disagreements on the legitimacy of particular uses of force are to be expected; and that a proper legal and moral evaluation of any particular use of force must be contextual – that is, it must take into account a wide range of factors, including the perceptions and utterances of decision makers, the nature of the policy choices they faced, and the many different legal, moral, and prudential considerations that were relevant to their decisions.

The obvious objection to a contextual approach is that it might risk reducing firm legal principle to infinitely elastic material; and it might make internationally agreed provisions vulnerable to endless interpretation within particular states and national traditions – with all the attendant hazards. This is indeed a danger – especially when law is interpreted as flexibly and as conveniently in support of US-led interventions, as it has been by some exponents of the 'New Haven School' of international law discussed earlier. However, this should not be taken as the only valid type of contextual approach.

A more rigorous contextual approach is one that recognizes that treaty-based rules have to be taken extremely seriously, but can sometimes be genuinely difficult to adapt to the facts of situations and indeed to each other. The strength of such a contextual approach is that it is based on a frank recognition of realities. It reflects an understanding of, if not necessarily agreement with, what actually happens in the decision-making processes of states. It could help to bring law to bear on the questions of *jus ad bellum* in a way that corresponds to the actual dilemmas faced by states and alliances. Most importantly, it reduces the danger of an important part of international law being dismissed as a set of utterly rigid non-interventionist rules, irrelevant to contemporary circumstances, imperfectly observed by states, and taking little or no account of some basic considerations of moral decency. Indeed, it could, paradoxically, help to restore the legitimacy of the norm of non-intervention, which remains fundamental.

Interventions are the outcome of enduring realities of the contemporary international political and legal system. There will certainly be new cases. Some may be legitimately viewed as occasional and exceptional necessities. Others, including Iraq since 2003, may be viewed as evidence that interveners have succumbed to the ancient sin of hubris, and must learn from their mistakes a respect for the difficulties of international relations. The questions that interventions raise need to be addressed less in terms of a purported general legal doctrine permitting intervention if certain criteria are satisfied, and more in terms of the particular nexus of legal, moral, and practical issues raised by each case.

Yet there has been a significant overall change in the practice of international intervention and in the ethics, law, and political debate relating to it. The character of the change is indicated by the improbability of any general definition of intervention in the twenty-first century being based on Hedley Bull's wording, namely 'dictatorial or coercive interference'. Although 'dictatorial' is no longer an appropriate general description of the nature of intervention as a general class of activity, the epithet 'coercive' retains its validity, and serves as a necessary reminder that interventionism has not changed out of all recognition. It remains as much a problem as a solution in international relations.

Notes

1 This chapter was completed in July 2005. It incorporates some material from 'Intervention: Suggestions for Moving the Debate Forward', a paper presented first at the International Commission on Intervention and State Sovereignty round-table meeting, London, 3 February 2001; and then at the conference on 'The International Ethics of Security', Peter Wall Institute for Advanced Studies, University of British Columbia, Vancouver, 5–7 April 2001.
2 Bull (1984), p. 1. Bull saw more clearly than most the likely direction of changes in the character and legitimacy of interventions, especially in his discussion of humanitarian intervention on pages 193 and 195.
3 On the complex story of British colonial administration in Sierra Leone, and the colony's role from the late eighteenth century onwards as a haven for freed slaves, see Peterson (1969).
4 For useful short accounts, see Woodhouse (1968), pp. 125–48; and Schevill (1922), pp. 337–9.
5 Woodward (1954), pp. 245–53.
6 The Covenant of the League of Nations, concluded in 1919 and entering into force in 1920, provided for possible authorizations by the League Council of the use of military force by states in articles 10, 11, and 16. However, the provisions of these articles were vague and permissive in character, and only applied in a restricted range of circumstances – essentially resort to aggressive war by the target state. In any case all members of the League Council had a veto. The system was ill-conceived and unworkable.
7 United Nations General Assembly Res. 2793 of 7 December 1971, on Question considered by the Security Council at its 1606th, 1607th, and 1608th meetings on 4, 5 and 6 December 1971.
8 Glennon (2001), p. 2.
9 See, for example, Reisman (1999), pp. 860–2.
10 For a critique of the New Haven approach, see Roth (2003), pp. 242–50.
11 Vincent (1974), p. 389.
12 Goulding (2002), p. 284, discussing United Nations Security Council Res. 689 of 9 April 1991, adopted under Chapter VII of the Charter.

13 United Nations Security Council Res. 743 of 21 February 1992, preamble and paragraph 3.

14 United Nations Security Council Res. 940 of 31 July 1994, passed with twelve votes in favour, two abstaining (Brazil and China) and one absent (Rwanda), was the first occasion on which the UN explicitly called for the overthrow of the functioning government of one of its members. It authorized member states to form a multinational coalition to use all necessary measures to facilitate the departure from Haiti of the military leadership, the return of the legitimately elected president, and the restoration of legitimate authorities.

15 Grotius (1925), book II, Chapter 20, section 40, 504. See also Chapter 25, sections 6 and 8. In the latter the word 'right' is again used.

16 For fuller discussion see Roberts (2000), pp. 3–51.

17 Writings on the issue reflecting experience since 1990 includes Murphy (1996); Wheeler (2000); Chesterman (2001); and Welsh (2004).

18 See, for example, the hesitant conclusions on the international legal basis of non-Security Council based military action in two post-Kosovo war reports: the independent Danish report, *Humanitarian Intervention: Legal and Political Aspects* (Copenhagen, Danish Institute of International Affairs, October 1999), 121–30; and the UK House of Commons, Foreign Affairs Committee (2000) HC 28-I), paragraph 132.

19 International Commission on Intervention and State Sovereignty (ICISS) (2001), p. 9.

20 ICISS (2001), pp. 16–17, 29.

21 Tesón (1988), p. 129. (a revised edition of his book was published in 1997).

22 Kalshoven (1999), pp. 3–61. The text of common Article 1 of the 1949 Geneva Conventions reads simply: 'The High Contracting Parties undertake to respect and to ensure respect for the present Convention in all circumstances.'

23 Simma (1999), p. 6.

24 Simma (1999), p. 22.

25 Cassese (1999), p. 25.

26 Cassese (1999), p. 25.

27 Neuhold (1999), p. 122.

28 Some key UN interpretations of the UN Charter address this matter, including the 1970 'Declaration on Principles of International Law concerning Friendly Relations and Co-operation among States in Accordance with the Charter of the United Nations.' Such documents reinforced the idea that external support for self-determination struggles might be legitimate.

29 UN Convention on the Safety of United Nations and Associated Personnel (1994), Article 7(3).

30 United Nations General Assembly Res. 56/1 of 12 September 2001. Statement in UN Press Release GA/9903, 12 September 2001.

31 United Nations Security Council Res. 1368 of 12 September 2001, passed unanimously, recognized 'the inherent right of individual or collective self-defence in accordance with the Charter'.

32 United Nations Security Council Res. 1373 of 28 September 2001, passed unanimously, requiring states to take seventeen specific measures against all those who support, directly or indirectly, all terrorist acts.

33 'Wars of Intervention: Why and When to Go In', *The Economist*, London, 8203 (6 January 2001), p. 22.

34 United Nations (2004), p. 67, available online at: www.un.org/secureworld (date accessed: 23 September 2005).

35 R. Jackson expounds on the ethical basis of the non-intervention principle as being intelligible in the value of freedom, see pp. 33–4.

10 Saving failed states

Trusteeship as an arrangement of security

William Bain

Insecurity is so much a part of daily life for many people on this planet that it has renewed interest in trusteeship as an arrangement of security in international society. Although the anti-colonial movement destroyed the legitimacy of trusteeship along with the great European empires in Africa and Asia, it did not simultaneously abolish the conditions to which trusteeship was a response. Indeed, daily life in some societies is so burdened by gross human rights abuses, mass murder, civil war, starvation, mutilation, slavery, and cannibalism that it is scarcely unlike the barbarism that self-proclaimed trustees of civilization set out to remedy in colonial Africa and Asia. The purpose of this chapter is to interrogate the character of trusteeship in the hope of assessing its suitability as an arrangement of security in contemporary international society. We shall proceed by examining the justification of trusteeship and its claim that one man may rule another, in lands that are not his own, so long as the power of dominion is directed toward the improvement of the weak and disadvantaged. This will lead into a discussion of one of the principal critiques of trusteeship, namely that its justification is confused by a conflict of obligation and interest. In the final section we shall explore the extent to which contemporary international society is hospitable to the resurrection of trusteeship. It will become evident as a result of this investigation that trusteeship is an unpromising arrangement of security in a pluralist international society that continues to value political independence, self-determination, and equality among its members.

The justification of trusteeship

When the first European explorers reached the New World they came into contact with people who were different in every way imaginable. Pizzarro, Cortes, and those who followed, encountered people who held vastly different beliefs about government, economy, and morality; they understood the notion of obligation, right, and good in wholly different terms; they acted in accordance with their own standards of courage, honour, and prudence; and they approached questions of community, religion, and family in ways that repelled or frightened most Europeans. This degree of difference, and the fact that it was not easily accommodated within existing European systems of value and knowledge, vastly complicated the task of determining the right by which the King of Spain laid claim to territories in the New World. The Spanish theologian Francisco de Vitoria responded to this problem by arguing that the Indians could not be arbitrarily dispossessed of their lands and property: they were barbarians, slow-witted and foolish, but they were nonetheless true masters entitled to the rights of dominion. Thus, he denied claims of universal dominion put forward on behalf of the Holy Roman Emperor and the supreme pontiff of the Roman Church; and he rejected the right of discovery, refusal to receive the Christian faith, and the commission of mortal sins as adequate reasons for occupying territory belonging to barbarians.[1] However, Vitoria admitted, albeit with considerable uncertainty, that just title might be secured if the Indians were unfit to administer a legitimate government by their own efforts. The Indians would then, he contended, be like children over whom it would be entirely lawful and appropriate for European princes to exercise authority, but only so long as 'everything is done *for the benefit and good of the barbarians, and not merely for the profit of the Spaniards*' (emphasis in original).[2]

This claim of dominion prefigures the emergence of trusteeship as a recognized and accepted practice during the latter part of the eighteenth century, a development that coincided with an important shift in Western thinking about the perfectibility of man. It is with reference to this shift that John Passmore argues that in the seventeenth century, man's primary duties were directed toward God; by the eighteenth century this emphasis shifts from God to his fellow man. It was then possible to speak of an alternative account of perfectibility: '[p]erhaps men could be perfected not by God, not by the exercise of their own free will, not even by some combination of the two, but by the deliberate intervention of their fellow-men'.[3] This principle, which is essential to any understanding of trusteeship, finds a secure footing in Edmund Burke's famous indictment of the East India Company and, particularly, its Governor-General, Warren Hastings. Burke did not deny the Company's right of commercial monopoly; nor did he dispute the Company's authority to administer the revenue of its Indian territories, to command an army of 60,000 men, and to rule over the lives of thirty million Indian subjects.[4] But the magnitude and extent of misrule in India, what he described as the egregious abuse of commercial and political rights, left him with little doubt that the Company had forfeited its claim to rule. Burke protested bitterly that the Company reduced to ruin every prince with whom it came into contact and that millions of Indians experienced neglect and despair at the hands of the Company's inept, and sometimes corrupt, administration: treaty obligations were ignored, rights of war and peace were abused, and young boys, intoxicated by the excesses of power, governed without sympathy for native interests. Moreover, he complained that, while conquerors of an earlier age left monuments of state and beneficence behind them, the Company's English masters had done nothing to compensate for the injustice of an ignominious rule. Indeed, Burke feared that '[w]ere we driven out of India this day, nothing would remain to tell that it had been possessed, during the inglorious period of our dominion, by anything better than the orangoutang or the tiger'.[5]

Burke understood the Company's abuse of commercial and political power as constituting a gross offence against the natural rights of men. Rights of this sort are not the products of human activity; they exist prior to the creation of positive rights and their fundamental character is not debased by an absence of formal recognition in positive instruments of law. Thus, Burke maintained that positive rights impose no obligation when they are repugnant to the authority of natural rights:

> self-derived rights, or grants for the mere private benefit of the holders ... are all in the strictest sense *a trust*: and it is the very essence of every trust to be rendered *accountable*, – and even totally to *cease*, when it substantially varies from the purposes for which alone it could have a lawful existence (emphasis in original).[6]

It is this notion of trust that underpinned Burke's conviction that the affairs of British India had to be placed under parliamentary supervision. Commercial and political privileges, he declared, are not rights of men; and the failure to discharge the duties assumed in possession of these rights violated the trust upon which the Company's claim to rule depended. Although Burke did not succeed in seeing the revocation of the Company's privileges, he registered the principle against which all subsequent governments in India would be judged:

> all political power which is set over men, and that all privilege claimed or exercised in exclusion of them, being wholly artificial, and for so much a derogation from the natural equality of mankind at large, ought to be some way or other exercised ultimately for their benefit.[7]

Success in this respect resulted in the passage of the India Act of 1784, which left the Company's commerce unmolested, but stipulated principles of good government that were intended to 'secure the happiness of the natives'.[8]

Burke's crusade against the East India Company succeeded in establishing the idea of trust as the principle that governed relations between the Company and its Indian subjects and, eventually, the relations between the so-called advanced and backward peoples throughout the British Empire. It is in this context that the idea of trusteeship assumes that a claim to rule must be subject to a test of fitness; for it accepts the proposition, expressed in Plato's *Republic*, that each man is endowed by nature to perform a particular task. Particular qualities of right conduct, that is, the virtues, are what render some men fit to rule; and it is to men endowed with these virtues – good memory, self-discipline, courage, morality, and a love of truth – that a republic should be entrusted.[9]

Thus the first justification of trusteeship consists in promoting the moral and material welfare of people who, on account of some infirmity, are incapable of directing their own affairs. However, trusteeship demands something more than the promotion of welfare; for it also recognizes the singular importance of security as a condition of life in society. Europeans typically regarded life in 'savage' and 'barbarian' societies as being retarded by chronic war and disorders of all kinds; and too often Europeans conducted their relations with the non-European world in ways that were antagonistic to the values they professed to cherish. Thus, the second justification of trusteeship consists in protecting dependent peoples from the rapacity of others. Together, these justifications of trusteeship join ruler and subject in a shared enterprise, an undertaking concerned foremost with the condition of the disadvantaged, whereby considerations of welfare and security vindicate rights of dominion. Indeed, it is in this context that William Pitt, the prime minister who presided over the passage of the India Act, argued that the success of the East India Company 'must chiefly depend on the establishment of the happiness of the inhabitants, and their being secured in a state of peace and tranquillity'.[10]

The idea of security that attaches to trusteeship, the idea to which Pitt refers, derives its principal justification from the fundamental sanctity of human personality. Hence, abolitionists like Thomas Fowell Buxton were apt to argue that the salvation of Africa required little more than establishing conditions favourable to the enjoyment of personal security. The people of Africa may have been mired in the darkest depths of ignorance and superstition, but still, he argued, they disclosed qualities that suggested a condition of conventional rather natural inferiority. Pervasive insecurity, the curse of predatory warfare, and systematic depopulation, was something born of slavery and of the slave trade, not of natural inferiority. Thus, for Buxton, the restitution of Africa and the elevation of the 'Negro mind' could not proceed in abeyance of the security afforded by legitimate commerce, the light of Christianity, and instruction in the arts of civilization; for no obstacle could stand before the righteous pursuit of this cause: 'whether we look to the great interests of humanity, or consult the prosperity and honour of the British empire, it is our duty to proceed, undeterred by difficulty, peril, or expense'.[11]

It is in the spirit of this duty that the relation of security and trusteeship comes into view: protecting the disadvantaged from harm outweighs other considerations, such as strategic interest or commercial advantage. For the moral weight of this principle demanded that the value of commerce, religion, and education, be judged by the extent to which they contribute to maintenance of public order and the dispensation of justice domestically, and the defence of dependent territories internationally.

Obligation and interest

While the claim of trusteeship stresses the overriding value of personal safety, it is also true that one of its enduring legacies is the consistency with which this claim is dismissed as being foolishly naive or utterly deceptive. This view holds that the argument of personal security is subordinate to other pressing interests or, alternatively, obscures less virtuous motives. For example, Ronald Robinson and John Gallagher submit that Africa was peripheral to British interests well into the latter part of the nineteenth century, apart from an enduring interest in extirpating the illegitimate commerce in human beings. Indeed, the Crown long regarded expansion in Africa, with its hostile climate, endemic warfare, and lack of organized economy, as a rather unpromising enterprise. Robinson and Gallagher concede that British officials had to respect the 'traditional shibboleths of trusteeship and anti-slavery', but they maintain nonetheless that Britain 'moved into Africa, not to build a new African empire, but to protect the old empire in India'.[12]

People who were once colonial wards may accept the underlying premise of this conclusion, but they are more likely to emphasize a history that is marked by acts of aggression, conquest, enslavement, deportation, and alien rule. Trusteeship is remembered by these people as the justification for racial segregation, forced labour, and loss of land, culture, and economic livelihood. This history betrays nothing but a brutal story of domination and exploitation that was underwritten by unbridled national greed. Indeed, it is in this vein that Kwame Nkrumah described the people of Africa as mere tools of European enrichment: they toiled in mines and on plantations while 'progressive' trustees of civilization kept the people of Africa in a depressed state of poverty, disease, and mass illiteracy. And so he could only disparage the many promises of protection and guardianship that were enshrined in the Berlin Act, the Covenant of the League of Nations, and the Charter of the United Nations, as platitudinous camouflage meant to disguise the exploitative nature of imperialism: '[b]eneath the "humanitarian" and "appeasement" shibboleths of colonial governments, a proper scrutiny leads one to discover nothing but deception, hypocrisy, oppression, and exploitation'.[13]

The principal thrust of Nkrumah's argument, and others like it, hinges on a conflict of obligation and interest, whereby protecting the disadvantaged and securing them in a state of peace and tranquillity is at some point incommensurable with the exigencies of empire and the pursuit of profit. Hence, the obligations of trusteeship pale before the high politics of imperial rivalry or they constitute mere rationalizations of oppression and servitude. It must surely be admitted that principles of trusteeship were sometimes twisted in order to attain ends that were in fact contrary to their true purpose. However, the character of trusteeship, the traits that enable us to recognize and to understand trusteeship in terms of an identity that is distinctly its own, discloses no contradiction of obligation and interest. In other words, the claims of trusteeship are justified in such a way that obligations owed to the disadvantaged coexist in perfect harmony with interests pertaining to the security of empire and the accumulation of wealth.

The most influential figures in the development of British colonial administration in Africa did not pretend as if they were engaged in a philanthropic enterprise that was wholly disinterested in questions of strategy and economy. For example, Buxton was certainly convinced of the certain truth of the Christian religion, but he was no less certain of the civilizing effects of a liberal and well-regulated commerce. Thus, he found no incoherence in satisfying the obligations of trusteeship through the propagation of commerce and Christianity:

> The extension of a legitimate commerce, and with it the blessings of civilization and Christianity, is worthy of the most strenuous exertions of the philanthropist, whilst to the mercantile and general interests of the civilised world it is of the highest importance.[14]

This unity of obligation and interest is even more pronounced in Lord Lugard's notion of the dual mandate, which invested the idea of trusteeship in nineteenth century Africa with a very simple, yet extraordinarily persuasive, justification: the exploitation of natural wealth should reciprocally benefit the people of Europe and Africa alike. Like Buxton, he finds no contradiction of obligation and interest:

> Let it be admitted at the outset that European brains, capital, and energy have not been, and never will be, expended in developing the resources of Africa from motives of pure philanthropy; that Europe is in Africa for the mutual benefit of her own industrial classes, and of the native races in their progress to a higher plane; that the benefit can be made reciprocal, and that it is the aim and desire of civilised administration to fulfil this dual mandate.[15]

Lugard justified the dual mandate by appealing to something like the Kantian idea of a universal right of mankind – *jus cosmopoliticum.* On this view, the wealth of the earth is by natural right the common inheritance of all men; and the fact that groups of human beings hold a juridically determined proprietary right to a portion of the earth's surface does not foreclose the exercise of this right. For this reason, Kant asserts that 'the possession of the soil upon which an inhabitant of the earth may live can

only be regarded as possession of a part of a limited whole and, consequently, as a part to which every one has originally a right'.[16] Thus,
rather than clothing naked ambition in the garb of humanitarian plati-
tude, Lugard argued that Europeans were entitled by right to a fair share
of Africa's natural wealth, an endowment wasted by the natives on account
of their inability to comprehend its value or proper use. Indeed, he asked:
'[w]ho can deny the right of the hungry people of Europe to utilise the
wasted bounties of nature, or that the task of developing these resources
was . . . a "trust for civilization" and for the benefit of mankind?'[17]

The claims of the dual mandate are fully intelligible in the proceedings
of the Berlin Conference of 1885. Signatories to the Berlin Act internationalized the principle of trusteeship when they agreed in Article 6 of the
treaty to 'watch over the preservation of the native tribes, and to care for
the improvement of the conditions of their moral and material well-being,
and to help in suppressing slavery, and especially the Slave Trade'.[18]
Although the star of free trade had dimmed somewhat toward the end of
the nineteenth century, the negotiations at Berlin reveal the firmly held
belief that the depressed state of the African would be served best by the
extension of complete and perfect commercial freedom. Free trade
advanced not only narrow national economic interests, but the cause of
humanity as well. The British representative, Sir Edward Malet, expressed
this sentiment when he impressed upon his colleagues that

> [t]he principle which will command the sympathy and support of Her
> Majesty's Government will be that of the advancement of legitimate
> commerce, with security for the equality of treatment of all nations,
> and for the well-being of the native races.[19]

And to ensure that the advantages of unrestricted commerce would be
enjoyed to the fullest extent possible, the conference felt it necessary to
adopt uniform rules for the recognition of future occupations and to
establish a system of neutrality in tropical Africa. Only these steps, the
parties agreed, would relieve the continent of Africa from the intrigues,
rivalries, and passions that all too easily lead to war.

The justification of these particular decisions, and of the Berlin Act
generally, is none too different from the reciprocal relation that underpins the dual mandate. And here too there is little evidence to suggest a
conflict obligation and interest as, again, they are fused in such a way as to
admit no contradiction. Thus, a report commissioned to study the prevention of war in tropical Africa observed:

> after having surrounded freedom of commerce and navigation in the
> centre of Africa with guarantees, and after having shown your solici-
> tude for the moral and material welfare of the populations which
> inhabit it, you are about to introduce rules into positive international

law which are destined to remove all causes of disagreement and strife from international relations.[20]

The justification of this conclusion is set out by the American representative, John Kasson, who argued that that it was not enough to safeguard European interests and property from the threat of war; to do so would be to transform tropical Africa into an estate in the service of the productive forces of Europe and America. Rather, as trustees of civilization, Europeans were duty-bound to introduce science, literature, the arts, and all other forms of useful knowledge; they were obliged to encourage the formation of productive labour; and they were responsible for assisting the native population of Africa in adapting to the customs and usages of civilization. This enterprise, he reminded fellow delegates, was fundamentally dependent on a condition of peace that must be enjoyed by trustee and ward alike; for 'war quickly lets loose every barbarous passion and destroys the progress of many years of civilisation'.[21]

The relation of obligation and interest that emerges out of the Berlin Conference is not altered in any fundamental way by the creation of the League of Nations mandates system. Critics derided the mandates experiment as a self-serving disguise, beneath which a thin veneer shrouded the selfish, pernicious, and dangerous principles of power politics. Perhaps a more accurate assessment is found in Quincy Wright's description of the creation and implementation of the mandates system as being 'mutilated in details, sullied by the spirit of barter, delayed in confirmation, and minified by the mandatories'.[22] Nonetheless, it is true that the mandates system was the result of a compromise between Woodrow Wilson's insistence on what he understood as 'the genuine idea of trusteeship'[23] and the annexationist ambitions of Australia, France, New Zealand, and South Africa. In this respect, the innovation of the system lies in the creation of supervisory machinery to ensure the performance of certain obligations, and in the confirmation of mandated peoples as subjects of international law. However, the mandates system did not, as David Lloyd George wished to impress upon the advocates of annexation, depart from the principles enshrined in the Berlin Act:

> there was no large difference between the mandatory principle and the principles laid down by the Berlin Conference, under which Great Britain, France, and Germany held many of their colonies. This Conference had framed conditions about the open door, the prohibition of the arms and liquor traffic, which resembled those President Wilson had in view in many respects, except that no external machinery had been provided for their enforcement.[24]

In reaching the compromise offered by the mandates system, the peacemakers who gathered at Versailles remained fixed on questions of national security; but in doing so, they accepted and gave positive expression to the principle that the search for security could not entail the neglect or maltreatment of dependent peoples. Thus, they agreed in Article 22 of the Covenant that 'there should be applied the principle that the well-being and development of such peoples form a sacred trust of civilisation and that securities for the performance of this trust should be embodied in this Covenant.'[25]

The substance of this principle is restated twenty-five years later in the Charter of the United Nations. Article 76 of the Charter proclaims that the objectives of the Trusteeship System consist in furthering international peace and security, promoting the political, economic, social, and educational advancement of the inhabitants of trust territories, upholding human rights and fundamental freedoms, and ensuring equal treatment in social, economic, and commercial matters for all members of the organization. That the furtherance of international peace and security is specified first among the objectives of trusteeship might be construed to mean the subordination of obligation to interest, especially since Article 84 stipulates that '[i]t shall be the duty of the administering authority to ensure the trust territory shall play its part in the maintenance of international peace and security'.[26] Indeed, H. Duncan Hall argues that historians have exaggerated the extent to which humanitarianism and liberal idealism account for the creation of the mandates system and the trusteeship system; they are, he argues, by-products of political relations and thus factors in the balance of power.[27]

But it would be a mistake of some considerable magnitude to suggest that these institutionalized forms of trusteeship subordinate the well-being of dependent peoples to the argument of national or international security. In the months leading up to the San Francisco Conference at which the United Nations Organization was established, Franklin Roosevelt refused to yield to the argument of national security when the War Department and United States Navy demanded the annexation of the Japanese mandated islands in the Pacific, just as Woodrow Wilson refused to bow to the argument of national security when discussing the disposal of German colonies at Versailles.[28] Indeed, a member of the American delegation to the San Francisco conference moved to disabuse the perception that international peace and security was superior to the obligations of trusteeship by saying: '[i]t was his Government's attitude that international peace and security and the welfare of dependent peoples, constituted twin objectives which could not be separated'.[29]

The international history of trusteeship provides scant evidence to support the allegation of a conflict of obligation and interest. However, this conclusion should not be taken to mean that the obligations of trusteeship were always fulfilled consistently and without controversy; nor does it mean that the performance of these obligations always withstood the scrutiny of the critical eye. For at times the discourse of trusteeship was surely used to obscure acts of oppression and exploitation as Nkrumah and others have alleged; but such criticism only impugns the conduct of those responsible for such acts, not the coherence of the obligations in terms of which trusteeship is intelligible. So when trusteeship is understood as an arrangement of security, it is in purpose, though not necessarily in its consequences, intelligible in a context of activity that is concerned with the general welfare of certain people, rather than in the meaning of motives and actions that are in so many ways elusive, contested, and unsettled.

The false promise of independence

The character of trusteeship and its relation to the idea of security is brought into sharper relief when it is considered against a backdrop of the idea that displaced it: political independence. Just before the Constituent Assembly of India adopted the state's newly drafted constitution in 1949, B. R. Ambedkar reminded his colleagues of the implications of acceding to such a status:

> [i]ndependence is no doubt a matter of joy. But let us not forget that this independence has thrown on us great responsibilities. By independence, we have lost the excuse of blaming the British for anything going wrong. If hereafter things go wrong, we will have nobody to blame except ourselves.[30]

In these brief and unusually candid words, we are able to make out the supreme dilemma of decolonization: independence held out the promise of emancipation, but entailed a frightening risk of failure. This promise of emancipation, of deliverance from poverty, ignorance, and oppression, is intelligible in theories that regard states as public arrangements which afford groups of human beings an opportunity to pursue and, if they are successful, to live the good life. Political independence endows a group of people with the authority to build a state of their own, a state directed toward the realization of ends that are of their own choosing and not those of their neighbours. And it is independence, and all the responsibility it entails, that makes it possible to speak of different conceptions of the good life.

But the many failed and quasi-states that have emerged out of decolonization offer powerful testimony to the reality that independence does not always result in emancipation. The problem with independence, as Margery Perham understood it, was that most colonial territories lacked nearly all the attributes of coherent and viable communities, the most important being the existence of an idea of community – civic, natural, or otherwise. Colonial societies were typically politically weak, economically underdeveloped, and socially divided, and their populations were ignorant of the obligations of citizenship and unfamiliar with the workings of modern government. It was this general condition of backwardness that hindered colonial development and which presented the greatest obstacle to the speedy granting of independence.[31] Thus, for Perham, and others who wished for the orderly transformation of empire, the granting of independence could not be separated from an estimate of ability. Conducting the affairs of state, they assumed, required a type of experience that is acquired slowly and only in the practice of doing things. Even the most sympathetic voices in support of colonial independence maintained, as did Arthur Creech Jones, that the extension of 'political freedom is an indifferent objective if the economic basis for the operation of that freedom is not properly laid'.[32] To proceed any other way was to embark upon an uncertain journey fraught with danger; for if the colonies were 'cut loose', Perham warned, 'they would presumably be set up as very weak units under an experimental world organization'.[33]

The hazards of which Perham spoke did not elude Ambedkar, who proved to be prophetically correct when he also warned that with independence 'there is a great danger of things going wrong'.[34] One of the distinctive features of post-colonial international society is that in some places things have gone wrong, as failed states – places where evidence of the good life is largely, if not totally, absent – are among decolonization's most conspicuous legacies. For in recent years daily life in places like Sierra Leone, Liberia, Rwanda, Congo, Somalia, Sudan, Angola, Cambodia, Burma, and East Timor calls to mind the most extraordinary conditions of insecurity. But these conditions should not be confused with being peculiarly African or Asian: the atrocities committed in Bosnia-Herzegovina and Kosovo ought to divest us of the idea that the moral and material achievements of Western civilization have rendered Europe immune to this kind of insecurity. The survival of failed states, and the patterns of violence to which they give rise, is underwritten in a rather perverse way by the constitutive norms of international society: the rights of political independence, territorial integrity, non-interference, and legal equality help sustain what are otherwise unviable states.[35]

That some states more closely resemble a state of nature casts considerable doubt on their worth as arrangements of security. Political independence, and its central assumption that self-determination is a fundamental prerequisite of the good life, has been for some people just as dangerous as Ambedkar feared. Historically, colonies or protectorates were established in territories affected by the type of violence and insecurity that is characteristic of failed states. It is in this sense that advocates of trusteeship, such as P. H. Kerr, proceeded on the belief that the 'decisive mark of a superior civilization is the readiness of its members to sacrifice themselves in order that their less fortunate fellows may learn how to share in their blessings'.[36] But the inequalities of wealth and power that sustained such thinking in the past have not disappeared with the end of empire, the expansion of international society, and the triumph of the sovereign state as the pre-eminent arrangement of security in the world today. The fact that groups of people continue to show themselves as being unable to effect the most minimum standards of public safety raises a question of supreme importance: in circumstances of grave human insecurity, is there a duty on the part of the strong to intervene on behalf of the weak? British Foreign Secretary Robin Cook answered this question in the affirmative by reverting to the paternal language of trusteeship: 'when faced with an overwhelming humanitarian catastrophe, which a government has shown it is unwilling or unable to prevent or is actively promoting, the international community should intervene'.[37]

In no other place has this proposition been put to a sterner test than in the context of NATO's intervention in Kosovo.[38] United Nations Security Council Resolution 1244 (1999) established an international presence in Kosovo, under the supervision of the United Nations, whose responsibilities include maintaining law and order, protecting human rights, performing basic administrative functions, and '[o]rganizing and overseeing the development of provisional institutions for democratic and autonomous self-government'.[39] Thus, Resolution 1244 transfers supreme civil authority in Kosovo from the Federal Republic of Yugoslavia to the United Nations sanctioned international presence and, thereby, transforms Kosovo into an international protectorate not substantially unlike the protectorates that were established in nineteenth century Africa. In other words Kosovo is in all but name a trust territory. Indeed, Strobe Talbott, the American Deputy Secretary of State in the Clinton administration, described Kosovo as a 'ward of the international community': '[i]t goes about the business of rebuilding itself under the day-in, day-out protection and supervision of a consortium of global and regional organizations'.[40]

Kosovo's status as a de facto trust territory lends weight to Peter Lyon's suggestion, made several years in advance of the latest war to convulse the Balkans, that pronouncements of the death of trusteeship may have been premature: the weak and disadvantaged peoples of the world continue to be disproportionately affected by persistent disorder, warfare, human misery, and acute shortages of welfare. And while he remains acutely attuned to the fact that any attempt to revive the legitimacy of trusteeship will certainly evoke unhappy memories of colonialism, he maintains nonetheless that 'a UN trusteeship would almost certainly be an improvement on the anarchical condition of the several quasi-states the world has now'.[41] This defence of trusteeship raises the obvious question: is contemporary international society in some way conducive to the resurrection of trusteeship as an arrangement of security?

Trusteeship in contemporary international society

One way of thinking about this question is to consider trusteeship in the context of two dispositions of association: *societas* and *universitas*.[42] Michael

Oakeshott understands *societas* as an association of persons who conceive themselves as being 'joined in the acknowledgement of the authority of a practice and not in respect of a common substantive purpose'.[43] In a *societas* of states there is little sense in speaking of the common good: states are associated in recognition of the authority ascribed to law rather than the pursuit of common, substantive ends. And the faithful subscription to obligations prescribed by this law, rather than the achievement of particular ends, are what inform the quality of conduct – that is, its goodness or badness. Thus, this mode of association conveys the image:

> not of pilgrims travelling to a common destination, but of adventurers each responding as best he can to the ordeal of consciousness in a world composed of others of his kind, each the inheritor of the imaginative achievements (moral and intellectual) of those who have gone before and some joined in a variety of prudential practices, but here partners in a practice of civility the rules of which are not devices for satisfying substantive wants and whose obligations create no symbiotic relationship.[44]

The contrasting idea of *universitas* expresses a form of corporate association: 'persons associated in respect of some identified common purpose, in the pursuit of some acknowledged substantive end, or in the promotion of some specified enduring interest'.[45] A society of states organized along these lines embraces all values, all peoples, and all jurisdictions. Law is endowed with purpose and its obligations are to be fulfilled only so long as they contribute to the realization of the common purpose of the association, whatever it might be. The members of such an association are not concerned with the adventure of negotiating a world marked by difference; instead they are concerned with the workings of a shared enterprise that is directed toward the achievement of this purpose. Thus, a *universitas* of states discloses one or more 'true' purposes or ends.

International society understood as a *societas* of states cannot accommodate the practice of trusteeship as it has been understood historically. The post-colonial *societas* of states is, against the claims of trusteeship, strictly anti-paternal. This view of international society is that of a voluntary association constituted by legal equals, who conduct their relations according to the principle of consent; it is an association in which orderly and peaceful relations depend on the principle of *pacta sunt servanda* – promises must be kept.[46] Thus, the procedural language of international society is not disclosed in the coercive and non-consensual vocabulary of trusteeship, but in a vocabulary that includes the words 'negotiation', 'persuasion', 'compromise', 'accommodation', and 'agreement'.

In this sort of world, a state, or portion thereof, cannot be subjected to a trustee and made a ward; for trusteeship, and its assumptions of inequality and interference, cannot be reconciled with a society of states that is founded upon the fundamental values of political independence, sovereign equality, territorial integrity, and non-interference.[47] Indeed, the revival of trusteeship would necessarily entail the revival of a suzerain system of the sort that distinguished the hierarchical relations of empire; and the reintroduction of a graded political status in international life would be nothing short of revolutionary. For it is nonsensical to suggest that a state can consent to being a ward; to do so is to confuse the characters of trusteeship and sovereignty. A trustee is someone who acts on behalf of someone else who is thought to be incapable of navigating the responsibilities of ordinary life, just as a parent acts on behalf of a child who is not yet ready to take on the responsibilities of adulthood. Indeed, it makes no sense whatsoever to speak of trusteeship if a state can consent to being a ward and, at the same time, possess the authority to terminate that status at its own choosing.[48]

But the idea of trusteeship may enjoy a rather secure place in an international society conceived as a *universitas* of states. Vaclav Havel evokes this solidarist understanding of association when he declares: 'our fates are merged together into one single destiny'.[49] Obstacles that render trusteeship morally dubious in a *societas* of states disclose a different disposition in an association ordered to the realization of substantive ends. The values of political independence, sovereign equality, territorial integrity, and non-interference can no longer be regarded as expressing procedural rules of mutual accommodation: in a *universitas* of states their value is derived from their contribution to the enjoyment of ends for which the association is instituted. Thus, trusteeship may be justified in instances where members of the association deviate from these ends (such as universal respect for human personality); and states that do so deviate – those which fall into unconscionable tyranny – shall be instructed and supervised in adequately subscribing to ends that make it a 'good' society.

A society of states founded upon this idea of association affords a ready and able response to modern day barbarism: the claims of individual human beings are superior to the claims of the communities in which they live. And affirming the sanctity of this principle is something for which it is right to wage war; for it accepts the proposition put forward by Grotius that human beings who are subjected to oppression that is 'odious to every just man' cannot be denied the 'right of all human society'.[50] Indeed, it this understanding of international society that underpins arguments used to justify the establishment of an international protectorate in Kosovo. Again, Havel articulates this conviction most clearly:

> [NATO] has acted out of respect for the law, for the law that ranks higher than the protection of the sovereignty of states. It has acted out of respect for the rights of humanity, as they are articulated by our conscience as well as by other instruments of international law.[51]

The distinction between *societas* and *universitas* is conceptually useful in bringing into focus the difficulties in resurrecting trusteeship as an arrangement of security in international society. Theorists who take their cues from the so-called English School or the international society approach to international relations attempt to get at this distinction by describing the world in terms of solidarism and pluralism. Of course, these categories are ideal types, which cannot by themselves describe the world as it really is. The problems of human insecurity, the jealousy, pride, and lust that are the wellspring of war and cruelty, inhabit the real world and care little for the clarity and tidiness afforded by intellectual categories. Still, there is an unhappy tendency in international relations scholarship, which too often leaves a lasting impression on the practitioners and participants in world affairs, of treating international society as if it consists in one image and not the other. The claims of solidarism and the claims of pluralism have never been totally absent in the practice of international society. Thus, academic theories that endeavour to defend a world of states against a world of peoples or, conversely, a world of peoples against a world of states, fail to make sufficient contact with the stuff that is the substance of human conduct.

It is well beyond the scope of this chapter to propose which mode of association, pluralism, or solidarism, provides a better account of contemporary international society, if such a judgement can be provided at all. But the introduction of these categories illuminates with sufficient clarity the obstacles set before any hope of resurrecting trusteeship as an arrangement of security in international society. To suggest that the claims of pluralism and solidarism are ever present in international society is not to minimize what surely must be the most vexing activity of human conduct: choosing well. Indeed, international society is marked by paradox, disagreement, and inconsistency that to some substantial degree defies rationalization; and in practice, that is, in the relations of states and in human conduct generally, it is inclusive – sometimes uneasily to be sure – of both a pluralist community of states and a solidarist community of human beings. Thus, it might not be inaccurate to approach and to understand the theory and practice of international relations in terms of an ongoing conversation between the voices of solidarism and the voices of pluralism. And, as well, the scholarly enterprise might be more profitably directed toward discerning the relation of these two modes of association at particular moments in history rather than asserting an academic understanding of one that does not take proper account of the other. It is here that we encounter contradiction, not in terms of obligation and interest, but in terms of conflicting obligations.[52]

Conclusion

There are times when the principles of pluralism and those of solidarism demand conflicting action, and it is therefore sometimes necessary that the claims of one yield to the claims of the other. It is the consequences of these decisions, and the need to justify them before the men and women of the world, which stand before the revival of trusteeship as an arrangement of security in international society. Robert Jackson has argued that '[i]nternational society is, by and large, a *societas* rather than a *universitas*: it is an association of independent and legally equal members states of varying substance, rather than a substantive and purposive enterprise in its own right'.[53] Thus, in exchange for security, advocates of trusteeship must accept the proposition that some people do not fully understand the responsibilities of liberty and that they are consequently unfit to rule themselves. Indeed, they must be prepared to overturn the normative settlement that emerged out of decolonization, a settlement that for better or worse accepts the advice offered by Satan in Milton's *Paradise Lost*: 'Better to reign in hell than serve in Heaven.'[54] The Ethiopian representative to the United Nations, Mr Alemayehou, expressed this conviction during the landmark debate on General Assembly Resolution 1514:

> But if, in spite of all, the question would be to choose between freedom with all its attendant economic difficulties and internal conflicts on the one hand, and the maintenance of colonial rule with all its attendant subjugation, exploitation, degradation and humiliation, and so on, on the other, I would right away and unequivocally say that the peoples, all peoples, under colonial rule prefer poverty in freedom to wealth in slavery, and they will definitely prefer fighting in freedom to peace in slavery.[55]

Personal security may be of little value if it is achieved at the expense of self-determination: the disposition to be the author of one's own actions and to exert one's effort in the pursuit of self-chosen ends. But in accepting the moral worth of this claim, the defenders of self-determination must be prepared to accept failure when people fall short of the mark.[56] They must be content, not to interfere and to set things aright, but to recognize tragedy and to express sympathy in the face of human suffering and cruelty.

Something too must be said of solidarism. Human beings may very well one day agree upon ends that are, without qualification, universally valid for the entire human family; and the society of states may one day more closely resemble a purposive association that is intelligible as a *universitas*. And while it cannot be denied that the universal ends expressed by the idea of humanity exert enormous influence in world affairs, the discourse and practice of contemporary international society suggests that in important respects the ends of life remain unsettled. That there continues to be considerable debate and disagreement over the proper ends of world affairs seems to confirm that our world is still one distinguished by difference that is appropriate of *societas*. But in a world where the fundamental ends of life remain unsettled, persons who are determined to act as if international society consists in a *universitas* of states are more likely to engender the insecurity that all too often accompanies moral crusading rather than lasting peace.

The moral crusader has certainly left a lasting imprint on the history of international society; for that history is rife with people who are so impressed with their own achievements that they assume that their habits, customs, traditions, and values constitute the standard of perfection for all. There are times when human beings love some thing more than life itself; they love an idea too much, or they love a group of their own kind too exclusively, that they are willing to justify cruelty and oppression for the sake of their cause.[57] It cannot be denied that human rights and international humanitarian law have altered and shaped our world in profound ways – indeed, they continue to do so. But in granting their signal importance, there is little reason to believe that most human beings have tempered their love of autonomy, their desire to be masters of their own affairs, to decide the ends of life for themselves, and to strive for them by their own efforts. Love of independence and of autonomy is a still very powerful aspiration in world affairs. The disparities in wealth and power that suggested the need for trusteeship historically have not disappeared with the expansion of international society; but the moral climate in which trusteeship thrived did disappear with the passing of the great European empires. And while insecurity is so much a part of daily life for many people on this planet, it seems as if trusteeship is a rather unpromising arrangement with which to respond to this most unsatisfactory state of affairs.

Notes

1 de Vitoria (1991), pp. 252–77.
2 de Vitoria (1991), pp. 290–1.
3 Passmore (2000), pp. 226–36.
4 Burke (1899), p. 439.
5 Burke (1899), pp. 447–64.
6 Burke (1899), p. 439.
7 Burke (1899), p. 439.
8 Pitt (1983), pp. 52–3.
9 Plato (1993), pp. 60, 196–212.
10 Quoted in Marshall (1968), p. 60.
11 Buxton (1967), pp. 310, 459, 530.
12 Robinson and Gallagher (1965), pp. 14–23, 464.
13 Nkrumah (1962), pp. xvi, 35.
14 Buxton (1967), p. 342.
15 Lugard (1929), p. 617.
16 Kant (1952), p. 456.
17 Lugard (1929), p. 615.
18 General Act of the Conference of Berlin, *Parliamentary Papers*, 1886 LXVII, mf. 92.353, p. 14.
19 Protocol No. 1 – Meeting of 15 November 1884, Protocols and the General Act of the West African Conference, *Parliamentary Papers*, 1885 LV mf. 91.435, p. 11.

20 Annex 1 to Protocol No. 8, Protocols and the General Act of the West African Conference, *Parliamentary Papers*, 1885 LV mf. 91.437, p. 217.
21 Annex 13 to Protocol No. 5, Protocols and the General Act of the West African Conference, *Parliamentary Papers*, 1885 LV mf. 91.437, pp. 163–4.
22 Wright (1930), p. 63.
23 'BC-12, Quai d'Orsay, January 27, 1919', *The Paris Peace Conference*, vol. III, (Washington: Government Printing Office, 1943), p. 740.
24 'BC-13, Quai d'Orsay, January 24, 1919', in Link (1986), pp. 310–11.
25 'Covenant Text in the Treaty of Versailles', in Miller (1928), p. 737.
26 'Charter of the United Nations', in Roberts and Kingsbury (1993), pp. 520–2.
27 Hall (1948), p. 8.
28 Louis (1977), pp. 373, 483.
29 United Nations Organization (1945), p. 440; see also Hull (1948), p. 1639.
30 Ambedkar (undated), p. 980.
31 Perham (1961), p. 26.
32 Jones (1959), p. 25.
33 Perham (1967), p. 267.
34 Ambedkar (undated), p. 980.
35 See Jackson (1990), Chapter 2.
36 Kerr (1916), p. 144.
37 Cook (2000).
38 See Roberts' contribution to this volume for an extended analysis of NATO's intervention in Kosovo and its implications, Chapter 9.
39 United Nations Security Council Resolution 1244 (1999), Adopted by the Security Council at its 4011th Meeting on 10 June 1999, S/RES/1244 (1999).
40 Talbott (1999), p. 5.
41 Lyon (1993), pp. 105–7.
42 This distinction provides the basis of R. Jackson's argument for a pluralist society of states. See Jackson (2000).
43 Oakeshott (1996), p. 242.
44 Oakeshott (1996), p. 243.
45 Oakeshott (1996), p. 203.
46 Crawford (1979) 79; and Mayall (1990), p. 37.
47 For an elaboration of this argument, see Bain (2003), pp. 59–77. A. Roberts argues in Chapter 9 that humanitarian intervention need not be conceived as being corrosive of the non-intervention principle. However, it would seem that trusteeship falls into a different category altogether because it extinguishes the political independence of a territory, and the people residing within it.
48 See Bain (2003), Chapter 6; and Bain (2004), pp. 6–14.
49 Havel (1999), p. 1.
50 Grotius (1949), p. 263.
51 Havel (1999), p. 5. On the issue of mixed motives in respect of intervention in Kosovo, see Roberts' chapter (pp. 162, 181–2).
52 Interestingly, Roberts addresses this conflict as being indicative, not of a conflict between ethics and law, but a conflict between different branches of law, see pp. 171–4.
53 Jackson (2000), p. 105.
54 Milton (1961), p. 44.
55 United Nations General Assembly, 928th Plenary Meeting, 30 November 1960, United Nations General Assembly Official Records, A/PV 928, 1021.
56 See J. Mayall's contribution to this volume for an extended analysis of the relation between security and self-determination.
57 Berlin (1969), p. 102; and Butterfield (1951), p. 49.

Bibliography

Ajami, F. 'Their Gilded Age – And Ours'. *National Interest.* 63 (Summer, 2001): 37–47.

Alcock, A. 'South Tyrol'. *Minority Rights in Europe: The Scope for a Transnational Regime.* Ed., H. Miall. London: Pinter Publishers for RIIA, 1994.

Ambedkar, B. R. *The Constituent Assembly Debates: Official Report.* Vol. 11. New Delhi: Lok Sabha Secretariat, undated.

American Civil Liberties Union. *Sanctioned Bias: Racial Profiling Since 9/11.* New York: ACLU, 2004.

Andreas, P. 'The Clandestine Political Economy of War and Peace in Bosnia'. *International Studies Quarterly.* 48.1 (2004): 29–52.

Angell, N. *The Great Illusion.* London: William Heinemann, 1911.

Annan, K. *'We the Peoples': The Role of the United Nations in the 21st Century.* New York: United Nations, 2000.

Arendt, H. *The Origins of Totalitarianism.* New York: Meridian, 1972.

Aron, R. *Peace and War: A Theory of International Relations.* London: Weidenfeld and Nicolson, 1966.

Aron, R. *On War: Atomic Weapons and Global Diplomacy.* London: Secker and Warburg, 1958.

Bacevich, A. *American Empire: The Realities and Consequences of U.S. Diplomacy.* Cambridge: Harvard University Press, 2002.

Bain, W. 'In Pursuit of Paradise: Trusteeship and Contemporary International Society'. *Tidsskriftet Politik.* 7.2 (2004): 6–14.

Bain, W. *Between Anarchy and Society: Trusteeship and the Obligations of Power.* Oxford: Oxford University Press, 2003a.

Bain, W. 'The Political Theory of Trusteeship and the Twilight of International Equality'. *International Relations.* 16.1 (2003b): 59–77.

Baldwin, D. 'The Concept of Security'. *Review of International Studies.* 23 (1997): 5–26.

Ballentine, K. and Sherman, J., Eds. *The Political Economy of Armed Conflict: Beyond Greed and Grief.* Boulder, CO: Lynn Rienner, 2003.

Barnhart, M. *Japan and the World Since 1868.* Oxford: Oxford University Press, 1995.

Bartlett, J. *Familiar Quotations,* 10th edn. Boston, MA: Little, Brown, and Company, 1919.

Bassiouni, C. 'Organized Crime and New Wars'. *Restructuring the Global Military Sector.* Vol. 1. Eds, M. Kaldor and B. Vashee. London and Washington: Pinter, 1997.

Beck, U. *What is Globalization?* Trans., P. Camiller. Polity Press: Cambridge, 1999.

Beloff, M. *The Great Powers: Essays in Twentieth Century Politics.* Westport, CT: Greenwood Press, 1979, 1959.

Bergson, F. 'Coming Investment Wars'. *Foreign Affairs.* 53.1 (1975): 135–52.

Berlin, I. 'In Pursuit of the Ideal'. *The Crooked Timber of Humanity.* Ed., H. Hardy. Oxford: Oxford University Press, 1990.

Berlin, I. 'Historical Inevitability'. *Four Essays on Liberty.* Oxford: Oxford University Press, 1969.

Bojicic, V. and Kaldor, M. 'The Political Economy of the War in Bosnia-Herzegovina'. *Restructuring the Global Military Sector.* Vol. I. Eds, M. Kaldor and B. Vashee. London and Washington: Pinter, 1997.

Boot, M. 'The Case for American Empire'. *Weekly Standard.* 7.5 (2001).

Booth, K. 'Critical Explorations'. *Critical Security Studies and World Politics.* Ed., K. Booth. Boulder: Lynne Rienner, 2005.

Booth, K. 'Cold Wars of the Mind', *Statecraft and Security: The Cold War and Beyond.* Ed., K. Booth. Cambridge and New York: Cambridge University Press, 1998.

Booth, K. 'Security and Emancipation'. *Review of International Studies.* 17 (1991a): 313–26.

Booth, K. 'War, Security, Strategy: Towards a Doctrine for Stable Peace'. *New Thinking About Strategy and International Security.* Ed., K. Booth. London: Harper Collins Academic, 1991b.

Braudel, F. *The Identity of France.* Vol. 1. Trans., S. Reynolds. London: Collins, 1988.

Bridge, F. R. and Bullen, R. *The Great Powers and the European States System, 1815-1914.* London: Longman, 1980.

Brownlie, I., Ed. *Basic Documents on Human Rights.* 3rd edn. Oxford: Clarendon Press, 1992.

Bull, H. 'Hobbes and the International Anarchy'. *Hedley Bull on International Society.* Eds, K. Alderson and A. Hurrell. Basingstoke: Macmillan, 2000.

Bull, H., Ed. *Intervention in World Politics.* Oxford: Clarendon Press, 1984.

Bull, H. *The Anarchical Society: a Study of Order in World Politics.* London: Macmillan, 1977.

Bull, H. 'Society and Anarchy in International Relations'. *Diplomatic Investigations.* Eds, M. Wight and H. Butterfield. London: George Allen and Unwin, 1966.

Bull, H., Kingsbury, B., and Roberts, A., Eds. *Hugo Grotius and International Relations.* Oxford: Clarendon Press, 1990.

Bullock, A. *Hitler: A Study in Tyranny.* Abridged edn. New York: Harper & Row, 1971.

Butterfield, H. *History and Human Relations.* London: Collins, St. James's Place, 1951.

Burke, E. 'Speech on Mr. Fox's East India Bill, December 1, 1783'. *The Works of the Right Honourable Edmund Burke.* Vol. II. Boston: Little, Brown, and Company, 1899.

Buxton, T. F. *The African Slave Trade and Its Remedy.* London: Frank Cass, 1967.

Buzan, B. *People, States, and Fear: An Agenda for International Security Studies in the Post-War Era.* 2nd edn. Boulder: Lynne Rienner, 1991.

Buzan, B., Waever, O., and de Wilde, J. *Security: A New Framework for Analysis.* Boulder: Lynne Rienner, 1998.

de Callières, F. *The Art of Diplomacy.* Eds, H. M. A. Keens-Soper and K. Sechweizer. Leicester: Leicester University Press, 1983.

Campbell, D. *Writing Security: United States Foreign Policy and the Politics of Identity.* Manchester: Manchester University Press, 1992.

Cassese, A. '*Ex iniuria ius oritur.* Are We Moving towards International Legitimation of Forcible Humanitarian Countermeasures in the World Community?' *European Journal of International Law.* 10.1 (1999): 23–30.

Chase, R., Hill, E., and Kennedy, P., Eds. *The Pivotal States: A New Framework for U.S. Policy in the Developing World.* New York: W. W. Norton, 1999.

Chesterman, S. *Just War or Just Peace? Humanitarian Intervention and International Law.* Oxford: Oxford University Press, 2001.

Churchill, W. S. *The Second World War: The Gathering Storm.* Vol. I. London: Cassell, 1948.

Cimbala, S. *The Politics of Warfare: The Great Powers of the 20th Century.* College Station, PA: Penn State University Press, 1996.

Clark, I. 'The Security State'. *Globalization and International Relations Theory.* Ed., I. Clark. Oxford: Oxford University, 1999.

Claude, I. *National Minorities: An International Problem.* Cambridge, MA: Harvard University Press, 1955.

von Clausewitz, C. *On War.* Eds, M. Howard and P. Paret. Princeton: Princeton University Press, 1984.

Cobban, A. *The Nation State and National Self-Determination.* New York: Thomas Crowell, 1970.

Coll, A. R. 'Normative Prudence as a Tradition of Statecraft'. *Ethics and International Affairs.* 5 (1991): 33–51.

Commission on Global Governance. *Our Global Neighbourhood: The Report of the Commission on Global Governance.* Oxford: Oxford University Press, 1995.

Commission on Human Security. *Human Security Now: Protecting and Empowering People.* New York, 2003.

The Compact Edition of the Oxford English Dictionary. Vol. II. Oxford: Oxford University Press, 1971.

Cook, R. 'Guiding Humanitarian Intervention'. Speech by the Foreign Secretary, American Bar Association Lunch, QE II Conference Centre. London, Wednesday 19 July 2000 (available at www.fco.gov.uk).

Cooper, R. 'The Post-Modern State'. *Re-Ordering the World: The Long Term Implications of 11 September.* Ed., M. Leonard. London: The Foreign Policy Centre, 2002.

Cornell, S. *Small Nations and Great Powers.* Richmond, Surrey: Curzon Press, 2000.

Cox, M. 'The Empire's Back in Town: Or America's Imperial Temptation – Again'. *Millennium.* 32.1 (2003): 1–27.

Cox, R. *Production, Power and World Order: Social Forces in the Making of History.* New York: Columbia University Press, 1987.

Craig, G. A. and George, A. L. *Force and Statecraft.* Oxford: Oxford University Press, 1983.

Crawford, J. *The Creation of States in International Law.* Oxford: Clarendon Press, 1979.

Cubban, B. 'The Duty of the Professional'. *Ethics in Public Services.* Ed., R. A. Chapman. Edinburgh: Edinburgh University Press, 1993.

Dalby, S. 'Geopolitical Change and Contemporary Security Studies: Conceptualizing the Human Security Agenda'. Institute of International Relations Working Paper. University of British Columbia, 2000.

Dayan, M. *Break-Through.* London: Weidenfeld and Nicolson, 1981.

Der Derian, J. *On Diplomacy*. Oxford: Basil Blackwell, 1987.

Desika Char, S.V., Ed. *Readings in the Constitutional History of India 1757–1947*. Delhi: Oxford University Press, 1983.

Dewitt, D., Haglund D., and Kirton, J., Eds. *Building a New Global Order: Emerging Trends in International Security*. Toronto: Oxford University Press, 1993.

Donnelly, J. *Universal Human Rights in Theory and Practice*. Ithaca: Cornell University Press, 1989.

Drinnon, R. *Facing West: The Metaphysics of Indian-hating and Empire Building*. Norman, OK and London: Oklahoma University Press, 1997.

Dunn, D. H. *Diplomacy at the Highest Level*. London: Macmillan, 1996.

Duyvesteyn, I. 'Contemporary War: Ethnic Conflict, Resource Conflict, or Something Else?' Paper presented at the Annual Meeting of the International Studies Association. Los Angeles, California, 15–18 March 2000.

Eayrs, J. *Diplomacy and Its Discontents*. Toronto: University of Toronto Press, 1971.

Eban, A. *An Autobiography*. New York: Random House, 1977.

Eichengreen, B. *International Monetary Arrangements for the 21st Century*. Washington: Brookings, 1994.

Enloe, C. *Bananas, Beaches, and Bases: Making Feminist Sense of International Politics*. Berkeley: University of California Press, 1990.

Fabry, M. 'International Norms of Territorial Integrity and the Balkan Wars of the 1990s'. *Global Society*. 16.2 (2002): 145–74.

Freedman, L. 'The Revolution in Strategic Affairs'. *Adelphi Paper 318*. Oxford: Oxford University Press, 1998.

Freeman, M. *Human Rights*. Cambridge: Polity Press, 2002.

Fukuyama, F. *The End of History and the Last Man*. New York: Free Press, 1992.

Gaddis, J. *We Now Know: Rethinking Cold War History*. Oxford: Clarendon Press, 1997.

Gallie, W. B. *Philosophy and the Historical Understanding*. New York: Schocken Books, 1968.

Gelb, L. 'Quelling the Teacup Wars'. *Foreign Affairs*. 73.6 (1994): 2–6.

Gellner, E. *Nationalism*. London: Weidenfeld and Nicolson, 1997.

Gellner, E. *Conditions of Liberty, Civil Society and its Rivals*. London: Hamish Hamilton, 1994.

Gellner, E. *Plough, Sword, and Book: The Structure of Human History*. London: Collins Harvill, 1988.

George, P. 'Dr Strangelove'. *The Cold War: A History in Documents and Eyewitness Accounts*. Eds, J. Hanhimaki and O. A. Westad. Oxford: Oxford University Press, 2003.

Gerth, H. H. and Wright, C., Eds. *From Max Weber*. London: Routledge, 1974.

Giddens, A. *The Consequences of Modernity*. Cambridge: Polity Press, 1990.

Gilpin, R. *War and Change in World Politics*. Cambridge: Cambridge University Press, 1981.

Glennon, M. J. *Limits of Law, Prerogatives of Power: Interventionism after Kosovo*. New York: Palgrave, 2001.

Goulding, M. *Peacemonger*. London: John Murray, 2002.

Government of the United States, *The Paris Peace Conference*. Vol. III. Washington: Government Printing Office, 1943.

Grotius, H. *De Jure Belli ac Pacis*. Trans., L. R. Loomis. Roslyn, NY: Walter J. Black, Inc., 1949.

Grotius, H. *De Jure Belli ac Pacis Libri Tres.* Trans., F. W. Kelsey. Oxford: Oxford University Press, 1925.

Gurr, T. R. *Peoples Versus States: Minorities at Risk in the New Century.* Washington: United States Institute of Peace Press, 2000.

Gutman, A. *Multiculturalism and the Politics of Recognition.* Princeton: Princeton University Press, 1992.

Halborn, H. 'Diplomats and Diplomacy in the Early Weimar Republic'. *The Diplomats, 1919–1939.* Eds, G. A. Craig and F. Gilbert. New York: Atheneum, 1968.

Hall, H. D. *Mandates, Dependencies, and Trusteeship.* London: Stevens & Sons Limited, 1948.

Hamish I. and Errington, E. J. *Great Powers and Little Wars.* Westport, CT: Praeger, 1993.

Hansard Society. 'Problems of Parliamentary Government in Colonies: A Report Prepared by the Hansard Society'. London: Hansard Society, 1953.

Harbour, F. V. *Thinking About International Ethics.* Boulder, CO: Westview, 1999.

Hare, J. E. and Joynt, C. B. *Ethics and International Affairs.* New York: St. Martin's Press, 1982.

Havel, V. Address of His Excellency Vaclav Havel, President of the Czech Republic to both Houses of Parliament in the House of Commons Chamber, Ottawa, on Thursday, 29 April 1999. Government of Canada, Department of Foreign Affairs and International Trade, 11 August 1999 (available at www.dfait.ca).

Hay, C. 'Globalization, Welfare Retrenchment and the Logic of No Alternative: Why Second Best Won't Do'. *Journal of Social Policy.* 27.4 (1998): 525–32.

Hay, C. and Marsh, D., Eds. *Globalization, Welfare Retrenchment and the State.* London: Macmillan, 2000.

Hay, C. and Marsh, D. 'Analysing and Explaining Postwar British Political Development'. *Postwar British Politics in Perspective.* Cambridge: Polity Press, 1999.

Held, D. *Democracy and the Global Order: From the Modern State to Cosmopolitan Governance.* Cambridge: Polity Press, 1995.

Held, D. and McGrew, A. G., Eds. *The Global Transformations Reader.* Cambridge: Polity Press, 2000.

Held, D. and McGrew, A. G. *Global Transformations: Politics, Economics and Culture.* Cambridge: Polity Press, 1999.

Helleiner, E. *States and the Reemergence of Global Finance: From Bretton Woods to the 1990s.* Ithaca: Cornell University, 1994.

Hendrickson, D. C. 'The Ethics of Collective Security'. *Ethics and International Affairs.* 7 (1993): 1–15.

Heraclides, A. 'The Ending of Unending Conflicts'. *Millennium: Journal of International Studies.* 26.3 (1997): 678–707.

Hirst, P. 'The Global Economy – Myths and Realities'. *International Affairs.* 73.3 (1997): 409–25.

Hirst, P. and Thompson, G. *Globalization in Question.* Cambridge: Polity Press, 1999.

Hobbes, T. *On the Citizen.* Eds. and trans., R. Tuck and M. Silverthorne. Cambridge: Cambridge University Press, 1998.

Hobbes, T. *Leviathan.* Ed., M. Oakeshott. Oxford: Basil Blackwell, 1960.

Hoffmann, S. *Duties Beyond Borders: On the Limits and Possibilities of Ethical International Politics.* Syracuse: Syracuse University Press, 1981.

Hollis M. and Smith, S. *Explaining and Understanding International Relations.* Oxford: Clarendon Press, 1990.

Holsti, K. J. 'From Khartoum to Quebec: Internationalism and Nationalism within the Multi-Community State'. *Nationalism and Internationalism in the Post-Cold War Era.* Eds, K. Goldmann, U. Hannerz, and C. Westin. London and New York: Routledge, 2000.

Holsti, K. J. *The State, War, and the State of War.* Cambridge: Cambridge University Press, 1996.

Holsti, K. J. *Peace and War: Armed Conflicts and International Order, 1648–1989.* Cambridge: Cambridge University Press, 1991.

Holsti, K. J. 'L'État et l'état de guerre'. *Études internationales.* 21.4 (1990): 705–17.

Hoogvelt, A. *Globalization and the Postcolonial World: The New Political Economy of Development.* London: Macmillan, 1997.

Howard, M. '*Temperamenta Belli:* Can War Be Controlled?' *Restraints on War: Studies in the Limitation of Armed Conflict.* Ed., M. Howard. Oxford: Oxford University Press, 1979.

Hull, C. *The Memoirs of Cordell Hull.* New York: Macmillan, 1948.

Huntington, S. *The Clash of Civilizations and the Remaking of World Order.* New York: Simon and Schuster, 1997.

Ignatieff, M. *The Warrior's Honour: Ethnic War and the Modern Conscience.* Toronto: Viking Press, 1998.

Ignatieff, M. *Blood and Belonging: Journeys into the New Nationalism.* Toronto: Penguin Books, 1993.

Ikenberry, G. J. 'America's Imperial Ambition'. *Foreign Affairs.* 81.5 (2002): 44–60.

Ikenberry, G. J. 'Getting Hegemony Right'. *National Interest.* 63 (Summer, 2001): 17–24.

International Commission on Intervention and State Sovereignty. *The Responsibility to Protect.* Ottawa: International Development Research Centre, 2001.

Jackson, R. *The Global Covenant: Human Conduct in a World of States.* Oxford: Oxford University Press, 2000.

Jackson, R. *Quasi-States: Sovereignty, International Relations and the Third World.* Cambridge: Cambridge University Press, 1990.

Jackson, J. 'The Great 1994 Sovereignty Debate: US Acceptance and Implementation of the Uruguay Round Results'. *Columbia Journal of Transnational Law.* 36.2 (1998): 157–88.

Jackson, R. and Rosberg, C. *Personal Rule in Black Africa.* Berkeley and London: University of California Press, 1982.

Jackson Preece, J. *Minority Rights: Between Diversity and Community.* Cambridge, UK: Polity Press, 2005.

Jones, A. *Genocide, War Crimes and the West.* London and New York: Zed Books, 2004.

Jones, A. C. 'The Labour Party and Colonial Policy 1945–51'. *New Fabian Colonial Essays.* Ed., A. C. Jones. London: Hogarth Press, 1959.

Kaldor, M. *New and Old Wars: Organized Violence in a Global Era.* Cambridge: Polity Press, 1999.

Kalshoven, F. 'The Undertaking to Respect and Ensure Respect in All Circumstances: From Tiny Seed to Ripening Fruit'. *Yearbook of International Humanitarian Law.* 2 (1999), 3–61.

Kant, I. 'Perpetual Peace: A Philosophical Sketch'. *Kant: Political Writings.* 2nd edn. Ed., H. Reiss, Trans., H. B. Nisbet. Cambridge: Cambridge University Press, 1991a.

Kant, I. 'The Metaphysics of Morals'. *Kant: Political Writings.* 2nd revised edn. Ed., H. Reiss, Trans., H. B. Nisbet. Cambridge: Cambridge University Press, 1991b.

Kant, I. 'On the Relationship of Theory to Practice in Political Right'. *Kant's Political Writings.* 2nd revised edn. Ed., H. Reiss, Trans., H. B. Nisbet. Cambridge: Cambridge University Press, 1970.

Kant, I. 'The Science of Right'. *Great Books of the Western World.* Vol. 42. Ed., R. M. Hutchins. Chicago: Encyclopedia Britannica, 1952.

Kapstein, E. *Governing the Global Economy.* Cambridge, MA: Harvard University Press, 1994.

Keiger, J. *France and the World in the 20th Century.* Oxford: Oxford University Press, 2001.

Kende, I. *Wars Since 1945.* Frankfurt am Mein: Friedens-und Konfliktforschung, 1982.

Kende, I. 'Twenty-Five Years of Local Wars'. *Journal of Peace Research.* 8.1 (1971): 5–22.

Kennan, G. F. *At a Country's Ending.* New York: Norton, 1996.

Kennan, G. F. *Around the Cragged Hill.* New York: Norton, 1993.

Kennan, G. F. *Memoirs, 1950–1963.* Boston: Little, Brown and Company, 1972.

Kennan, G. F. *Russia and the West Under Lenin and Stalin.* London: Hutchison, 1961.

Kennedy, P. *The Rise and Fall of the Great Powers.* New York: Vintage, 1989.

Kennedy, P. and Andreopoulos, G. 'The Laws of War: Some Concluding Reflections'. *The Laws of War: Constraints on Warfare in the Western World.* Eds, M. Howard, G. Andreopoulos, and M. Schulman. New Haven and London: Yale University Press, 1994.

Kennedy-Pipe, C. *Russia and the World, 1917–1991.* Oxford: Oxford University Press, 2001.

Keohane, R. 'Hobbes's Dilemma and Institutional Change in World Politics'. *The Global Transformations Reader.* Eds, D. Held and A. G. McGrew. Cambridge: Polity Press, 2000.

Kerr, P. H. 'Political Relations Between Advanced and Backward Peoples'. *An Introduction to the Study of International Relations.* London: Macmillan, 1916.

Kissinger, H. 'America at the Adex'. *National Interest.* 64 (Summer, 2001): 9–17.

Kissinger, H. *Diplomacy.* New York: Simon and Schuster, 1994.

Krasner, S. 'Compromising Westphalia'. *The Global Transformations Reader.* Eds, D. Held and A. G. McGrew. Cambridge: Polity Press, 2000.

Krasner, S. *Sovereignty: Organized Hypocrisy.* Princeton: Princeton University Press, 1999.

Krasner, S. *Structural Conflict: The Third World Against Global Liberalism.* Berkeley, CA: University of California Press, 1985.

Krause, K. and Williams, M. 'Broadening the Agenda of Security Studies: Politics and Methods'. *Mershon International Studies Review.* 40.2 (1996): 229–54.

Krauthammer, C. 'The Unipolar Moment Revisited'. *National Interest.* 70 (Winter, 2002/2003): 5–17.

Kymlicka, W. *Multicultural Citizenship.* Oxford: Clarendon Press, 1995.

Ledda, G. *Padre Padrone.* Milan: Feltrenelli, 1975.

LeFebvre, G. *The Coming of the Revolution.* Trans., R. R. Palmer. Princeton: Princeton University Press, 1988.

Licklider, R. 'Early Returns: Results of the First Wave of Statistical Studies on Civil War'. *Civil Wars.* 1.3 (1998): 120–32.

Liddel Hart, B. H. *The Strategy of Indirect Approach.* London: Faber and Faber, 1941.

Link, A. 'The Higher Realism of Woodrow Wilson'. *Ethics and Statecraft: The Moral Dimension of International Affairs.* Ed., C. J. Nolan. Westport, CT: Praeger, 1993.

Link, A. S., Ed. *The Papers of Woodrow Wilson,* Vol. 54. Princeton: Princeton University Press, 1986.

Lipsey, R. G. 'Globalization and governments' policies'. *States Against Markets.* Eds, R. Boyer and D. Dracher. London: Routledge, 1996.

Louis, W. R. *Imperialism at Bay, 1941–1945: The United States and the Decolonization of the British Empire.* Oxford: Clarendon Press, 1977.

Lucas, J. R. 'Freedom and Prediction'. *Aristotelian Society.* 41 (1967): 163–72.

Lugard, F. D. *The Dual Mandate in British Tropical Africa.* 4th edn. London: William Blackwood & Sons, 1929.

Lundestad, G. *Empire by Integration.* Oxford: Oxford University Press, 1998.

Lundestad, G. *The American 'Empire'.* Oslo: Norwegian University Press, 1990.

Luttwak, E. *Turbo-Capitalism.* New York: Basic Books, 1999.

Lyon, P. 'The Rise and Fall and Possible Revival of International Trusteeship'. *Journal of Commonwealth and Comparative Politics.* 31.1 (1993): 96–110.

Lyons, G. M. and Mayall, J., Eds. *International Human Rights in the 21st Century: Protecting the Rights of Groups.* Boulder, CO: Rowan and Littlefield, 2003.

Machiavelli, N. *The Prince.* New York: Norton, 1977.

Mallaby, S. 'The Reluctant Imperialist: Terrorism, Failed States, and the Case for American Empire'. *Foreign Affairs.* 81.2 (2002): 2–7

Mannheim, K. *Ideology and Utopia.* New York: Harcourt, Brace and Co., 1936.

Marshall, P. J., Ed. *Problems of Empire, 1757–1813.* London: George Allen and Unwin, 1968.

Martin, W. and Winters, A. *The Uruguay Round and the Developing Countries.* Cambridge, MA and New York: Cambridge University Press, 1996.

Mayall, J. 'National Self-Determination and International Order: The Asian Experience'. *Asian Nationalism.* Ed., M. Leifer. London: Routledge, for LSE Asia Centre, 2000.

Mayall, J. *Nationalism and International Society.* Cambridge: Cambridge University Press, 1990.

Mayer, A. E. *Islam and Human Rights.* London: Pinter, 1995.

Maynes, C. 'Contending Schools'. *National Interest.* 63 (Spring, 2001): 49–58.

Michie, J. and Grieve Smith, J., Eds. *Managing the Global Economy.* Oxford and New York: Oxford University Press, 1995.

Mill, J. S. *Utilitarianism, On Liberty, Considerations on Representative Government.* London: Everyman, 1999.

Mill, J. S. *Considerations on Representative Government.* Amherst, NY: Prometheus Books, 1991.

Mill, J. S. 'A Few Words on Non-Intervention'. *Essays on Politics and Culture by John Stuart Mill.* Ed., G. Himmelfarb. New York: Anchor Books, 1963.

Miller, D. H., Ed. 'Covenant of the League of Nations'. *The Drafting of the Covenant.* New York: G. P. Putnam's Sons, 1928.

Milton, G. *Nathaniel's Nutmeg.* London: Hodder and Stoughton, 1999.

Milton, J. *Paradise Lost and Other Poems.* New York: Mentor Books, 1961.

Moorehead, A. *Darwin and the Beagle.* Harmondsworth: Penguin Books, 1971.

Moran, T. H. 'Multinational Companies and Dependency'. *International Organization.* 32.1 (1978): 79–100.

Morgenthau, H. *Politics Among Nations: The Struggle for Power and Peace.* 6th Edn. New York: Alfred Knopf, 1985.

Morwood, J., Ed. *The Pocket Oxford Latin Dictionary.* Oxford: Oxford University Press, 1995.

Mowat, R. B. *Diplomacy and Peace.* London: William and Norgate, 1935.

Mueller, J. 'Does War Still Exist?' Paper delivered at the conference on 'The Waning of Major War'. University of Notre Dame, 6–8 April 2001.

Mueller, J. *Retreat From Doomsday: The Obsolescence of Major War.* New York: Basic Books, 1989.

Murphy, S. D. *Humanitarian Intervention: The United Nations in an Evolving World Order.* Philadelphia, PA: University of Philadelphia Press, 1996.

Musgrave, T. *Self Determination and National Minorities.* Oxford: Oxford University Press, 1997.

Nafziger, W., Stewart, F., and Väyrynen, R., Eds. *War, Hunger and Displacement: The Origins of Humanitarian Emergencies.* London: Oxford University Press, 2000.

NATO Handbook. Brussels: NATO Office of Information and Press, 1995.

Nehru, J. *The Discovery of India.* London: Meridian Books, 1946.

Neuhold, H. 'The Foreign-Policy "Cost-Benefit Analysis" Revisited'. *German Yearbook of International Law, 1999.* 42 (1999): 84–124.

Newman, B. *The New Europe.* London: Macmillan, 1943.

Nicolson, H. *The Congress of Vienna.* London: Methuen, 1970.

Nicolson, H. *Peacemaking 1919.* London: Methuen, 1967.

Nicolson, H. *The Evolution of Diplomatic Method.* London: Cassell, 1954.

Nish, I. 'Nationalism in Japan'. *Asian Nationalism.* Ed., M. Leifer. London: Routledge, for LSE Asia Centre, 2000.

Nkrumah, K. *Towards Colonial Freedom: Africa and the Struggle Against World Imperialism.* London: Heinemann, 1962.

Nolan, C. J. 'The United States, Moral Norms, and Governing Ideas in World Politics'. *Ethics and International Affairs.* 7 (1993a): 223-39.

Nolan, C. J. *Principled Diplomacy: Security and Rights in U.S. Foreign Policy.* Westport, CT: Greenwood, 1993b.

Nolan, C. J. 'La liberté est-elle divisible? Comment rapprocher les concepts de mission et de sécurité dans la politque étrangère américane'. *Études Internationales.* 22.3 (1991): 509-31.

Nye, J. *The Paradox of American Power: Why the World's Only Superpower Can't Go it Alone.* Oxford: Oxford University Press, 2002.

Nye, J. 'International Conflicts After the Cold War'. *Managing Conflict in the Post-Cold War World.* Aspen: Aspen Institute, 1996.

Oakeshott, M. *On Human Conduct.* Oxford: Clarendon Press, 1996.

Oakeshott, M. *On History and Other Essays.* Oxford: Blackwell, 1983.

Oakeshott, M. 'The Vocabulary of a Modern European State'. *Political Studies.* 23.2/3 (1975): 197–219.

Ohmae, K. *The Borderless World: Power and Strategy in the Global Marketplace.* London: Harper Collins, 1992.

Olafson, F. A. *Ethics and Twentieth Century Thought.* Englewood Cliffs: Prentice Hall, 1973.

Oren, N. 'Statecraft and the Academic Intellectuals'. *Intellectuals in Politics.* Ed., N. Oren. Jerusalem: Magnes, 1984.

Owens, M. T. 'Technology, the RMA, and Future War'. *Strategic Review.* 26.2 (1998): 63–70.

Pagden, A. *Lords of All the World: Ideologies of Empire in Spain, Britain, and France c. 1500–c. 1800.* New Haven: Yale University Press, 1995.

Parker, G. 'Early Modern Europe'. *The Laws of War: Constraints on Warfare in the Western World.* Eds, M. Howard, G. Andrepoulos, and M. Schulman. New Haven and London: Yale University Press, 1994.

Passmore, J. *The Perfectibility of Man.* 3rd edn. Indianapolis: Liberty Fund, 2000.

Pastor, R. *A Century's Journey: How the Great Powers Shape the World.* New York: Basic Books, 1999.

Perham, M. *Colonial Sequence, 1930–1949.* London: Methuen & Co., 1967.

Perham, M. *The Colonial Reckoning.* London: Collins, 1961.

Peterson, J. *Province of Freedom: A History of Sierra Leone 1787–1870.* London: Faber & Faber, 1969.

Pitt, W. 'William Pitt on his First East India Bill'. *Readings in the Constitutional History of India 1757–1947.* Ed., S. V. Desika Char. Delhi: Oxford University Press, 1983.

Planze, O. 'Realism and Idealism in Historical Perspective: Otto von Bismarck'. *Ethics and Statecraft: The Moral Dimension of International Affairs.* Ed., C. J. Nolan. Westport, CT: Praeger, 1993.

Plato. *Republic.* Trans., R. Waterfield. Oxford: Oxford University Press, 1993.

Polanyi, K. *The Great Transformation.* New York: Octagon Books, 1944.

Pollis, A. and Schwab, P. 'Human Rights: A Western Construct with Limited Applicability'. *Human Rights: Cultural and Ideological Perspectives.* Eds, A. Pollis and P. Schwab. New York: Praeger, 1979.

Popper, K. *Conjectures and Refutations.* London: Routledge and Kegan Paul, 1963.

Porter, T. *States, Markets and Regimes in Global Finance.* Houndmills, UK: Macmillan, 1993.

Protocols and the General Act of the West African Conference, *Parliamentary Papers,* 1885 LV mf. 91.435.

Ratner, S. R. 'Drawing a better line: *Uti Possidetis* and the borders of New States'. *American Journal of International Law.* 90.4 (1996): 590–624.

Rawls, J. *Political Liberalism.* New York: Columbia University Press, 1999.

Raz, J. *The Morality of Freedom.* Oxford: Oxford University Press, 1986.

Raza, M. *Wars and No Peace Over Kashmir.* New Delhi: Lancer Publishers, 1996.

Reisman, W. M. 'Kosovo's Antinomies'. *American Journal of International Law.* 93.4 (1999): 860–2.

Roberts, A. 'The So-Called "Right" of Humanitarian Intervention'. *Yearbook of International Humanitarian Law.* 3 (2000): 3–51.

Roberts, A. and Kingsbury, B., Eds. *United Nations, Divided World.* Oxford: Clarendon Press, 1993.

Robinson R. and Gallagher, J., with Denny, A. *Africa and the Victorians: The Official Mind of Imperialism.* London: Macmillan, 1965.

Ron, J. 'Boundaries and Violence: Repertoires of State Action along the Bosnia/Yugoslav Divide'. *Theory and Society.* 29.5 (2000): 609–49.

Ross, G. M. *Leibniz.* Oxford: Oxford University Press, 1984.

Roth, B. R. 'Bending the Law, Breaking it, or Developing it? The United States and the Humanitarian Use of Force in the post-Cold War Era'. *United States*

Hegemony and the Foundations of International Law. Eds, M. Byers and G. Nolte. Cambridge: Cambridge University Press, 2003.

Rothenberg, G. 'The Age of Napoleon'. *The Laws of War: Constraints on Warfare in the Western World*. Eds, M. Howard, G. Andreopoulos, and M. Schulman. New Haven and London: Yale University Press, 1994.

Rothschild, E. 'What Is Security?' *Daedalus*. 124.3 (1995): 53–98.

Rovere R. A. and Am Schlesinger, A. *The General and the President*. New York: Farrar, Straus and Young, 1951.

Rummel, R. *Death by Government*. London: Transaction Publishers, 1994.

Saurin, J. 'The End of International Relations? The State and International Theory in the Age of Globalization'. *Boundaries in Question: The Expansion of International Theory*. Eds, A. Linklater and J. Macmillan. London: Pinter, 1995.

Schechtman, J. *European Population Transfers 1939–1945*. New York: Oxford University Press, 1946.

Schevill, F. *History of the Balkan Peninsula: From the Earliest Times to the Present Day*. New York: Harcourt Brace, 1922.

Scholte, J. *The International Relations of Social Change*. Buckingham: Open University, 1993a.

Scholte, J. 'From Power Politics to Social Change: An Alternative Focus for International Studies'. *Review of International Studies*. 19.1 (1993b): 3–21.

Shaw, M. *War and Genocide: Organized Killing in Modern Society*. Cambridge: Polity Press, 2003.

Shaw, M. 'The Heritage of States: The Principle of *Uti Possidetis Juris* Today'. *British Yearbook of International Law*. 67 (1996): 75–154.

Shaw, M. *Global Society and International Relations*. Cambridge: Polity Press, 1994.

Shklar, J. Legalism. Cambridge, MA: Harvard University Press, 1964.

Simma, B. 'NATO, the UN and the Use of Force: Legal Aspects'. *European Journal of International Law*. 10.1 (1999): 1–22.

Smith, S. 'The Contested Concept of Security'. *Critical Security Studies and World Politics*. Ed., K. Booth. Boulder: Lynne Rienner, 2005.

Smith, S. 'The Increasing Insecurity of Security Studies: Conceptualizing Security in the Last Twenty Years'. *Critical Reflections on Security and Change*. Eds, S. Croft and T. Terriff. London: Frank Cass, 2000.

Snow, D. *Uncivil Wars: International Security and the New Internal Conflicts*. Boulder, CO: Lynne Rienner, 1996.

Snow, D. and Benford, R. 'Master Frames and Cycles of Protest'. *Frontiers in Social Movement Theory*. Eds, A. Morris and C. M. McClurg. New Haven, CT: Yale University Press, 1992.

Sorenson, G. 'An Analysis of Contemporary Statehood: Consequences for Conflict and Cooperation'. *Review of International Studies*. 23.3 (1997): 253–69.

Steiner, B. S. 'Another Missing Middle: Diplomacy and International Theory'. Paper presented at the Annual Convention of the International Studies Association. Los Angeles, 14–18 March 2000.

Strange, S. *The Retreat of the State: The Diffusion of Power in the World Economy*. Cambridge: Cambridge University, 1996.

Sunkel, O. 'Big Business and Dependencia'. *Foreign Affairs*. 50.3 (1978): 517–31.

Talbott, S. 'The Balkan Question and the European Answer'. Address at the Aspen Institute, Aspen, Colorado, 24 August 1999 (available at www.state.gov).

Taylor, A. J. P. *The Struggle for Mastery in Europe*. Oxford: Clarendon Press, 1971.

Taylor, A. J. P. *Europe: Grandeur and Decline.* Harmondsworth: Penguin, 1967a.

Taylor, A. J. P., 'Bismarck's Morality'. *Europe: Grandeur and Decline.* London: Pelican Books, 1967b.

Taylor, A. J. P. *Bismarck, the Man and the Statesman.* New York: Alfred A. Knopf, 1955.

Tesón, F. R. *Humanitarian Intervention: An Inquiry into Law and Morality.* Dobbs Ferry, New York: Transnational Publishers, 1988.

Thomson, D. *Europe Since Napoleon*, revised edn. London: Penguin Books, 1990.

Thornberry, P. *International Law and the Rights of Minorities.* Oxford: Clarendon Press, 1991.

Tickner, J. A. *Gender in International Relations: Feminist Perspectives on Achieving Global Security.* New York: Columbia University Press, 1992.

Ulam, A. *Expansion and Coexistence.* New York: Praeger, 1974.

Ullman, R. 'Redefining Security'. *International Security.* 8.8 (1983): 129–53.

UK House of Commons, Foreign Affairs Committee. 'Fourth Report – Kosovo'. *Report and Proceedings of the Committee.* Vol. I. London: Her Majesty's Stationery Office, 2000.

United Nations Development Programme. *Human Development Report.* New York and Oxford: Oxford University Press, 1994.

United Nations Organization. *A More Secure World: Our Shared Responsibility – Report of the Secretary-General's High-level Panel on Threats, Challenges and Change.* New York: United Nations, 2004.

United Nations Organization. *Documents of the United Nations Conference on International Organization.* Vol. X. London: United Nations Information Organizations, 1945.

Vagts, A. *Defense and Diplomacy.* New York: King's Crown Press, 1956.

Valls, A. *Ethics in International Affairs.* Lahman: Rowman and Littlefield, 2000.

Van Creveld, M. *The Transformation of War.* New York: The Free Press, 1991.

Vasquez, J. A. *The War Puzzle.* Cambridge: Cambridge University Press, 1993.

Vaughn, C. E. *The Political Writings of J. J. Rousseau.* Vol. I. Cambridge: Cambridge University Press, 1915.

Vincent, R. J. *Nonintervention and International Order.* Princeton: Princeton University Press, 1974.

de Vitoria, F. 'On the American Indians (*de Indis*)'. *Political Writings.* Eds, A. Pagden and J. Lawrance. Cambridge: Cambridge University Press, 1991.

De Waal, A. 'Contemporary Warfare in Africa'. *Restructuring the Global Military Sector.* Vol. I. Eds, M. Kaldor and B. Vashee. London and Washington: Pinter, 1997.

Wachtel, H. *The Money Mandarins: The Making of a New Supranational Economic Order.* New York: Pantheon, 1986.

Waever, O. 'The EU as a Security Actor: Reflections from a Pessimistic Constructivist on Post-Sovereign Security Orders'. *International Relations Theory and the Politics of European Integration: Power, Security and Community.* Eds, M. Kelstrup and M. Williams. London: Routledge, 2000.

Wallensteen, P. and Sollenberg, M. 'Armed Conflicts, Conflict Termination, and Peace Agreements, 1989–1996'. *Journal of Peace Research.* 34.3 (1997): 339–58.

Walt, S. 'The Renaissance of Security Studies'. *International Studies Quarterly.* 35.2 (1991): 211–39.

Waltz, K. *Theory of International Politics.* New York: McGraw Hill, 1979.

Waltz, K. *Man, The State, and War: A Theoretical Analysis*. New York: Columbia University Press, 1959.

Walzer, M. *Just and Unjust Wars*. 2nd edn. New York: Basic Books, 1992.

Waters, M. *Globalization*. London: Routledge, 1995.

Watson, A. *The Evolution of the International Society*. London: Routledge, 1992.

Weber, M. *The Theory of Social and Economic Organization*. Trans., A. Henderson and T. Parsons. New York: Oxford University Press, 1947.

Welch, D. A. 'Can We Think Systematically About Ethics and Statecraft?' *Ethics and International Affairs*. 8 (1994): 23–37.

Welsh, J. M., Ed. *Humanitarian Intervention and International Relations*. Oxford: Oxford University Press, 2004.

Wheeler, N. *Saving Strangers: Humanitarian Intervention in International Society*. Oxford: Oxford University Press, 2000.

Wiener, A. 'Constructivism and the Social in Political Science'. Paper delivered at the 42nd International Studies Association Annual Convention. Chicago, 20–4 February 2001.

Wight, M. *International Theory: The Three Traditions*. Leicester and London: Leicester University Press, 1991.

Wight, M. *Power Politics*. Harmondsworth: Penguin and the Royal Institute of International Relations, 1986.

Wight, M. *Systems of States*. Leicester: Leicester University Press, 1977.

Wight, M. 'Western Values in International Relations'. *Diplomatic Investigations*. Eds, H. Butterfield and M. Wight. London: George Allen and Unwin, 1966.

Wilmot, E. *The Great Powers, 1814-1914*. Walton-on-Thames, Surrey: Nelson, 1992.

Wilson, W. *The Papers of Woodrow Wilson*. Vol. 54. Ed., A. Link. Princeton: Princeton University Press, 1986.

Wright, Q. *Study of War*. Chicago: University of Chicago Press, 1965.

Wright, Q. *Mandates Under the League of Nations*. Chicago: University of Chicago Press, 1930.

Woodhouse, C. M. *The Story of Modern Greece*. London: Faber, 1968.

Woodward, E. L. *The Age of Reform: 1815–1870*. Oxford: Oxford University Press, 1954.

Wyn Jones, R. *Security, Strategy and Critical Theory*. Boulder, CO: Lynne Rienner, 1999.

Young, I. M. *Justice and the Politics of Difference*. Princeton: Princeton University Press, 1990.

Young, J. *Britain and the World in the 20th Century*. Oxford: Oxford University Press, 1997.

Zacher, M. 'The Territorial Integrity Norm'. *International Organization*. 55.2 (2001): 215–50.

Index

Smith, S. 3, 117
social contract 20, 24, 27
societas 200–1; *see also* Oakeshott, M.
society of states *see* international society
Sofer, S. 10
solidarism 32, 38, 57, 59n48, 114, 160,
   181–3, 202–3
sovereign state 18, 23, 25; equal rights
   31; failure 30; freedom 34; liberal
   character 22; monopoly on violence
   20–1; recognition 25–6, 31; retreat
   119; postmodern 21
sovereignty 6, 15, 112, 125; alliances
   27–8; fundamental norms 30–1;
   institution 28; negative 32–3;
   normative content 21, 23; popular
   99–100; responsibility 56–7; self-help
   23–4; *see also* security
Soviet Union *see* Russia
Snow, D. 47
standard of civilization 26, 90n8; *see also*
   barbarians
state of nature *see* Hobbes, T.; Kant, I.
Strange, S. 118–20, 124–5, 126, 135
Sudan 103, 149
system of states 24

Taylor, A. J. P. 61, 63, 78
Teson, F. 171
Thirty Years War 39–41
trusteeship 33; contemporary
   international society 199–202;
   justification 189–92, 203–4; obligation
   192–7; self-interest 3, 192; United
   Nations 13, 31, 110; *see also* security
tutelage 31; *see also* trusteeship

unconditional surrender 45
unequal treaties 92n22
United Kingdom 25, 60–1, 73, 83, 125,
   129, 143, 161–2, 182, 189–91
United Nations 26, 48–9, 74, 84, 110,
   113, 147–8, 151, 175–6, 165, 175,
   178–80, 182, 192; Charter 31, 40, 54,
   108, 148, 159, 164, 172, 174, 187n28,
   196; General Assembly 165, 169–71,
   176, 203; reform 56–7, 179; Security
   Council 160, 163, 166–8, 170, 175–6,
   179, 83–4, 187n14; trusteeship system
   13, 110; *see also* intervention
United Nations Development Report
   126
United States of America 11, 21, 73, 85,
   87, 90n8, 93n31, 109, 126, 139, 162,

177, 195; balance of power 84;
   constitution 20; Cuban Missile Crisis
   176; foreign policy 7; military
   intervention 162, 165–8, 174, 176,
   180–3, 185; neoimperialism 6–7;
   open world 7; post-war order 83–5;
   war 42; war against terror 162
universitas 200–1; *see also* Oakeshott, M.;
   societas
uti possidetis see self-determination

Vasquez, J. 66
Versailles peace settlement 45, 195
Vietnam War 42, 46, 74, 163
Vincent, R. J. 166
de Vitoria, F. 189

Walt, S. 8
Waltz, K. 104, 125
war 18, 20, 99; black economy 47;
   chivalry 39; Clausewitzian conception
   37, 46, 50, 53, 55, 58n6;
   contemporary 37, 41–4, 46–7, 50;
   discriminate 41, 43; duration 46–7;
   Enlightenment image 37–9, 41, 50;
   ethnic 12, 37, 42–3, 44, 47, 52, 103,
   120–2; extermination 42; human
   nature 104; humanitarian 34; *jus ad
   bellum* 41, 159, 183; *jus in bello* 40–1;
   just war tradition 178; limited 39;
   medieval 39, 52; moral rules and
   norms 39–40, 44; national
   debilitation 10, 43, 47–9, 51–2, 54, 58;
   nationalist 102; NGOs 49; right of 28;
   settlement 50–1; technological
   development 52–3; total 45; treaties
   and conventions 40, 45; vocabulary 54
war against terror 5, 144, 162, 176
Watson, A. 107
weapons of mass destruction:
   proliferation 5
Weber, M. 21
Westphalian order 5, 9, 13, 71, 75, 83,
   89n2, 106, 142, 146
Wight, M. 64, 68, 70n60
Williams, M. 3
Wilson, W. 11, 45, 85, 95, 109, 113, 146,
   195; *see also* liberalism
World Trade Organization (WTO) 95,
   126; *see also* GATT

Yugoslavia *see* Balkans

Zedong, M. 43, 73, 106

Printed in Poland
by Amazon Fulfillment
Poland Sp. z o.o., Wrocław